FEDERAL ESTATE AND GIFT TAXATION

IN A NUTSHELL®

TENTH EDITION

JOHN K. McNULTY
Late Roger J. Traynor
Professor of Law, Emeritus
University of California, Berkeley

GRAYSON M.P. McCOUCH
Clarence J. TeSelle Professor of Law
University of Florida

WEST ACADEMIC

860 Blue Gentian Road, Suite 350
Eagan, MN 55121
1-877-888-1330

Published in the United States of America

ISBN: 979-8-31770-247-2

PREFACE

This book, now in its tenth edition, provides an introduction to the federal law of estate and gift taxation in the United States. It is thus a companion to Lathrope, Yamamoto & McNulty, Federal Income Taxation of Individuals in a Nutshell (9th ed. 2023), and McCouch, Federal Income Taxation of Estates, Trusts, and Beneficiaries in a Nutshell (4th ed. 2026). It is intended to be used by lawyers, students and scholars from other legal systems, as well as by law students in this country as a supplement to usual law school courses and materials, and perhaps as a refresher or orientation for members of the bar. It attempts to summarize the law, frequently mentioning the purposes of, and sometimes the alternatives to, existing legal rules. Only occasionally does it attempt a critical evaluation, or a history, or full justification, of the existing law. Chapters on some fundamentals of estate and gift and generation-skipping transfer tax planning, and on reform of and fundamental alternatives to the federal transfer tax system, have been included.

The book is organized in a way that parallels many courses and teaching materials. It begins with an introduction to the gift tax, the estate tax and the generation-skipping transfer tax as separate components of the transfer tax system. After the introductory chapters, however, the book follows a "transactional" approach, taking up both the estate tax and the gift tax (and, where appropriate, the generation-skipping transfer tax) treatment of particular kinds of transfers, dispositions and situations.

Very little attention has been given to the matter of filling out required tax returns or forms or to other questions of compliance and administration of the tax laws. These matters fall outside the scope of a short volume of this kind.

The statutory provisions themselves form the core of the subject matter, and readers of this book should have a current copy of the Internal Revenue Code at hand. Much the same can be said for the Treasury Regulations under the transfer taxes. Frequent references to sections of the Code (often cited as "I.R.C. §" to distinguish them from cross references to other sections of this book) and the Regulations (cited as "Reg. §") are given throughout the text. Rulings and other administrative pronouncements are cited to the volume and page of the Cumulative Bulletin (abbreviated as "C.B.") or the Internal Revenue Bulletin (abbreviated as "I.R.B.").

Reference is also made to leading cases, revenue rulings, and collateral sources. These citations are intended to offer access to some central areas of authority without attempting to cover all relevant or helpful material.

This short book is intended to provide an introduction, review or overview of the subject matter of federal wealth transfer taxation in the United States. Nevertheless, it cannot substitute for, but at best can supplement, a thoroughgoing examination and analysis of the Code, regulations, rulings and cases, which are the principal sources of federal wealth transfer tax law and which must be emphasized in the study of that law by students in law school courses.

I note with sadness the passing of the original author of this book, Jack McNulty, who died in 2020. Jack was a good friend and a gracious collaborator, and I am grateful to him for inviting me to join as a co-author of this book beginning with the sixth edition. This tenth edition continues to reflect his thorough knowledge and expertise in the area of federal taxation which laid the groundwork for previous editions.

GRAYSON M.P. MCCOUCH

June, 2026

OUTLINE

TABLE OF CASES

References are to Pages

TABLE OF INTERNAL REVENUE CODE SECTIONS

References are to Pages

TABLE OF TREASURY REGULATIONS

References are to Pages

TABLE OF REVENUE RULINGS

References are to Pages

FEDERAL ESTATE AND GIFT TAXATION

IN A NUTSHELL®

TENTH EDITION

CHAPTER 1

INTRODUCTION

§ 1 NATURE OF THE FEDERAL ESTATE, GIFT, AND GENERATION-SKIPPING TRANSFER TAXES

Taxation of property transferred by an individual to others at death is one of the oldest and most common forms of taxation, at least in societies where property is privately owned. Death transfer taxes often take the form of an *estate* tax, which is an excise tax levied on the privilege of transferring property at death and usually is measured by the size of the decedent's estate. Or, a death tax can be configured as an *inheritance* tax, an excise tax levied on the privilege of receiving property from the decedent and usually measured by the amount of property received by each particular recipient, rather than by the amount of the total estate, and by the recipient's relationship to the decedent. The federal estate tax, as its name suggests, is an example of the former; several *state* death taxes are cast in the form of an inheritance tax. Both forms of tax usually, but not necessarily, employ a graduated rate scale; the larger the estate or the larger an inheritance received, the higher the *marginal* tax rates (the rates charged on the last $1 of taxable property) applied, and consequently the higher the *effective* or *average* rate of tax paid. The effective tax rate consists of the total tax paid divided by the total taxable estate or inheritance and is therefore lower than the top marginal rate.

Since a transfer tax imposed at death can so easily be avoided by lifetime gifts—"inter vivos" gifts, made between living persons—a federal transfer tax is imposed on the making of gifts during life. Some states also impose a gift tax to back up their death transfer taxes. Gift taxes also can be progressive; the rate of tax varies with the amount of taxable transfers previously made during the donor's lifetime. Gift taxes and death taxes in the form of estate or inheritance taxes are known as "transfer taxes." Transfer taxes can be combined or integrated so that, for example, the rate of tax on transfers made at death is affected by the aggregate amount of gift transfers made during life.

The U.S. Constitution requires that all "direct taxes" imposed at the federal level must be apportioned among the several states according to their respective populations. (After the income tax was held to be a direct tax, the Sixteenth Amendment was passed to exempt the income tax from this apportionment rule.) The federal estate and gift taxes are not viewed as direct taxes. They are excise taxes, imposed on an event or a transaction (a gift or transfer of property at death), as distinguished from direct taxes, which are imposed on a person (a "poll tax") or on property itself (whether or not it has been transferred or otherwise made the subject of a transaction or an event). Consequently, the federal estate and gift taxes fall outside the apportionment requirement.

§ 2 HISTORY AND EVOLUTION OF THE FEDERAL ESTATE, GIFT, AND GENERATION-SKIPPING TRANSFER TAXES

Throughout the nation's early history, federal taxes on transfers at death were imposed primarily to provide revenue in time of actual or threatened war. From 1797 to 1802 Congress levied a stamp tax on receipts of legacies and probate of wills, to finance a naval buildup in response to French attacks on American ships. An inheritance tax was enacted in 1862, during the Civil War, and repealed in 1870 after the end of the war. In 1894 Congress enacted an income tax which included gifts and inheritances in income, but this tax was struck down as unconstitutional the next year. In 1898 Congress instituted a mixed estate and inheritance tax to finance the Spanish-American War. This tax was progressive with the size of the estate and also graduated with respect to the relationship between the decedent and the recipient. It survived an attack on constitutional grounds but was repealed in 1902.

In 1916 a federal estate tax was enacted, in part to raise revenue as the United States prepared to enter World War I, and in part to attack undue concentrations of inherited wealth. The constitutionality of this tax was upheld in New York Trust Co. v. Eisner, 256 U.S. 345 (1921); it was viewed as an *indirect tax,* an excise tax which did not have to be apportioned among the states. Meanwhile, many states had adopted estate or inheritance taxes. Some had not, however, and rates varied widely from state to state. These disparities created an inducement for wealthy people to change domicile for tax purposes. To promote greater uniformity, Congress in 1924 enacted a credit against the federal estate tax for death taxes paid at the state level. As a result, states were induced to enact death transfer taxes and to bring their rates up to the maximum amount allowable as a credit against the federal tax. Many states enacted such "pick-up" or "sponge" taxes geared to the full amount of the credit against the federal tax.

To avoid the federal and state taxes on transmission or receipt of property at death, some property owners made large inter vivos transfers. To counteract this technique and partly for political reasons, the federal gift tax was introduced in 1924. (It was repealed in 1926 but reinstated in 1932.) This gift tax was imposed on lifetime gifts at rates equal to three-quarters of the estate tax rates on equivalent transfers made at death. The gift tax was, and is, progressive and cumulative over a donor's lifetime—the tax on a taxable gift of a given amount is higher if the donor has made many or large taxable gifts previously, even in prior years. Today's federal estate and gift taxes retain many of the essential features of their 1916 and 1932 forebears. In the intervening years, however, the taxes have evolved in several significant ways.

The *marital deduction* originated as an attempt to achieve roughly equal tax treatment of married couples in community property states and separate property states. Under community property law, the estate of a deceased husband (if he is the first to die) includes only one-half of the couple's community property, whereas in a separate property state the husband's estate generally includes all property titled in the decedent's name, which may well represent the bulk of the couple's wealth. To eliminate the tax advantage of automatic estate-splitting for couples in community property states, Congress amended the estate tax in 1942 to provide that the husband's estate would include almost all of the couple's community property. In 1948, Congress reversed course and reinstated the original treatment of community property while allowing a marital deduction for one-half of the value of separate property passing from the decedent to the surviving spouse. Thus, if a deceased husband left all of his property to his surviving spouse, only one-half of the value of the couple's wealth would be subject to estate tax at the husband's death, regardless of whether the couple lived in a separate property state or a community property state. Parallel treatment was afforded for lifetime gifts under the federal gift tax.

For many years, the separate lower rates on lifetime gifts, and the fresh start up the progressive rate ladder provided by separate taxation of the estate at death, offered substantial tax benefits for wealthy families that could afford to make large inter vivos gifts. In an effort to curtail the advantages of inter vivos giving resulting from the separate gift and estate tax structures, Congress restructured the estate and gift taxes in the Tax Reform Act of 1976, P.L. 94–455 (the "1976 Act"). Instead of two separate taxes, with two different rate schedules and a fresh start up the progressive rate ladder for the taxable estate at death, the 1976 Act adopted a unified tax structure, using only one rate schedule which applies to cumulative taxable transfers made during life and at death.

The 1976 Act also adopted a *unified credit* (often referred to as an "exemption equivalent") to replace the separate gift and estate tax exemptions of prior law ($30,000 deduction for cumulative lifetime gifts, $60,000 deduction for the taxable estate). By casting the new exemption in the form of a credit rather than a deduction, Congress ensured that the dollar savings would be uniform for all taxpayers, regardless of their marginal tax brackets. As a result of subsequent legislation, the exemption equivalent has grown by leaps and bounds, reaching $1 million in 2002, $3.5 million in 2009, $5 million in 2010, $10 million in 2018, and $15 million in 2026. Moreover, under current law the amount of the exemption equivalent is subject to automatic annual adjustment for inflation. Under the unified rate schedule in I.R.C. § 2001(c),* assuming a top marginal rate of 40 percent, a credit of $5,945,800 is equal to the tax that would be imposed on a transfer of $15 million and thus is equivalent to a $15 million exemption; hence

* Section numbers of the Internal Revenue Code (I.R.C.) cited in this book correspond to section numbers of Title 26 of the United States Code (U.S.C.) and the United States Code Annotated (U.S.C.A.). The federal estate, gift, and generation-skipping transfer taxes are found in Chapters 11 through 14 of the Internal Revenue Code. (The federal income tax appears in Chapter 1 of the Internal Revenue Code.)

the use of the term "exemption equivalent" to describe the amount sheltered from tax by the unified credit. In effect, a credit of $5,945,800 produces an effective tax rate of zero on the first $15 million of cumulative taxable transfers made during life or at death.

The 1976 Act also introduced for the first time a tax on *generation-skipping transfers,* to supplement the estate and gift taxes. Under prior law it was possible for a transferor to avoid estate and gift taxes by creating trusts that spread the beneficial enjoyment of property temporally across several generations. For example, a trust to pay income to the grantor's child for life, with remainder to grandchildren, gave the child the immediate use and enjoyment of the property, but occasioned no additional estate tax on the corpus when the property passed to the grandchildren. Consequently the property, although of course taxed in the estate of the original grantor, could be passed through one (or more) succeeding generations with no further estate or gift tax liability. The only limit was imposed indirectly by applicable state law in the form of a rule against perpetuities or a similar rule, with the result that property held in trust might be sheltered from transfer taxes for 100 years or more. The generation-skipping provisions enacted in 1976 closed this avenue of tax avoidance by taxing the entire property *as though* it had passed through the estate of the skipped generation (the grantor's child, in the example above). However, those provisions were flawed by administrative complexity and other shortcomings, and they were eventually replaced in

1986 by an entirely new generation-skipping transfer (GST) tax. The revised GST tax, contained in Chapter 13 of the Internal Revenue Code (I.R.C. §§ 2601–2663), is described in §§ 6 and 15, *infra.*

The 1976 Act also amended some *income tax* provisions which have great importance for estate planning and administration. The most important of these was an attempt to equalize the treatment of accrued but unrealized appreciation (or decrease) in the value of property gratuitously transferred. The old law was that the donee of an inter vivos gift took the donor's basis in the property ("carryover" basis), while the recipient of a testamentary gift took a new basis stepped up (or down) to fair market value at the date of the transferor's death ("fresh-start" basis). Under the 1976 Act, for all post-1976 transfers, both inter vivos and testamentary, the recipient was to take the transferor's basis ("carryover" basis), subject to various adjustments. However, the 1976 carryover basis provisions were postponed in 1978 and then repealed in 1980, without ever having gone into general effect. See former I.R.C. § 1023. Accordingly, the "old law" rules of carryover basis for inter vivos transfers and fresh-start basis for testamentary transfers remain in effect today. See I.R.C. §§ 1014 and 1015.

The Economic Recovery Tax Act of 1981, P.L. 97–34 (the "1981 Act"), expanded the marital deduction by removing the limitations on the amount of property that can be transferred between spouses during life or at death without incurring estate or gift taxes. The 1981 Act also relaxed the restrictions on the types of transfers that qualify for the marital deduction. Broadly speaking, the adoption of an *unlimited* marital deduction has the effect of treating a married couple as a single unit for estate and gift tax purposes, thus relieving most inter-spousal transfers from transfer tax liability. See I.R.C. §§ 2056 and 2523.

The Tax Reform Act of 1986, P.L. 99–514 (the "1986 Act"), made several income tax changes which have continuing significance for estate planning. For example, the income tax rates for estates and trusts were lowered and the rate brackets were compressed, so that estates and trusts with taxable income above a rather low threshold are now subject to tax at the maximum marginal rate. See I.R.C. § 1(e). In addition, the 1986 Act curtailed the use of so-called "*Clifford* trusts" as an income-shifting technique (see I.R.C. § 673), and introduced the "kiddie tax" of I.R.C. § 1(g), which makes the "net unearned income" over a specified amount (including trust or custodianship income) of a child under the age of 18 (or older, in some cases) taxable at special rates. For further discussion of these and other income tax provisions, see the companion text, Lathrope, Yamamoto & McNulty, Federal Income Taxation of Individuals (9th ed. 2023).

The Economic Growth and Tax Relief Reconciliation Act of 2001, P.L. 107–16 (the "2001 Act"), as amended in 2010, reduced the top marginal rate from its pre-2001 level of 55% to 45% in 2007 and then to 35% in 2010. At the same time the exemption equivalent increased dramatically, reaching $1 million in 2002, $3.5 million in 2009, and $5 million in 2010; moreover, the $5 million figure was indexed for inflation beginning in 2012.* Legislation enacted in 2012 set the top marginal rate at 40%. Subsequent legislation raised the exemption equivalent to $10 million (indexed for inflation) for decedents dying (and gifts made) after 2017 and then to $15 million (indexed for inflation) for decedents dying (and gifts made) after 2025. As a result, under present law, the gift and estate taxes are imposed at a flat rate of 40% on cumulative taxable transfers, whether made during life or at death, in excess of the inflation-indexed $15 million exemption equivalent.**

In its original form, the 2001 Act called for the repeal of the estate tax (but not the gift tax) and introduced a modified carryover basis regime to replace the traditional fresh-start basis rules for testamentary transfers. Although these changes were scheduled to take effect in 2010, the 2010 legislation retroactively reinstated the estate tax (with a top marginal rate of 35% and an exemption equivalent of $5 million) along with the fresh-start

---

* For gift tax purposes, the exemption equivalent was frozen at $1 million from 2002 through 2010, but this disparity ended in 2011 and the exemption equivalent is now the same for both gift and estate tax purposes.

** When a married decedent fails to exhaust his or her exemption equivalent, the decedent's executor may elect to pass on the unused amount to the surviving spouse to be added to the spouse's own exemption equivalent. This "portability" provision, which applies to decedents dying in 2011 or later years, offers married couples considerable flexibility in tax planning and reduces the need for "credit shelter" bequests and lifetime gifts to avoid wasting the unified credit.

basis rules and made the carryover-basis-without-estate-tax provisions optional for decedents dying in 2010. Accordingly, the executor of a decedent who died in 2010 could opt out of the estate tax and accept the carryover basis regime set forth in former I.R.C. § 1022. Under that provision, property passing from a decedent generally took a basis in the recipient's hands equal to the lesser of the decedent's basis or the value of the property at death. Nevertheless, in the case of appreciated property owned by the decedent at death, the statute allowed a tax-free basis increase of up to $1.3 million, regardless of the relationship (if any) between the decedent and the recipient, as well as a separate basis increase of up to $3 million for property passing in qualifying form to the decedent's surviving spouse. For very large estates, the ability to avoid an immediate estate tax, even at the cost of foregoing a fresh-start basis, provided substantial tax savings. For most estates of small or moderate size, however, the advantages of a $5 million exemption equivalent coupled with an unlimited basis step-up for appreciated property proved irresistible. One way or another, the vast bulk of property passing from decedents in 2010 emerged undiminished by any immediate estate or income tax liability. The optional carryover-basis-without-estate-tax provisions applied only to decedents dying in 2010 and are not available for decedents dying in subsequent years. Under present law, property acquired from a decedent generally takes a fresh-start basis in the recipient's hands under I.R.C. § 1014.

The 2001 Act also brought major changes in the design of state death taxes. The federal estate tax credit for state death taxes, originally enacted in 1924, provided a powerful incentive for states to impose "pick-up" or "sponge" taxes equal to the maximum allowable credit, and by 2001 all of them had done so. The 2001 Act phased out the credit and replaced it with a deduction for state death taxes beginning in 2005. This change removed the underpinning for the longstanding system of pick-up taxes and forced many states to choose between reconfiguring their existing death taxes and abandoning them altogether.

Despite years of turmoil following the 2001 Act, the federal estate, gift, and GST taxes have proved remarkably resilient. Legislative wrangling over rates and exemptions is likely to continue for years to come, but the prospect of major structural reform or outright repeal remains as nebulous as ever. In the meantime, the primary focus of this book is on the structure and operation of the taxes as they exist under present law.

§ 3 REVENUE AND OTHER ROLES OF THE TRANSFER TAXES

The federal estate and gift taxes do not raise very large amounts of revenue now, nor have they ever done so. In fiscal year 2024, they accounted for about $32 billion, or less than one percent of federal budget receipts, a smaller percentage by far than the corresponding figures for the individual income tax (48.7%), the corporate income tax (11.6%), the employment or payroll taxes (36.3%), or even the excise taxes (1.59%). Rates are low and exemptions are high, and, as a result, the vast majority of people are not subject to federal estate or gift taxes; among those who are taxable, many pay relatively small amounts in tax.

The transfer taxes were not enacted merely to raise revenue. In part they are designed to prevent people from accumulating large blocks of wealth and then transmitting those blocks undiminished from generation to generation. Also, these taxes make an important contribution to the progressivity of the entire tax system. Wealth and high income are closely associated, and estate and gift taxes mainly affect families with relatively high annual incomes.

For taxpayers whom the transfer taxes do affect, the impact can be great, so the prospect of these taxes looms large for such taxpayers and their lawyers. The transfer taxes, as presently structured, offer enormous opportunities for planning. Several features of the taxes can produce erratic results; often the taxes can be legally and easily avoided or drastically reduced by steps (such as regular annual gifts to children) that are perfectly acceptable on non-tax grounds. For society at large and for the finance of government, reform and revitalization of these taxes pose significant and difficult issues of revenue collection, economic efficiency, and equitable distribution of benefits and burdens.

§ 4 INTRODUCTION TO THE ESTATE TAX

As with all other taxes, the basic computation of the estate tax takes this form: the *tax payable* equals the tax *rate* times the tax *base*, minus *credits* (if any). The difficulty comes, for the most part, in determining the tax base.

Under the estate tax, the beginning point for determining the tax *base* is a concept labeled the *gross estate* (see I.R.C. § 2031). From the gross estate are subtracted allowable *deductions* to determine the *taxable estate* (see I.R.C. § 2051), to which the tax *rates* must be applied (see I.R.C. § 2001).

The *gross estate* includes, at a minimum, the value of all property owned by the decedent at death which passes to someone else by will or intestacy. The gross estate includes more than this, however. It also includes some life insurance proceeds and some jointly-owned property. It may even include some property given away by the decedent during life but treated by the law as if retained until death. So the *gross estate* for tax purposes is not the same as the "probate estate" under state law or an individual's "wealth" or "estate" in common usage.

Once the gross estate has been determined, allowable *deductions* may be taken to arrive at the *taxable estate.* See I.R.C. §§ 2051–2058. Such deductions include allowances for transfers to a surviving spouse (*marital deduction*), contributions to charity (*charitable deduction*), and certain *debts* and *expenses.* After subtracting these items from the gross estate, the *taxable estate* (if any) remains.

Statutory, graduated rates apply against the sum of the taxable estate and all post-1976 taxable gifts not included in the gross estate, to determine a "tentative tax." From this amount are subtracted the taxes already paid on those lifetime gifts, as well as any allowable *credits* (including the immensely important *unified credit,* which can be likened to an exemption) to arrive at the actual *tax payable.* See I.R.C. §§ 2001 and 2010–2015.

Prior to 1977, the rate of estate tax was not affected by the amount or number of transfers made during life, unless those transfers were drawn back into the gross estate and treated as transfers made at death. See Chapters 3 and 5, *infra.* That is, there were two separate trips up the graduated rate schedules, once for cumulative lifetime gifts, and once for the taxable estate at death. Now, for decedents dying after 1976, the taxable estate is cumulated with post-1976 gifts, thus exposing it to progressively higher rates as a function of the *total* amount of post-1976 taxable transfers. Thus, in effect, the taxable estate is treated as one final gift occurring at death. This is one aspect of the "unified" estate and gift tax system.

§ 5 INTRODUCTION TO THE GIFT TAX

The gift tax is a companion tax to the estate tax. For pre-1977 gifts, its rates were lower, three-quarters of the estate tax rates. Now its rates are the same as those of the estate tax, and this is a second aspect of the 1976 "unification" of the two taxes. See I.R.C. § 2502. The gift tax applies to all gratuitous transfers of property made during life, since such transfers serve to reduce the estate subject to the estate tax at death. See I.R.C. §§ 2501 and 2511. However, the two taxes do not fit together perfectly. As a result, some lifetime transfers that were subject to the gift tax are nevertheless includable in the gross estate, but for gifts made before 1977, a credit for gift taxes paid attempts to eliminate any actual "double tax." See I.R.C. § 2012. For post-1976 gifts, this credit is inapplicable, since the gift taxes imposed on lifetime gifts are automatically taken into account in the unified estate tax computation. See I.R.C. § 2001(b)(2). Other overlaps, gaps or conflicts may arise from the lack of complete "integration" of the two taxes.

The gift tax is imposed and reported on a calendar-year basis and the appropriate tax rate is applied to the total taxable gifts made during each year. Each year's taxable gifts are cumulated with taxable gifts made in prior years and are taxed at progressively higher marginal rates under the graduated rate schedule. This system is explained more fully below.

Each year, a donor (any individual) is entitled to an *annual exclusion* for gifts in amounts up to $10,000 (indexed for inflation, $19,000 in 2026) to *each* donee, without limitation as to the total number of donees. See I.R.C. § 2503(b). A separate exclusion is allowed for unlimited amounts paid on behalf of a donee directly to an educational institution for tuition or to a health care provider for medical expenses. See I.R.C. § 2503(e). Only when the donor gives more than the excludable amount to a donee in one year will the gift be taxable. Even then no tax may be payable because the donor may use up part (or all) of the available *unified credit* against any tax otherwise due. See I.R.C. § 2505. Once the available exclusions and the unified credit are exhausted, any additional gifts are fully taxable. The tax liability is determined by cumulating all prior taxable gifts, adding the current year's taxable gifts, applying the graduated rates to this total, and subtracting from this "tentative tax" the taxes attributable to the prior taxable gifts. The result is the tax on the current year's taxable gifts. See I.R.C. §§ 2502 and 2504. Accordingly, except for changes in value over time, and apart from annual exclusions, the amount of gift tax payable on a donor's lifetime transfers will be the same whether the gifts are all made at one time or are spread out over many years. The timing of the tax may vary, however, and that may represent an important planning consideration.

For a given year, the gift tax *base* consists of gross transfers or *aggregate gifts* minus allowable *exclusions* and *deductions* (see I.R.C. §§ 2522–2524) to arrive at *taxable gifts* (see I.R.C. § 2503), against which tax *rates* are applied in the cumulative manner described above. The result is the current year's gift tax liability, which is reduced by any remaining portion of the donor's *unified credit* to arrive at the tax actually payable.

§ 6 INTRODUCTION TO THE GENERATION-SKIPPING TRANSFER TAX

The gift and estate taxes apply to gratuitous *transfers* of property. Holding a life estate, which expires at the holder's death, therefore causes no additional tax burden on the deceased holder's estate, since there is no transfer of property by the decedent—nothing "passes" at death from the decedent to any other person. The remainder interest which does then accrue to the next successive taker is treated as "passing" directly from the original grantor, where it was of course taxed, and not through the estate of the deceased life tenant. (See § 16, *infra.*) Thus, for example, a gift (whether inter vivos or testamentary) by a grandparent of property in trust, with income to a child for life, remainder to grandchild, would be taxed as a gratuitous transfer by the grandparent, but the shift in possession of the property to the grandchild at the child's death would occasion no further gift or estate tax.

This general rule, that interests terminating at death do not produce an estate tax, is the basis of much estate planning. The disposition illustrated in the example above accomplishes what is known as "generation skipping," and has been a source of some controversy in connection with proposals for reform of the estate tax.

By careful use of this slack in the gift and estate taxes, substantial tax savings could be accomplished. For this purpose, one might compare the taxes that would be paid if property were transferred outright through several generations with the tax savings that could be accomplished by creating a trust with successive beneficial interests. For example, a grandparent could transfer property in trust to pay income to a child for life, with the child as trustee. In addition, the child could be given a non-general testamentary power of appointment over the property. (See § 45, *infra.*) To that could be added a non-general lifetime power of appointment. In addition, the child could be given a power to invade the corpus of the trust to the extent necessary for the child's health, education, maintenance, or support. Moreover, the child could be given the power to withdraw up to $5,000 or 5% of the corpus per year, whichever is greater, and that power, if it remained unexercised, would not cause the child to be treated as the owner of the property for transfer tax purposes. If another trustee were appointed to act with the child, the other trustee could be given a power to invade the trust still further for the child's benefit.

Although the child would have nearly the equivalent of outright ownership of the property, no estate tax would be imposed when the property passed on to other beneficiaries at the child's death. Still further, the trust could provide that at the child's death the property would pass to a grandchild and then to a great-grandchild with powers similar to those held by the child. In each case, after the grandparent's initial transfer in trust, the property could pass from one generation to another without any further transfer taxes, as long as the interest held by each generation did not exceed those described. Subject only to state law limitations (e.g., a rule against perpetuities), this kind of generation-skipping disposition could go on indefinitely. Even under those rules, the kind of outright transfer that would trigger a transfer tax usually could be postponed for a period ranging anywhere from 50 to 150 years. In a sense, then, a wealthy family could choose whether to pay the tax or not, because the dispositions of property that could be made without payment of the tax would often suffice for family financial purposes.

Allowing the use and enjoyment of large amounts of property to pass to successive generations free of transfer taxes undermines the goal of uniformity in the operation of the taxing system. From a revenue-raising point of view, reasonably periodic collection of taxes is desirable. Also, horizontal equity (as between estates of the same size) demands that *all* such estates be taxed with the same frequency, and therefore that the timing of the imposition of the tax not depend on the *form* of the donor's gift (in trust versus outright), since then the donor in effect could choose whether or not to subject the property to further transfer taxes. In addition, although all donors theoretically have similar choices, actually only very large estates can afford to use generation-skipping trusts, since the income alone of smaller estates often is not sufficient for the needs of the "skipped" generation. Vertical equity, therefore, demands that the progressivity of the transfer tax rates not be defeated by a device available only to the very wealthy. Still another undesirable effect of pre-1977 law was that many transfers in trust were motivated solely by tax considerations. Ideally, however, the tax law should be "neutral" and should not influence primary activities in an unintended manner. People should not be "forced" or induced to alter their own dispositive plans because of a taxing system which provides more favorable treatment for certain types of transfers than for other similar types (unless, perhaps, there is a conscious public policy to encourage the favored type of transfer).

One way of dealing with the kind of generation-skipping transfer described above would be to impose an additional tax on the original transfer (by the grandparent, in the example). Another possibility would be to impose a tax at the death of the skipped generation's representative (the child, in the example). Imposing a tax at that time would more nearly resemble the tax treatment of a non-generation-skipping disposition, one in which the grandparent made an outright gift of the property to the child who consumed the income but preserved the property intact and passed it on at death to the grandchild. Both of these approaches, as well as variations and combinations thereof, were elaborated in separate proposals put forward in the late 1960s by the Treasury Department and the American Law Institute. See U.S. Treasury Department, Tax Reform Studies and Proposals, House Comm. on Ways and Means, Senate Comm. on Finance, 91st Cong., 1st Sess. (1969); American Law Institute, Federal Estate and Gift Taxation: Recommendations and Reporters' Studies (1969).

The proposals of the Treasury Department and the American Law Institute laid the groundwork for the tax on generation-skipping transfers, which was initially enacted in 1976 and was then completely rewritten in 1986. The GST tax appears in Chapter 13 of the Internal Revenue Code (I.R.C. §§ 2601–2663). This supplementary tax is entirely separate from the gift and estate taxes, and is implemented via a multitude of specially defined terms and concepts.

The GST tax is imposed on "generation-skipping transfers" which, subject to important exceptions, are transfers of property made by a transferor to a transferee who is two or more generations younger (a "skip person") without incurring gift or estate tax at the intervening generation(s). See I.R.C. §§ 2601, 2611–2613, and 2651.

To be subject to tax, a transfer must fit within one of the three defined types of generation-skipping transfers: (1) a "direct skip" (a transfer, either outright or in trust, that is subject to estate or gift tax and is made to a skip person); (2) a "taxable distribution" (a distribution of trust income or corpus to a skip person); or (3) a "taxable termination" (a shift to a skip person of the beneficial enjoyment of property held in trust). For example, a gift or bequest from a grandparent to a grandchild is a direct skip. If the grandparent creates a trust to pay income to a child for life with remainder to a grandchild, a distribution of trust income or corpus to the grandchild during the child's life is a taxable distribution; at the child's death, a taxable termination will occur with respect to any property remaining in the trust. See I.R.C. § 2612.

The GST tax is aimed at removing incentives to make gifts and bequests to persons more than one generation removed from the transferor in a manner that avoids estate and gift taxation of the transferred property in the intervening generations. In some ways, the GST tax actually creates incentives for transferors to ensure that property *will* be subject to estate or gift tax in the intervening generations.

Though closely linked to the estate and gift taxes, the GST tax operates separately from—and in important respects differently from—those taxes. The GST tax is a flat tax; its rate is fixed for *all* taxpayers at the highest marginal estate tax rate (40% since 2013). See I.R.C. § 2641. Unlike the estate and gift taxes, the GST tax does not make use of the unified credit. Instead, each transferor is allowed a special exemption which shelters up to $15 million of property transferred either in the form of direct skips or in generation-skipping trusts having skip persons as beneficiaries. See I.R.C. § 2631. The amount of the GST exemption is equal to the amount sheltered from the estate and gift taxes by the unified credit; since 2012, both exemptions have been indexed for inflation.

Many lifetime transfers that are excluded from gift tax under I.R.C. § 2503 are also exempt from GST tax. For example, a grandparent can make direct payments for a grandchild's tuition or medical care without incurring any tax if the payments come within the gift tax exclusion of § 2503(e). Finally, transfers to individuals *more than* two generations removed from the transferor are subject to only one application of the GST tax. (Thus, a transferor pays the same tax on a direct skip to a great-grandchild as on a direct skip to a grandchild.)

This complex system will be described in more detail (and perhaps with greater comprehensibility) in later chapters. See especially § 15, *infra.*

§ 7 REPORTING AND PAYMENT OF THE TAXES

The most important requirement is that an *estate tax return* (Form 706) must be filed within nine months after the decedent's death, if any return is required. I.R.C. § 6075. Payment of tax normally is due with the return. I.R.C. § 6151. An extension of time for filing the return can sometimes be obtained for a period up to six months (I.R.C. § 6081), and an extension of time for payment of tax of up to twelve months (I.R.C. § 6161), or sometimes up to fourteen years if more than 35% of the decedent's adjusted gross estate consists of an interest in a closely-held business (I.R.C. § 6166). I.R.C. § 6018 requires that a return be filed in any instance when the gross estate of a U.S. citizen or resident exceeds the amount sheltered from estate tax by the decedent's remaining, unused unified credit. (See § 72, *infra.*) If the decedent was a nonresident and non-citizen, a return (Form 706 or 706NA) must be filed if that part of the gross estate situated in the United States exceeds $60,000 reduced by certain lifetime gifts. I.R.C. § 6018. As a consequence of these rules and the exemptions they contain, a return need not be filed for every decedent. Furthermore, not every estate that is required to file a return will owe any tax; in 2023, only a small number of decedents, fewer than two in a thousand, incurred any federal estate tax liability.

A *gift tax return* must be filed by any U.S. citizen or resident who in any calendar year makes a gift of property that is not fully covered by the gift tax exclusions of § 2503, the charitable deduction of § 2522, or the marital deduction of § 2523. See I.R.C. § 6019. Thus, a return must be filed if the donor makes any taxable gifts, even if no gift tax is actually payable as a result of the unified credit. (Even if there are no taxable gifts, the donor may have to file a gift tax return in order to elect gift-splitting treatment under § 2513 or to claim a marital deduction for qualified terminable interest property under § 2523(f).) Gift tax returns normally must be filed before April 15 following the close of the calendar year of the reportable gift. I.R.C. § 6075(b). An extension of up to six months may be granted under § 6081.

The tax, if any, is due with the return. I.R.C. § 6151. Extensions sometimes can be obtained. See I.R.C. § 6161. For further details about filing the returns and paying the taxes, see Chapter 14, *infra*.

With regard to the GST tax, I.R.C. § 2662 specifically authorizes the promulgation of Treasury regulations specifying the person who must file the return and the time of filing. The regulations provide generally that the return must be filed by the party primarily liable for the tax under § 2603, i.e., the distributee in the case of a taxable distribution, the trustee in the case of a taxable termination or a direct skip from a trust, or the transferor (or his executor) in the case of any other direct skip. In the case of a direct skip, the regulations require that the return be filed on or before the date on which an estate or gift tax return is due in connection with the transfer. Filings for other generation-skipping transfers normally are to be made by April 15 following the close of the calendar year of the transfer. See Reg. § 26.2662–1.

§ 8 LEGISLATION AND THE LEGISLATIVE PROCESS

Although the federal estate, gift, and GST tax laws are not altered as frequently as is the income tax, legislative changes must be expected from time to time. Congressional action traditionally results from Presidential recommendations, filtered through the Treasury Department, though sometimes the initial proposals come from within Congress itself.

In Congress, the legislative process begins with a hearing before the Committee on Ways and Means of the House of Representatives, because the Constitution requires all revenue legislation to originate in the House of Representatives. (As a practical matter, important legislation can begin in the Senate where it may be attached to a revenue bill as an amendment, after which House action and Conference Committee action would have to follow.) At the Ways and Means Committee hearing, the President's proposals are presented by officials of the Treasury Department. Representatives of various private and public groups also appear to present their views of the proposed legislation. Eventually, a tax bill and a committee report are reported to the House of Representatives. There the bill is debated and possibly passed in some form by the House. Next, similar hearings are begun in the Committee on Finance of the Senate, which considers the House bill. Eventually, the House bill, as amended by the Senate committee, and a Senate committee report are brought to the floor of the Senate. If passed by the Senate, the bill with Senate amendments goes to a Conference Committee of the House and Senate which irons out the differences between the two legislative chambers. The action of the Conference Committee is reported in a Conference Report, which then is usually approved by the House and the Senate. The legislation then goes to the President for approval or veto. These various processes, and others that fill the gaps, provide rich legislative history for a tax lawyer or judge to use in understanding and interpreting the legislation.

§ 9 ADMINISTRATION AND THE ADMINISTRATIVE PROCESS

Revenue laws are administered under the Treasury Department by the Internal Revenue Service (I.R.S.), an agency headed by the Commissioner of Internal Revenue. The principal office of the I.R.S. is in Washington, D.C., but there is a field office in most cities of substantial size throughout the country. (The Treasury Department is mainly responsible for tax policy within the government; the Commissioner, appointed by the

President, is delegated the task of assessing and collecting federal taxes.)

For many years the I.R.S. was organized based on a structure of national, regional and district offices. The national territory was divided into regions, and each region was in turn divided into districts, with each district office having primary responsibility for taxpayers within its jurisdiction. Under the Internal Revenue Service Restructuring and Reform Act of 1998, P.L. 105–206, the I.R.S. was reorganized into four operating divisions, and the division known as "Small Business/Self-Employed" was given jurisdiction over estate and gift tax returns throughout the country. (The other three divisions are called "Large Business and International," "Wage and Investment," and "Tax Exempt and Government Entities.") The basic examination and audit functions, however, are still conducted in much the same way as before the reorganization. In the event a tax return is examined or becomes the subject of an audit, a conference will be held with an I.R.S. Revenue Agent or Estate Tax Examiner in a field or office audit or other inquiry. Later, if agreement cannot be reached, disputed items can be reviewed with an Appeals Officer. If the dispute has not been settled by then, it is necessary to "go to law." (See § 10, *infra.*)

Many disputes between the taxpayer and the Internal Revenue Service never reach litigation in court, as a result of procedures by which I.R.S. representatives and the taxpayer may discuss and settle the controversy administratively. When a tax return is first filed with the appropriate I.R.S. Service Center, it is checked for form, execution and mathematical accuracy. The return is then screened by computer, using the "discriminant inventory function system" and other techniques to identify returns with a high probability of error. The I.R.S. uses this screening process to decide which returns will ultimately be selected for audit. The return may be audited either in the local I.R.S. office (an "office audit") or at the taxpayer's premises (a "field audit"). During and after the audit, opportunities exist for the controversy to be settled or dropped as part of the administrative process. If the taxpayer so requests, the case will be referred to the Appeals Office, which will afford the taxpayer an opportunity for a conference. The determination by the Appeals Office is final, so far as the administrative appeal process within the Service is concerned. After the I.R.S. issues a notice of deficiency, the taxpayer may petition the Tax Court for review, or pay the tax. If the tax is paid, the taxpayer may still file a claim for refund and eventually go to court. (See § 10, *infra*.)

Administrative interpretations of the tax laws are reported in general rules and policies announced by the Treasury Department and also are reflected in the administrative practices and litigation practices of the I.R.S. with respect to individual tax returns. The most important form of general administrative guidance is that made by the Treasury Department in the form of Treasury regulations, specifically "Estate Tax Regulations" and "Gift Tax Regulations," authorized by Congress in I.R.C. § 7805. In addition, I.R.C. § 2663 specifically authorizes regulations to be promulgated to implement the purposes of the GST tax. When a regulation is promulgated or amended, the text of the regulation, along with an explanatory preamble, is issued as a "Treasury Decision" (abbreviated "T.D.").

Treasury regulations are presumed to be valid; occasionally, however, a court may invalidate a regulation as unreasonable, unauthorized, or inconsistent with law. These regulations appear in the publication entitled "Internal Revenue Bulletin" (I.R.B.), as well as in the Code of Federal Regulations (C.F.R.) and the Federal Register (Fed.Reg.). Other authoritative pronouncements on tax law also appear in several forms in the Internal Revenue Bulletin—Treasury Decisions, Proposed Regulations, Revenue Rulings, and Revenue Procedures.

Some, but not all, revenue rulings are published by the Internal Revenue Service. These rulings amount to decisions on given facts which usually involve a problem that is likely to recur frequently. Generally such rulings are issued pursuant to a request for a ruling by a particular (unnamed) taxpayer on an uncertain or difficult point of interpretation. Published rulings are referred to as Revenue Rulings (Rev. Rul.) and are cited "2026–1," the first number referring to the year of the ruling and the second number designating the ruling number for that year. Not all rulings are published; "private letter rulings" and "technical advice memoranda," issued in response to requests from taxpayers or from I.R.S. offices, reach the light of day, if at all, only in privately published compilations or if disclosure is obtained by request or demand. I.R.C. § 6110 now provides for public inspection of I.R.S. "written determinations" (including private letter rulings and technical advice memoranda, as well as "chief counsel advice"), with a few exceptions.

Regulations and revenue rulings are binding on the Internal Revenue Service and are followed by the I.R.S. in handling particular controversies and cases. Published rulings are applied retroactively unless they explicitly state to the contrary, and they can be revoked retroactively, unless doing so is held to be an abuse of discretion. See I.R.C. § 7805(b)(8). A private letter ruling ordinarily will not be revoked or modified retroactively as to the particular taxpayer to whom it was issued or as to someone else directly involved.

The I.R.S. sometimes publishes a notice of "acquiescence" or "non-acquiescence" when it loses a case in the Tax Court, in order to indicate whether the Service will accept that case as authority in the future or not. Also, in some revenue rulings the Service lets it be known whether or not it will follow a decision or line of cases in a federal Circuit Court of Appeals as to other taxpayers or other years.

§ 10 JUDICIAL PROCESS AND PROCEDURE

If proceedings are carried beyond the administrative stage and into the courts, the taxpayer has a choice of tribunals. He or she may choose not to pay the tax deficiency (in which event interest will accrue at a statutorily determined rate) and to petition the United States Tax Court for redetermination of the deficiency. Or, the taxpayer may pay the tax and file a claim for refund, after adverse action on which he or she may then sue for a refund in the federal District Court or in the Court of Federal Claims. In the District Court, the taxpayer may request a trial by jury. In the Tax Court or in the Court of Federal Claims, the case will be heard by a judge without a jury. From the Tax Court or the District Court, the case may be appealed to the appropriate Circuit Court of Appeals; appeals from the Court of Federal Claims lie to the Court of Appeals for the Federal Circuit. From there, review may ultimately be sought in the United States Supreme Court.

The Tax Court (formerly known as the Board of Tax Appeals) was once technically an agency in the executive branch of the government. As a result of 1969 legislation, it now has the standing of an "Article I Court" under the Legislative Article of the United States Constitution. It handles appeals from deficiencies in tax which have been determined by the Commissioner. It does not have jurisdiction over refund cases. (But, in a deficiency case the Tax Court may order a refund as the proper remedy in the proceeding.) The Tax Court now follows Court of Appeals precedents in cases that would be appealed to that Court of Appeals. See Golsen v. Commissioner, 54 T.C. 742 (1970). The "regular" and "court reviewed" decisions of the Tax Court are reported in the official Tax Court Reports, but its "memorandum" decisions are published only in unofficial form by the tax services. An informal procedure is available in the Tax Court for cases involving small amounts.

§ 11 SUPPLEMENTARY MATERIALS

The main sources of law and interpretation of the law are the federal estate, gift, and GST tax statutes themselves and the Treasury regulations thereunder as well as reports of cases decided by the Tax Court, the Circuit Courts of Appeals, and other federal courts. Revenue rulings issued by the I.R.S. also provide helpful guidance and analysis. In addition, there are several useful books and treatises concerning the federal estate and gift taxes.

These include Bittker & Lokken, Federal Taxation of Income, Estates and Gifts, Vol. 5 (2d ed. 1993 & Supp.); Harrington, Plaine, Kwon & Zaritsky, Generation-Skipping Transfer Tax (2d ed. 2001 & Supp.); and Stephens, Maxfield, Lind & Calfee, Federal Estate and Gift Taxation (9th ed. 2013 & Supp.).

A fine set of essays on succession law and transfer taxation is collected in a volume entitled Death, Taxes and Family Property (Halbach ed., 1977).

Perspectives on the economics of transfer taxation are collected in Rethinking Estate and Gift Taxation (Gale, Hines & Slemrod eds., 2001), and in Does Atlas Shrug? The Economic Consequences of Taxing the Rich (Slemrod ed., 2000). For a provocative and insightful analysis of the political controversy surrounding the taxation of inherited wealth, see Graetz & Shapiro, Death by a Thousand Cuts (2005).

Numerous articles published in law reviews and professional journals address various practical and theoretical aspects of the transfer taxes. In addition, digests and analysis of cases and rulings under the estate and gift tax laws are available through various on-line data bases.

§ 12 CONSTITUTIONALITY OF THE TRANSFER TAXES

The constitutionality of the early federal "death duty" was tested in Knowlton v. Moore, 178 U.S. 41 (1900) and the (then inheritance) tax was upheld as an excise tax, not a direct tax, valid despite its progressive rates. The present federal estate tax was upheld in New York Trust Co. v. Eisner, 256 U.S. 345 (1921), again as an indirect tax not subject to the apportionment requirement for federal direct taxes. The tax also was held to comply with the requirement of Art. I, § 8 of the Constitution that taxes be uniform throughout the United States.

Because the estate tax is an excise tax on a transfer of property, not a direct tax on the property itself (however thin the line between these two categories, especially when the excise tax is geared to the value of the property transferred), the tax can apply to a transfer of property that itself might be exempt from federal tax. So, state and local municipal bonds, whose interest is free from income tax, can be included in the base of the estate tax. Similarly, property that is exempt by federal statute from direct tax (e.g., certain federal housing agency bonds) may nevertheless give rise to estate (or gift) tax liability.

See United States v. Wells Fargo Bank, 485 U.S. 351 (1988). Foreign real estate may be included in the base of the transfer taxes without constitutional objection.

The federal gift tax was held to be constitutional in Bromley v. McCaughn, 280 U.S. 124 (1929), over arguments based on the apportionment clause, the uniformity requirement, and the due process clause.

There is no reported case challenging the constitutionality of the GST tax. The federal estate and gift tax precedents cited above would appear to protect this more recent transfer tax from constitutional attack.

When the estate and gift taxes first appeared, questions of unconstitutional retroactivity often presented themselves if a tax was levied on a transfer made before the tax was enacted. Such taxpayer objections, based on the due process clause, were successful in a few early cases. See Nichols v. Coolidge, 274 U.S. 531 (1927) (estate tax); Untermyer v. Anderson, 276 U.S. 440 (1928) (gift tax). More recently, however, the Supreme Court has announced a more lenient standard, requiring only "a legitimate legislative purpose furthered by rational means." United States v. Carlton, 512 U.S. 26 (1994). Accordingly, some degree of retroactivity, in the form of increased rates or technical modifications, is constitutionally permissible. See Milliken v. United States, 283 U.S. 15 (1931); NationsBank of Texas, N.A. v. United States, 269 F.3d 1332 (Fed.Cir. 2001), cert. den., 537 U.S. 813 (2002). Sometimes difficult questions arise about which event is the key one for determining whether a new tax rule is retroactive, when some events preceded its enactment and others occurred later. See United States v. Jacobs, 306 U.S. 363 (1939); United States v. Irvine, 511 U.S. 224 (1994).

The gift tax explicitly applies only to post-enactment gifts. I.R.C. § 2502(c). In contrast, the estate tax contains a general rule looking in the direction of retroactivity. I.R.C. § 2045.

The GST tax contains very specific effective date provisions. The original GST tax enacted in 1976 has been repealed retroactively. The revised GST tax enacted in 1986 generally applies to transfers made after October 22, 1986, but this general rule is subject to some rather significant exceptions. See Tax Reform Act of 1986, P.L. 99–514, § 1433(b); Reg. § 26.2601–1.

CHAPTER 2

THE FEDERAL ESTATE, GIFT, AND GENERATION-SKIPPING TRANSFER TAX LAWS IN OUTLINE

§ 13 OUTLINE OF THE ESTATE TAX

The federal estate tax occupies a small number of sections of the Internal Revenue Code of 1986. The estate tax is the lineal descendant of the 1916 legislation which in turn became a portion of the 1939 Internal Revenue Code and later the Internal Revenue Code of 1954. The estate tax begins with I.R.C. § 2001, which sets forth the method of computation and rates of tax. Perhaps better starting points, however, are §§ 2031 and 2033.

Section 2031 provides that the value of the gross estate of the decedent shall be determined by including "the value at the time of his death of all property, real or personal, tangible or intangible, wherever situated." Section 2033 makes it clear that the value of the gross estate shall include the value of "all property"—to the extent of any interest in that property held by the decedent at the time of death.

Section 2032 provides for an alternate valuation date. Under this section, the executor may elect to value the property included in the gross estate as of a date *six months after* the decedent's death (or, in the case of property already sold or otherwise disposed of by the estate, at the date of disposition), instead of at the date of death. Real property used in a farm or a closely held business may be eligible for "special use" valuation under § 2032A. (Valuation will be covered in greater detail in Chapter 10, *infra.*)

Under § 2034, the value of the gross estate includes all of the property of the decedent *without* any reduction for an interest in the nature of dower or curtesy or a statutory elective share in favor of a surviving spouse.

These basic sections defining the *gross estate* of the decedent are supplemented by additional sections which provide for the inclusion of some property interests held by the decedent at death and also for the inclusion of some property interests transferred before death, transfers which are treated for estate tax purposes as substitutes for testamentary dispositions. As a result of these latter sections, the *gross estate* may exceed the wealth actually held by the decedent at the time of his death. For example, § 2040 provides that in some cases jointly-owned property will be taxed in the estate of the first of the joint owners to die.

Under § 2035, the gross estate includes the value of some property that was gratuitously transferred by the decedent within three years of death.

Sections 2036(a)(2) and 2038 deal with interests gratuitously transferred by the decedent in trust or otherwise during life subject to retained powers to alter or amend or revoke the transfer. If the decedent retained any of the specified powers, the property is includable in his gross estate at death. Under § 2036(a)(1) a similar rule applies to property gratuitously transferred by the decedent during life if he retained a life estate in the property or a right to the income of the property for his life or for a period which does not in fact end before his death or which is not ascertainable without reference to his death. Again, such property is includable in the gross estate because of the retained interest.

Under § 2037, interests gratuitously transferred by the decedent during life but taking effect at death are includable in the gross estate if the decedent retained a reversionary interest of more than a minimal value.

Section 2042 provides that the gross estate will include the proceeds of insurance on the decedent's life—but only if the proceeds are receivable by the executor *or* if the decedent at his death possessed any of the incidents of ownership of the life insurance.

Section 2039 provides that the decedent's gross estate includes the value of an annuity or other payment receivable by a surviving beneficiary under a contract or agreement if the decedent had the right to receive an annuity or other payment for his life or for a period which does not in fact end before his death or which is not ascertainable without reference to his death.

Under § 2041, property over which the decedent had a general power of appointment, as defined in the statute, is includable in the gross estate even if the power was not actually exercised and thus terminated at death.

Section 2043 deals with the problem of defining transfers made for insufficient consideration. In particular, § 2043(b) provides that marital property rights relinquished by a spouse shall not be considered to be consideration "in money or money's worth" for purposes of the estate tax, except in the case of property settlement agreements entered into within a few years of a divorce.

The tax rates set forth in I.R.C. § 2001 are applied against the *taxable estate* of every decedent who was a citizen or resident of the United States. The *taxable estate* is defined by § 2051 to consist of the *gross estate,* as defined by §§ 2031 and 2033 and the other inclusion sections, minus allowable *deductions.* The *deductions* are set forth in §§ 2053 through 2058. Section 2053 allows deductions for funeral and administrative expenses, claims against the estate, and unpaid mortgages or other indebtedness in respect of property included in the gross estate. Section 2054 provides a deduction for uncompensated casualty or theft losses arising during settlement of the estate. Section 2055 allows a deduction for transfers made for public, charitable and religious uses. Section 2056 grants an unlimited deduction for qualified transfers to a surviving spouse. Section 2058 allows a deduction for state death taxes, replacing the credit for such taxes formerly provided in § 2011.

After the *taxable estate* has been determined by subtracting deductions from the *gross estate,* the tax is determined by applying the rates and computation method of I.R.C. § 2001 to the base (i.e., the taxable estate). Prior to 1977, the rate of tax on the taxable estate was independent of the size and number of any inter vivos gifts the decedent had made. Under the unified rate schedule of § 2001, however, those prior gifts may push the taxable estate into progressively higher rate brackets, depending on their cumulative size.

There is no longer a separate trip up the rate schedule for the taxable estate at death. This result is achieved in a manner very like the cumulative computation of the gift tax. To the taxable estate are added all *adjusted taxable gifts,* defined in § 2001(b) as the decedent's taxable gifts made after 1976 and not otherwise included in the gross estate. (Only post-1976 gifts are cumulated under § 2001, so the 1976 "unification" of the gift and estate taxes operates only prospectively.) This grand cumulative total is then subjected to the rate schedule of § 2001(c), and the result is a "tentative tax," from which is subtracted a second tentative tax (using the same progressive rate schedule) on the decedent's post-1976 lifetime gifts.

The result is the estate's tax liability, which amounts to a tax on the value of the taxable estate, at the progressive rates reflecting not just the taxable estate but also the decedent's cumulative post-1976 taxable gifts. However, the amount thus ascertained is not the final tax liability, for certain *credits* are allowed against the tax otherwise payable. The *unified credit* provided in I.R.C. § 2010 eliminates the estate tax on taxable transfers up to an *applicable exclusion amount* (also known as the "exemption equivalent") which was set at $15 million in 2026 and is indexed for inflation. Credits are also allowed for gift taxes paid on pre-1977 gifts that are included in the gross estate (§ 2012), for estate tax paid on prior transfers (§ 2013), and for foreign death taxes (§ 2014). These credits are subtracted from the tax liability determined by applying the rates and computational mechanics of § 2001 against the taxable estate. The amount remaining after subtracting these credits is the tax that must actually be paid.

Income Tax Basis. For income tax purposes, I.R.C. § 1014(a) sets forth the basic "fresh-start" basis rule for property acquired from a decedent. Under this rule, the recipient of such property takes a basis equal to the fair market value of the property at the decedent's death. (Alternatively, if the executor elects to use the alternate valuation date under § 2032 or the special valuation method under § 2032A, the recipient's basis must be determined accordingly.) In other words, the recipient gets a basis that has a "fresh start" rather than a "carryover" basis determined by reference to the basis in the hands of the decedent. This rule applies for all property acquired by bequest, devise or inheritance, or by the decedent's estate from the decedent. See I.R.C. § 1014(b). It also applies to other property includable in the gross estate—for example, property that was transferred by the decedent during life but is drawn back into the gross estate because of retained strings, such as a life estate, power of revocation, etc. The fresh-start basis, a *higher* basis in the case of appreciated property with a fair market value exceeding its basis in the hands of the decedent, provides a loose linkage between the income and estate taxes and gives income tax basis for value included in the gross estate. In light of this understanding of the rule of § 1014, the next step becomes somewhat surprising.

If decedent and his or her spouse owned community property, one half of the property passes to the decedent's successors by will or intestacy at the decedent's death, and the other half belongs to the surviving spouse by virtue of community property law. The one-half share passing from the decedent takes a fresh-start basis in the recipient's hands, under the general rule discussed above. Under § 1014(b)(6), the surviving spouse's one-half share of the property also receives a fresh-start basis. Thus, for income tax purposes, both halves of the community property receive a fresh-start basis, even though only one half of the property is includable in the decedent's gross estate. Accordingly, if the decedent leaves his or her one-half share to the surviving spouse, the entire property takes a fair-market-value basis in the spouse's hands—even though no estate tax is payable at the decedent's death, due to the unlimited marital deduction. No comparable treatment is available for other forms of joint ownership (with or without right of survivorship), even though they may bear a close functional resemblance to community property.

Section § 1014(c) specifies that the fresh-start basis rule does *not* apply to property that constitutes a right to receive income in respect of a decedent under § 691.

Section 1014(e) blocks one device for improperly obtaining an advantageous fresh-start basis. If an owner of appreciated property transfers it to a person nearing death, with assurance that the imminent decedent will bequeath the property back to the original owner, § 1014(e) will fend off the § 1014(a) step-up if the first transfer occurs within one year before the decedent's death. Unless and until that period elapses, the death will result in retention of the property's old basis.

International Aspects. A decedent who was a U.S. citizen or resident is subject to estate tax on all property owned at death, wherever located (the "world-wide" estate). I.R.C. § 2031(a). If property is located in another country, or if the decedent was a citizen of another country, or if another country—applying its own rules of residency—treats the decedent as a resident of that country, some (or all) of the decedent's property may be subjected to estate tax or "capital transfer tax" by the other jurisdiction, as well as by the United States. Such "international double taxation" of a transfer can occur under the gift tax as well.

International double taxation is eliminated or ameliorated by two main devices. One is the statutory *credit* for foreign taxes, in I.R.C. § 2014. (Alternatively, the § 2053(d) *deduction* for foreign death taxes may provide some lesser relief.) The other main device consists of bilateral tax treaties between the United States and other countries, under which—typically—the country of citizenship (or domicile or residence) agrees to allow a tax credit (with some limitations) for foreign death taxes paid to the country of situs or source. The treaties define situs, and other key terms, in an effort to provide certainty and to fend off different or inconsistent applications of the treaty by the two countries. Some treaties provide a foreign tax credit of their own.

The United States has entered into transfer tax treaties with a number of countries, but with many more there is no treaty, and so the § 2014 foreign tax credit becomes the crucial source of relief from double taxation. That credit uses the "situs" rules of I.R.C. §§ 2104 and 2105 to determine the location of property in question. Sometimes both the § 2014 (statutory) credit and a treaty could apply. In that event, the taxpayer may choose the most favorable relief. (Usually any tax credit leaves in place the higher of the two competing death taxes.)

The United States also taxes non-resident aliens, but only on their property situated in the United States. See I.R.C. §§ 2103–2106. The estate of the non-resident alien decedent may be entitled to a credit or other relief in the country of citizenship (or domicile or residence) under a tax treaty or under internal, domestic law.

As to gift transfers by nonresident aliens, and some major exemptions, see I.R.C. §§ 2501(a) and 2511.

If a U.S. citizen expatriates (gives up citizenship and residence) to avoid U.S. estate tax, the trick won't necessarily work. Prior to 2008, I.R.C. § 2107 imposed U.S. estate tax on the estate of a nonresident alien who died within ten years after losing U.S. citizenship, subject to limited exceptions; similar rules applied for the gift and income taxes. See I.R.C. §§ 2501(a)(3) and 877. In 2008 Congress replaced the ten-year lookback rule with a completely different approach. Transfers made during life or at death by a "covered expatriate" are no longer subject to gift or estate tax. Instead, § 2801 imposes a tax on receipt by a U.S. citizen or resident of gifts and bequests from a covered expatriate, subject to a few limited exceptions. For income tax purposes, the covered expatriate is treated as selling all his or her property and realizing any built-in gain or loss at the time of expatriation. § 877A.

§ 14 OUTLINE OF THE GIFT TAX

The federal gift tax is set forth in a brief sequence of statutory provisions, beginning with I.R.C. § 2501. The brevity and occasional vagueness and incompleteness of these sections leaves much to be determined without the benefit of direct statutory command.

Section 2501(a) imposes a tax on the "transfer of property by gift" during the calendar year by any individual. Section 2511 goes further in providing that the tax imposed by § 2501 shall apply "whether the transfer is in trust or otherwise, whether the gift is direct or indirect, and whether the property is real or personal, tangible or intangible."

In general, the gift tax applies to any transfer made without consideration or an equivalent value received in return, without regard to the form of the transfer or the subjective intent of the parties. In other words, the common law requirement of donative intent is not a necessary element of a taxable gift for federal gift tax purposes. Thus, a transfer made without adequate consideration *in money or money's worth* will be taxable, except for business or arm's-length transfers, transactions required by or made under compulsion of law (such as alimony), and incomplete transfers (such as a revocable trust).

Section 2512 requires that the *valuation* of any gift be made at the date of the gift. When property is transferred for less than an adequate and full consideration in money or money's worth, the amount of the gift is the amount by which the value of the property transferred exceeds the value of the consideration received.

The method of computing the gift tax is set forth in § 2502. The rates are the same as the progressive estate tax rates of § 2001(c), and the tax is applied cumulatively to taxable gifts made over the donor's lifetime.

Every donor is allowed an *annual exclusion* for a specified amount of gifts made to each donee. See I.R.C. § 2503(b). The amount of the annual exclusion was set at $10,000 in 1981 and was indexed for inflation beginning in 1998; in 2026, it was $19,000. In addition, an unlimited exclusion is allowed for amounts paid on behalf of a donee directly to an educational institution for tuition payments, or to a health care provider for medical expenses, without regard to the relationship between donor and donee.

See I.R.C. § 2503(e). An unlimited *charitable deduction* is granted by § 2522. In addition, an unlimited *marital deduction* is found in § 2523.

Under § 2513, a gift by a husband or wife *to a third party* may be considered as made one-half by each spouse. This is the so-called *split-gift* provision, which attributes one-half of the gift to the donor's spouse, if the spouse consents to such treatment. This split-gift provision enables spouses, in effect, to combine their separate lifetime unified credits and annual exclusions for gifts made by either or both of them during life.

Gifts may occur in disguised or subtle forms; some of these are subject to special statutory rules. Section 2514 provides that the exercise or release of a *power of appointment* may give rise to a taxable gift. Under § 2516, some *property settlements* made in connection with divorce are *not* treated as taxable gifts; in contrast, transfers not made in compliance with the conditions of § 2516 are subjected to the more general rules in determining whether there has been a transfer for full and adequate consideration in money or money's worth or a taxable gift. (Compare § 1041 which, for *income tax* purposes, treats transfers between spouses, and property settlements between ex-spouses incident to a divorce, as nontaxable gifts.)

The federal gift tax, then, has a structure that resembles that of the federal estate tax, although the statutory language tends to obscure this resemblance. The gift tax begins with the notion of a net transfer—the value of the total gift under § 2512, minus any applicable exclusions under § 2503—

which is reduced to the concept of a *taxable gift* by subtracting the deductions allowed under §§ 2522 and 2523. There is only one *credit* available against the gift tax, the *unified credit* of § 2505. This is a cumulative credit, and in any given year only the amount not used in previous years may be taken. Moreover, the use (and consequent exhaustion) of this credit is not elective, since § 2505(a) specifies that in computing the amount allowed as a credit in any given year, the full amount of the credit must be reduced by any amounts "allowable" (as opposed to "allowed") in previous years.

The computation of the gift tax is further complicated by the fact that it is *cumulative* over the donor's lifetime as well as *progressive*. To make the tax cumulative in this way, the tax for the current year's gifts must be determined in the following fashion. First, total taxable gifts made since the enactment of the gift tax to the end of the current taxable year must be aggregated and a "tentative tax" on that amount computed at current rates. From the tax so determined must be subtracted another "tentative tax," again computed at present rates, on the total taxable gifts made prior to the beginning of the current year. The difference is the amount of gift tax on gifts made in the current year. I.R.C. § 2502. The progressive rates and this cumulative computation of the gift tax result in taxing larger gifts or gifts made in succeeding years at progressively higher rates, up to the maximum rate under the unified rate schedule. Beginning in 2026, the gift tax in effect is imposed at a flat 40% rate on all taxable gifts in excess of the inflation-indexed $15 million exemption equivalent, since the unified credit will eliminate any tax that would be imposed at lower rates.

One subtle but significant difference between the gift tax and the estate tax involves the measurement of the tax base. For gift tax purposes, the amount of a gift is defined as the value of the transferred property, excluding any gift tax imposed on the transfer. Accordingly, the gift tax is said to be computed on a "tax-exclusive" base; there is no "tax on the tax." In contrast, the estate tax base includes the value of all the property owned at death (including any amount used to pay the estate tax), not just the property that actually comes into the hands of the beneficiaries. The estate tax must be paid from "after-tax" dollars, and the estate tax base is therefore said to be "tax-inclusive." As a result of this difference in the measurement of the tax base, the *effective* rates of the gift tax are lower than those of the estate tax, even though both taxes share the same *nominal* rate schedule. To illustrate, suppose that both taxes are imposed at a flat 50% rate. A donor who makes an inter vivos gift of $1,000 will incur a (tax-exclusive) gift tax of $500, bringing the total out-of-pocket cost of the transfer to $1,500. However, a decedent who dies leaving an estate of $1,500 will incur a (tax-inclusive) estate tax of $750, leaving only $750 for the heirs after tax. Here, the gift tax is $250 less than the estate tax on a comparable transfer—precisely the amount saved by excluding the gift tax from the gift tax base ($500 × 50%). Another way to understand the difference is to observe that a $500 gift tax on a net transfer of

$1,000, conventionally viewed as a 50% tax on a tax-exclusive base of $1,000, is equivalent to a 33⅓% tax on a tax-inclusive base of $1,500.

Income Tax Basis. As to gifts of property made during life, I.R.C. § 1015 provides that for income tax purposes, the basis of the gift property in the hands of the donee shall be the same as its basis in the hands of the donor (carryover basis), except that if such basis is *greater* than fair market value at the time of the gift, then the basis for purposes of determining *loss* (only) shall be such fair market value. (This means that if the donee sells for a price below carryover basis but above the fair market value limitation, a "gray area" results, with no gain or loss to the donee. See Reg. § 1.1015–1(a)(2).)

Section 1015(d) entitles the donee to step up the § 1015(a) basis by the portion of the gift tax allocable to "net appreciation" in the value of the gift property.

§ 15 OUTLINE OF THE GENERATION-SKIPPING TRANSFER TAX

The generation-skipping transfer (GST) tax, completely revised in 1986, appears in Chapter 13, beginning with I.R.C. § 2601. These statutory provisions are very complicated and contain a multitude of new terms with mutually dependent and interlocking definitions. An overview of the GST tax was given in § 6, *supra.* Now comes the more detailed and technical treatment of the statute which implements the scheme.

This outline is organized in four parts: (1) *What is a generation-skipping transfer?* (2) *How is the tax on generation-skipping transfers determined?* (3) *Who pays the tax?* (4) *What basis effects and other consequences follow a generation-skipping transfer?* The simplicity of this outline belies the morass of specially defined terms which implement the scheme. It may be tempting for students (and for instructors) to pay scant attention to the GST tax. After all, today only a very small number of households pay estate or gift taxes. Given the structure of the transfer taxes and the generous scope of the available exemptions, it appears that even fewer will ever pay any GST tax. With the population living longer and longer (and the elderly becoming increasingly wealthy), however, a well-drawn estate plan must consider its effects not only on the transferor's children, but also on grand- and great-grandchildren and unborn generations. Accordingly, practitioners involved in planning all but the simplest and smallest estates are remiss if they do not take the time to become familiar with the basic structure and operation of the GST tax.

(1) What Is a Generation-Skipping Transfer?

I.R.C. § 2601 purports to impose a tax on every "generation-skipping transfer." Section 2611(a) generally defines a generation-skipping transfer as either a *direct skip,* a *taxable termination,* or a *taxable distribution.* These three types of generation-skipping transfers are the exclusive triggering events for imposing the GST tax.

Direct Skips. A major innovation of the revised GST tax enacted in 1986 was the taxation of "direct skips." The classic direct skip is a bequest or inter vivos gift from a transferor to a grandchild. Had the property been transferred first to the transferor's child, there would be some additional estate or gift tax consequences when and if the property passed from the transferor's child to the grandchild. At least, some or all of the child's annual exclusion or unified credit might be used, and perhaps some estate or gift tax would have to be paid.

By "skipping a generation" and transferring property directly to a grandchild, the transferor (prior to the 1986 Act) could be sure that no adverse transfer tax consequences would be incurred that might diminish the gift or reduce the estate and gift tax planning options available to members of the "skipped" generation.

Example: D dies and leaves her entire estate of $30 million to her wealthy son, S. D's estate will incur a federal estate tax of $6 million [$11,945,800 tax under § 2001 less $5,945,800 unified credit under § 2010], leaving S with a net bequest of $24 million (assuming no state death tax). (To simplify the computation, the unified credit is assumed to be equivalent to a $15 million exemption, without any adjustment for inflation.) Ten years later, S dies and leaves his entire estate to his daughter. Since S's estate includes other property in addition to the bequest from D, his inheritance—assuming it enlarges his estate, directly or indirectly, by $24 million—will exhaust S's unified credit (again, equivalent to a $15 million exemption), incur a federal estate tax of $3,600,000, and "push" the rest of S's estate into the 40% bracket. Prior to 1986, D and other members of wealthy families could avoid such consequences by making gifts or bequests directly from grandparent to grandchild.

The revised GST tax enacted in 1986 applies to a direct skip, which is defined as a transfer otherwise subject to estate or gift tax which transmits an interest in property to a "skip person" (generally a person two or more generations below the transferor). I.R.C. § 2612(c). The precise definition of "skip person" is discussed more fully below.

Example: A makes an outright inter vivos gift of $100,000 to her grandchild, B. The transfer is *subject to* gift tax (though the annual exclusion and the unified credit may shield the transfer from actual taxation) and the transferee is two generations below the transferor. Therefore, this is a direct skip. (Nevertheless, the GST exemption, discussed below, may allow this generation-skipping transfer to escape actual taxation).

Taxable Terminations. Unlike direct skips, taxable terminations were made subject to the original GST tax when it was first enacted in 1976. (The computation of the tax on terminations, however, was significantly changed in the 1986 revision.)

Prior to 1976, a grantor could save tax by setting up a trust that paid income to a child for life, then income to a grandchild for life, then income to a great-grandchild for life, etc. Even though beneficial enjoyment of the trust property would be shifted at each death, there would be no estate (or gift) tax consequence upon the death of the child, grandchild, or great-grandchild. Such a trust could give a wealthy family a great deal of estate planning flexibility. (Recall the discussion of the pre-1986 tax avoidance motivation for direct skips, above.)

The GST tax closes this loophole by treating such an arrangement as a series of taxable terminations. Section 2612(a) defines "taxable termination" as "the termination (by death, lapse of time, release of power, or otherwise) of an *interest in property held in a trust*" (emphasis added), unless immediately after such termination a non-skip person holds an *interest* in the property or no subsequent distributions can be made from the trust to any skip person.

The term "interest," as it relates to trust property, has a specially defined meaning for GST tax purposes. I.R.C. § 2652(c) states that "[a] person has an interest in property held in trust if (at the time the determination is made) such person has a *right* (other than a future right) to receive income or corpus from the trust" or "is a *permissible* current recipient of income or corpus" (emphases added).

Example: A creates a trust to pay income to her son B for life, with remainder to her grandchild C. Upon B's death, B's interest terminates and C becomes entitled to receive the trust corpus. This is a taxable termination. Notice that no estate or gift tax is incurred when B's interest terminates. If, upon B's death, the trust income became payable to B's spouse, there would be no taxable termination since B's spouse is a non-skip person. (See discussion below.) If the remainder passed to C at the death of

B's spouse, there would be a taxable termination at that time, because C is a skip person.

Estate planners might be tempted to create nominal or token interests in non-skip persons so as to avoid causing a taxable termination upon the expiration of a life estate. See I.R.C. § 2612(a)(1)(A). With this possibility in mind, § 2652(c)(2) permits the I.R.S. to disregard "an interest which is used primarily to postpone or avoid any [GST tax]."

Anticipating efforts to avoid the tax on terminations (or distributions) by creating non-trust arrangements that are "trust equivalents," Congress has defined "trust" broadly to include "any arrangement (other than an estate) which, although not a trust, has substantially the same effect as a trust." I.R.C. § 2652(b)(1). Congress specifically contemplated "arrangements involving life estates and remainders, estates for years, and insurance and annuity contracts." I.R.C. § 2652(b)(3).

Taxable Distributions. If a distribution from a trust to a skip person is neither a direct skip nor a taxable termination, it is a taxable distribution.

Example: Grandparent A creates a trust to pay income (and principal, in the trustee's discretion) to son S, daughter D, and their children as long as any of them are alive. The remainder goes to A's favorite charity. Payments of trust income or principal to the grandchildren are taxable distributions subject to GST tax. Payments to S and D are *not* taxable distributions, of course, because S and D are not "skip persons."

Who Is a Skip Person? All three types of generation-skipping transfers involve transfers of property to "skip persons." Since a skip person is an integral part of the definition of a generation-skipping transfer, it is important to have a precise definition of "skip person." In most cases, it suffices to say that a skip person is a person who is two or more generations younger than the transferor. Sections 2613 and 2651 fill in the details.

Section 2613 defines a skip person as an individual "assigned to a generation which is 2 or more generations below the generation assignment of the transferor." A trust may also be a skip person if all of the interests in the trust are held by skip persons or if only skip persons can receive distributions (including distributions on termination) from the trust. Note that, in the case of trusts, the definition of skip person requires reference to the § 2652(c) definition of "interest" (discussed above).

The definition of skip person requires reference to § 2651 in order to determine a transferee's generation assignment relative to that of a transferor. Section 2651 divides transferees into two categories—those who have some family relationship with the transferor and those who do not.

Family Member Transferees. The most common generation-skipping transfers are those made within the family, either directly between family members or with a trust as an intermediary.

Section 2651(b) gives the generation assignment rules for an individual who is a lineal descendant of a *grandparent of the transferor* (or a grandparent of the transferor's *spouse*). They require one to compare the number of generations between the grandparent and the individual with the number of generations between the grandparent and the transferor. The difference is the number of generations between the transferor and the individual. Adopted children and half-blood relatives are treated as full family members. I.R.C. § 2651(b)(3).

Section 2651(c) gives the rules for an individual who is (or was) married at any time to the transferor or to a family member described in § 2651(b). The transferor's spouse is assigned to the transferor's generation. The spouse of a § 2651(b) family member is assigned to the same generation as that family member.

Special Rule for Transfers to Grandchild with Predeceased Parent. I.R.C. § 2651(e) provides a special rule in the case of a transfer to a grandchild of the transferor (or of the transferor's spouse) if, at the time the transfer is made, the grandchild's parent is no longer living and that parent was a child of the transferor (or of the transferor's spouse). Such a grandchild is reassigned to the deceased parent's generation and is treated as a child of the transferor (not a skip person). Thus, an outright gift or bequest from a grandparent to a grandchild does not constitute a generation-skipping transfer if the parent in the intervening generation is already deceased at the time of the transfer.

This rule also applies to lineal descendants in more remote generations. For example, if a great-grandchild's parent and grandparent have predeceased a great-grandparent transferor so as to leave two "holes" in the line of descent from great-grandparent to great-grandchild, the great-grandchild is treated as a child of the transferor (not a skip person) in determining whether a generation-skipping transfer has occurred. The predeceased parent rule also applies to collateral relatives descended from the parents of the transferor (or of the transferor's spouse), but only if the transferor had no living descendants at the time of the transfer. I.R.C. § 2651(e)(2).

The predeceased parent rule applies only if the transferee's parent (or other appropriate lineal ancestor) is deceased *at the time of the transfer giving rise to gift or estate tax.* This determination normally coincides with the time of the potential generation-skipping transfer, in the case of a direct skip. In the case of a taxable termination or a taxable distribution, however, the rule applies only if the transferee's parent was already deceased when the original transfer in trust became complete for gift or estate tax purposes.

Example: A dies, leaving property in trust for her surviving spouse B, her surviving child C, and C's descendants. One year later, C dies. Because C was living when the trust was created at A's death, C's descendants are skip persons and any distributions made to them during B's lifetime will be taxable distributions. By contrast, if C predeceased A, C's descendants would all move up one generation, with the result that C's children would not be skip persons and distributions to them would not be subject to GST tax.

Transferees Outside the Family. Sometimes the transferee is an individual who has no close family relationship to the transferor. Such a person is not a lineal descendant of a grandparent of the transferor (or the transferor's spouse); nor has such a person been married to the transferor or to any lineal descendant of a grandparent of the transferor (or the transferor's spouse). Section 2651(d) gives the generation assignment rules for such strangers to the transferor. The generation assignment is made by comparing the date of the individual's birth with the date of the transferor's birth and applying a simple formula. "[A]n individual born not more than 12½ years after the date of birth of the transferor" is assigned to the transferor's generation. I.R.C. § 2651(d)(1). "[A]n individual born more than 12½ but not more than 37½ years" after the transferor is assigned "to the first generation younger than the transferor." I.R.C. § 2651(d)(2). An individual born more than 37½ years but not more than 62½ years after the transferor is assigned to the second generation younger than the transferor, and so on, with a new generation at each 25-year interval. I.R.C. § 2651(d)(3).

It is conceivable that several different generation assignment rules could apply to the same individual, placing him or her in more than one generation. Section 2651(f)(1) anticipates this possibility by assigning the individual "to the youngest such generation."

Section 2651(f)(2) deals with the possibility that people may try to avoid tax by channeling transfers through "an estate, trust, partnership, corporation, or other entity." In such a case, the veil of such a purportedly separate entity will be pierced, and "each individual having a beneficial interest in such an entity shall be treated as having an interest in such [transferred] property and shall be assigned to a generation" under the generation assignment rules described above.

Certain transfers to charitable organizations or trusts are effectively exempted from the GST tax by assigning these entities to the transferor's generation. See I.R.C. § 2651(f)(3).

The GST tax applies only if property is shifted from a transferor to a skip person at least two generations below the transferor, without imposition of a gift or estate tax at the intervening "skipped" generation. Thus, to determine whether a generation-skipping transfer has occurred, it is important to identify the *transferor*. Under I.R.C. 2652(a), the transferor is generally defined as the decedent in the case of property subject to estate tax, or the donor in the case of property subject to gift tax. For this purpose, any property which is includable in the decedent's gross estate or transferred by gift during life is deemed to be "subject to" estate or gift tax, without regard to exemptions, exclusions, deductions or credits. Reg. § 26.2652–1(a). As a result, whenever property becomes subject to gift or estate tax in the hands of a donor or decedent, the generation assignment of the new transferor must be examined to determine whether the transferees are skip persons.

To illustrate, suppose grandmother transfers property in trust to pay income to her child for life (second generation), with remainder at the child's death to a grandchild (third generation). This would ordinarily give rise to a GST tax, since the transfer skips the second generation and triggers a taxable termination at the child's death. But, if the child has a power to invade the trust for his or her own benefit so as to draw the trust property into the child's gross estate (e.g., under § 2041), the transfer to the third generation at the death of the second generation will *not* be taxable as a generation-skipping transfer, since the child is now the transferor and the grandchild is only one generation below the child. The planning implications of incurring a gift or estate tax in order to avoid the GST tax are discussed in § 81, *infra*.

(2) Computing the Tax

I.R.C. § 2602 presents a (deceptively) simple formula for computing the GST tax on a direct skip, a taxable termination, or a taxable distribution. In each case, the tax is equal to the *taxable amount* multiplied by the *applicable rate*.

Taxable Amount. For direct skips, the taxable amount is the value of the property *received* by the transferee. I.R.C. § 2623. If $100,000 is transferred by direct skip and the applicable rate is 40%, the *transferor* must pay $40,000 of GST tax. I.R.C. § 2603(a)(3). The GST tax on direct skips is *tax exclusive*. The $40,000 tax is not considered to be part of the direct skip. Thus, there is no "tax on the tax." (For *gift tax* purposes, however, the payment of the GST tax itself is treated as a taxable gift, in addition to the gift of the property transferred. See I.R.C. § 2515.)

Compare with direct skips the treatment of taxable distributions and taxable terminations. Suppose a grandparent creates a trust to pay income to a child for life with remainder to a grandchild. At the child's death the trust property is worth $166,667 and a taxable termination occurs with respect to that amount. At a 40% rate, the trustee must pay a *tax-inclusive* $66,667 GST tax from the trust property. Thus, the grandchild receives property worth $100,000 following this $166,667 taxable termination. To understand the difference between tax-inclusive and tax-exclusive taxes, note that for the grandchild to receive $100,000 after tax, the trust property must be worth $166,667 at the time of the taxable termination. This tax is tax inclusive. In contrast, for grandchild to receive $100,000 by *direct skip,* grandparent can transfer $100,000 to grandchild and then pay 40% tax on $100,000, which totals only $40,000. Thus, grandparent needs to start with only $140,000 to ensure that grandchild ends up with $100,000. This tax is tax exclusive.

Like the tax on taxable terminations, the tax on taxable distributions is *tax inclusive.* There *is* a tax on the tax. (What if a trustee attempts to circumvent this rule by paying the tax directly from the trust property? Section 2621(b) blocks this gambit by treating any GST tax paid from the trust as an additional taxable distribution.) Clients planning generation-skipping transfers may wish to favor direct skips over taxable terminations and distributions in order to gain the benefits of tax exclusivity. The disparate treatment given to direct skips, as opposed to the other two generation-skipping transfers, is not unique in the federal transfer tax system. The gift tax also is tax exclusive, while the estate tax is tax inclusive.

For taxable terminations and distributions, the taxable amount may be reduced by certain deductions. See I.R.C. §§ 2622 and 2621(a).

In general, property is valued at the time of the generation-skipping transfer. I.R.C. § 2624. For the purpose of computing the taxable amount, the value of the property is reduced by the amount of any consideration provided by the transferee. I.R.C. § 2624(d).

Alternative valuation and special use valuation elections may apply to certain direct skips and taxable terminations. See I.R.C. §§ 2624(b)–(c), 2032, and 2032A.

Section 6166(i) grants an option to defer payment of GST tax arising on a "direct skip" that occurs at the death of a transferor who owns an interest in a closely-held business.

Applicable Rate. The applicable rate is "the product of (1) the *maximum Federal estate tax rate,* and (2) the *inclusion ratio* with respect to the transfer." I.R.C. § 2641 (emphases added).

Section 2641(b) states that the maximum federal estate tax rate is the maximum rate imposed by § 2001 on the estates of decedents dying at the time of the generation-skipping transfer. Since 2013, the maximum rate has been 40%. I.R.C. § 2001(c).

Inclusion Ratio. The inclusion ratio (IR) for taxable terminations and distributions is defined as "the excess (if any) of 1 over . . . the *applicable fraction* determined for the trust from which such transfer is made"; for direct skips, the IR is "the excess (if any) of 1 over . . . the *applicable fraction* determined for such skip." I.R.C. § 2642(a)(1) (emphases added). The applicable fraction depends on the amount of GST exemption allocated to a transfer and the value of the property transferred.

GST Exemption. Section 2631 grants every individual a GST exemption of $15 million (indexed for inflation), which may be allocated by the individual (or his executor) to any property for which the individual is the transferor. Once an allocation of GST exemption is made, the allocation is irrevocable. I.R.C. § 2631(b). Section 2632 gives rules for allocating the GST exemption in the event that the transferor (or the transferor's executor) does not make an allocation. A married couple may elect to treat a lifetime transfer by either spouse as made one-half by each, and thus they can "double" the $15 million individual GST exemption as well as the gift tax annual exclusion. See I.R.C. § 2652(a)(2).

Absent a contrary election by the transferor, the GST exemption applies first to lifetime direct skips and to certain inter vivos trusts from which a generation-skipping transfer might occur, then—after the transferor's death—to testamentary direct skips, and finally to other trusts from which a taxable termination or a taxable distribution might occur. See I.R.C. § 2632(b)–(e). It will often be important for the transferor (or the executor of a deceased transferor) to elect out of this scheme. Reg. § 26.2632–1 prescribes the time and manner for making an allocation of the GST exemption.

Computing the IR. The IR (inclusion ratio) is simple to compute in the case of a direct skip. In general, the IR is 1 minus the applicable fraction—the numerator of which is the amount of the GST exemption allocated to the transferred property and the denominator of which is the value of the property involved in the direct skip (reduced by any federal estate tax or state death tax paid from the property and by any charitable deduction allowed with respect to the property). I.R.C. § 2642(a). The IR can be expressed as follows:

$$\text{IR} = 1 - \frac{\text{GST exemption allocated to transferred property}}{\begin{array}{c}\text{Value of transferred}\\ \text{property}\end{array} - \begin{array}{c}\text{Federal estate tax}\\ \text{and state death tax}\end{array} - \begin{array}{c}\text{Charitable}\\ \text{deduction}\end{array}}$$

Thus, for example, suppose a grandparent transfers \$100,000 in a direct skip to a grandchild. Grandparent allocates \$100,000 of GST exemption to this gift. The IR is equal to 1 − (\$100,000 ÷ \$100,000), or zero. With the IR equal to zero, no GST tax will be payable, but the grandparent will have used up \$100,000 of his or her GST exemption, leaving the balance of the exemption available to shelter future lifetime or testamentary generation-skipping transfers from GST tax.

Computing the IR for the other two types of generation-skipping transfers is a bit more complicated. A trust's IR is ordinarily established *when there is a completed transfer of property to the trust.* This IR continues for the duration of the trust, unless the trust receives additional contributions of property or supplementary allocations of the transferor's GST exemption. The trust's IR determines the applicable rate of GST tax for subsequent taxable terminations and taxable distributions. (This general rule does not apply to charitable lead annuity trusts. See I.R.C. § 2642(e).)

When a trust is established, its IR equals 1 minus the applicable fraction—the numerator of which is the amount of the GST exemption allocated to the trust and the denominator of which is the value of the property transferred to the trust (reduced by any federal estate tax or state death tax paid from the trust and by any charitable deduction allowable with respect to the trust property).

Example: A transfers $15 million to an irrevocable inter vivos trust. A elects to allocate her entire $15 million exemption to the trust. Twenty years later, when the trust is worth $30 million, the trustee makes a $100,000 distribution of trust income to A's grandchild, B. Does this taxable distribution incur a GST tax liability? No. The inclusion ratio was determined *at the inception of the trust,* not at the time of the subsequent taxable distribution. In this case, the inclusion ratio is zero, and hence the applicable rate is also zero (40% × 0). A generation-skipping transfer has occurred, but no tax is payable.

In the above example, suppose A allocated only $6 million of her GST exemption to the trust. The IR then would be 60%, producing an applicable rate of 24% (40% × 60%). A taxable distribution of $100,000 would leave B with $76,000, after paying a tax of $24,000.

Several insights flow from these simple examples:

(1) From a tax computation point of view, if the IR is equal to zero, it is unnecessary to determine whether or not a particular transferee is a skip person. No matter who receives the income or corpus of such an "exempt trust," there will be no GST tax to pay. As a matter of trust management, however, it is desirable that corpus and income of such an exempt trust go only to skip persons, if other non-exempt funds are available for non-skip beneficiaries, since only transfers to skip persons can incur GST tax liability. A well-advised transferor can avoid "wasting" the GST exemption by creating a non-exempt trust (with an IR of 1) to provide for the needs of his or her spouse, children, and other non-skip beneficiaries. As a general rule, trusts should be either wholly exempt or wholly non-exempt, with no IR between zero and 1.

(2) Since the applicable fraction is determined at the time of the transfer to the trust, much more than $15 million can ultimately be sheltered in an exempt trust. In the first example, A transferred $15 million and completely exempted this property from future

GST taxes by allocating $15 million of her GST exemption to the trust. So long as no subsequent additions are made to this trust, all distributions of income or corpus (including distributions on termination) will be exempt from GST tax. If A was 30 years old when she made the transfer and the property grows by 6% per year (as a result of income accumulations and capital appreciation) until A's death at age 70, the trust will grow to more than $150 million. This entire amount (as well as further income and appreciation after A's death until the trust terminates) will be available for tax-free generation-skipping transfers. In theory, the exempt trust can grow (and shelter generation-skipping transfers) for as long as it is permissible to hold property in trust under the perpetuities rules of applicable state law.

If a transferor contributes additional property to an existing trust, the trust's IR may have to be recalculated. See I.R.C. § 2641(d).

Section 2642(c) provides special rules for determining the IR in the case of a *nontaxable* gift. A nontaxable gift is defined as a § 2503(b) annual exclusion gift or a § 2503(e) educational or medical exclusion gift. I.R.C. § 2642(c)(3). In general, a nontaxable gift that constitutes a direct skip automatically receives an IR of zero and therefore escapes GST tax, without the need to use any of the transferor's GST exemption. I.R.C. § 2642(c)(1). In the case of a transfer in trust, however, this rule applies only if the trust is exclusively for the benefit of a single individual and will be includable in that individual's gross estate should he or she die before the termination of the trust. I.R.C. § 2642(c)(2). (The most common example of a trust that meets these requirements is a § 2503(c) trust for a minor beneficiary. See the discussion in § 57, *infra.*) In all other cases, a nontaxable gift in trust is *not* eligible for an automatic IR of zero; to avoid GST tax, the transferor must allocate a portion of his or her GST exemption to the trust.

Example: A makes an outright inter vivos gift of $10,000 to her grandchild, B. The gift is nontaxable for gift tax purposes by virtue of the annual exclusion (see I.R.C. § 2503(b)), but it meets the definition of a direct skip for GST tax purposes because it is "subject to" gift tax and is made to a skip person. See I.R.C. § 2612(c). Nevertheless, the transfer automatically receives an IR of zero and therefore incurs no GST tax. See I.R.C. § 2642(c); Reg. § 26.2642–1(d) (Example 2). The same result would follow if A made a § 2503(e) qualified transfer to pay for B's tuition or medical care.

Example: A makes an inter vivos transfer of $30,000 in trust to pay discretionary income to her three grandchildren. Each grandchild has the right to withdraw $10,000 from the trust, so A's transfer is nontaxable for gift tax purposes under § 2503(b). For GST tax purposes, the transfer is a direct skip because it is "subject to" gift tax and is made to a skip person (the trust). See I.R.C. §§ 2612(c) and 2613. The transfer is not eligible for a zero inclusion ratio unless A allocates $30,000 of GST exemption to the trust. See I.R.C. §§ 2641 and 2642.

GST Exemptions and Exclusions. Overall, the GST tax has several exemptions or exclusions. The first is the $15 million GST exemption (indexed for inflation), which is freely allocable to transfers made by an individual transferor during life or at death. See I.R.C. § 2631(a). The second is for certain transfers excluded from gift tax by the § 2503(b) annual exclusion or the § 2503(e) educational and medical exclusion. See I.R.C. § 2642(c). The third is for qualified educational and medical expenses, paid at the transferor's death or from a trust, which would have qualified for the § 2503(e) exclusion "if made inter vivos by an individual." I.R.C. § 2611(b)(1). In addition, once property is subject to GST tax, a subsequent transfer of the property to a transferee in the same or a higher generation will be exempt from a second level of GST tax. See I.R.C. § 2611(b)(2). And, as mentioned, a married couple may share their individual GST exemptions with respect to lifetime transfers by electing, under § 2513, to have gifts by either spouse considered as made one-half by each spouse. See I.R.C. § 2652(a)(2).

(3) Who Pays the Tax?

Once the tax is computed, I.R.C. § 2603(a) gives the rules for who is personally liable for the tax. The tax on a *direct skip* (other than a direct skip from a trust) is to be paid by the transferor. The tax on a taxable *termination* (or a direct skip from a trust) is to be paid by the trustee. The tax on a taxable *distribution* is to be paid by the transferee.

Unless otherwise directed by a specific reference in the governing instrument, the GST tax is charged to the property constituting the transfer. I.R.C. § 2603(b). (Recall the tax exclusivity of direct skips as compared with the tax inclusivity of taxable terminations and taxable distributions, in the discussion of the taxable amount, above.)

(4) Consequences Following a Generation-Skipping Transfer

Multiple Skips. It is important not to lose sight of the purpose of the GST tax. It is designed to fill in gaps in the estate and gift tax system by ensuring that family wealth will be taxed at least once per generation. In addition to the generous shelters offered for pre-existing trusts, the inflation-indexed $15 million GST exemption, and incorporation of § 2503 exclusions, the GST tax is inherently "leaky" inasmuch as a direct skip is taxed only once—regardless how many generations are skipped.

Example: A makes a lifetime transfer of $100,000 to her great-grandchild, B. The tax on this gift will be identical to the tax on a gift to a grandchild. If A had instead transferred $100,000 to A's grandchild, the parent of B, there would have been an additional gift or estate tax when B's parent transferred the property to B.

Except for direct skips, the GST tax aims (with some success) to ensure that there will be a transfer tax each time the benefits of trust property shift from one generation to the next. Application of the GST tax more than once to the same generation, however, would lead to harsh results, especially since the tax is imposed at a relatively high, flat rate.

Section 2653 helps to ensure that property which has been subjected to GST tax at a particular generation level will not be subject again to GST tax on a subsequent transfer to a transferee at the same generation level. In the case of a direct skip free of trust, there is no problem. Section 2652(a)(1) defines "transferor" as the decedent, in the case of a transfer subject to estate tax, or the donor, in the case of a transfer subject to gift tax. If a donor makes a direct skip, the donee's subsequent transfer of the property to members of the same generation (or the one immediately below) will *not* be a generation-skipping transfer because: (1) application of gift or estate tax will convert the original donee into a new "transferor" for GST tax purposes and (2) none of the new transferees will be skip persons relative to the donee transferor.

As to property that continues to be held in trust following a generation-skipping transfer, however, trust distributions or terminations will not incur a gift or estate tax unless a trust beneficiary has an inter vivos or testamentary general power of appointment. See Chapter 9, *infra*. Without § 2653, a subsequent distribution or termination would give rise to an additional GST tax even if the beneficiaries of the trust were in the same generation as the skip person involved in the initial generation-skipping transfer, since those beneficiaries would continue to be skip persons relative to the original transferor.

Section 2653 handles this situation by treating the trust "as if the transferor of such property were assigned to the 1st generation above the highest generation of any person who has an interest [see § 2652(c)] in such trust immediately after the transfer." § 2653(a). An example illustrating the effect of § 2653 appears in § 81, *infra*.

Effect on Basis. If property with an inclusion ratio of 1 is transferred in a taxable termination occurring at the same time as, and as a result of, an individual's death, the property receives a fresh-start basis, by analogy to § 1014. If the inclusion ratio of such property is less than 1, any increase (or decrease) in basis called for by § 1014 is limited by multiplying the increase (or decrease) by the inclusion ratio. Thus, the termination (at death) of an exempt trust (with an IR of zero) will result in no change of basis. See I.R.C. § 2654(a)(2).

The basis effects of other generation-skipping transfers are governed by I.R.C. § 2654(a)(1). Transferred property retains its prior basis, adjusted (but not in excess of its fair market value) by an amount equal to that portion of the GST tax which is attributable to the excess value of such property over its adjusted basis immediately before the transfer. Section 2654 is to be applied after any basis adjustment under § 1015 (relating to property acquired by gift).

CHAPTER 3

THE ESTATE AND GIFT TAXES APPLIED TO TRANSFERS AT DEATH AND DURING LIFE

§ 16 APPLICATION OF THE ESTATE TAX TO TRANSFERS OF PROPERTY AT DEATH

The *gross estate* is determined or defined under I.R.C. §§ 2031 and 2033. Section 2031(a) states that the decedent's "gross estate" shall be determined by including the value at the time of his death of "all property, real or personal, tangible or intangible, wherever situated." To make it clear that an interest in property will be included in the gross estate of the decedent even if he does not own legal title or all of the bundle of rights in the property, § 2033 goes on to state that the gross estate shall include the value of all property "to the extent of the interest therein of the decedent at the time of his death." Not just property in the probate estate or subject to claims of creditors or distributed as part of the administration of the decedent's estate, but much more, can fall within the tax concept of the gross estate.

However, not every item of wealth or every economic resource of the decedent becomes part of the gross estate under § 2033. (Some potentially difficult questions about the scope of § 2033 have not arisen because the arrangements and transactions to which it arguably might apply are clearly covered by later sections, such as §§ 2039, 2041, and 2042. Other questions have arisen in contexts where the inclusion must occur under § 2033 if at all, or in cases that came up before the enactment of the later, more specific sections.)

Thus, the general question arises: What will be included in the gross estate of a decedent under the terms of § 2033? The statute, the cases and the regulations (see Reg. § 20.2033–1) shed some illumination. Obviously, the gross estate includes property owned by the decedent in the form of real estate, bank accounts, stocks and bonds (including dividends whose record date occurred on or before the date of death), causes of action that survive the decedent's death, claims against debtors (including accounts receivable), patent and copyright royalties, interests in an unincorporated business, and the decedent's interest in community property or a tenancy in common. Reg. § 20.2033–1(b). In contrast, § 2033 does not reach property held by the decedent in the form of a joint tenancy with right of survivorship (or a tenancy by the entirety), since the decedent's interest expires at death; such interests are governed instead by § 2040. Similarly, special rules in § 2042 govern the proceeds of insurance on the decedent's life. But, if the decedent owned an insurance policy on the life of *another* person, who survived the decedent, the value of the decedent's interest in the policy is includable in the gross estate under § 2033.

Legal title to property or an interest in property is not necessary or determinative for inclusion in the gross estate. For example, property held by the decedent as trustee or guardian or in some other fiduciary capacity will not be included in the gross estate under § 2033. The decedent's interest must be a *beneficial* interest to result in inclusion. Any beneficial interest, however, will do. For example, if the decedent held a vested remainder in a trust established by someone else, the value of that interest is includable in the gross estate. Even a contingent remainder held by the decedent will be included if that remainder is not destroyed by the death of the decedent and if it passes from him or her to someone else at or by reason of the decedent's death. Thus, § 2033 embraces a broad range of interests owned at death.

Can Congress limit the scope of §§ 2031 and 2033 by enacting a statute outside the estate tax code? Yes it can, but it must do so unambiguously. This is the import of a Supreme Court case, United States v. Wells Fargo Bank, 485 U.S. 351 (1988). The background is this: In 1937, Congress passed a housing act authorizing local authorities to issue tax-free obligations, termed "Project Notes." The Project Notes were exempted by statute "from all taxation now or hereafter imposed by the United States." The executors contended that the notes could be transferred without federal estate tax liability. After reviewing the legislative history, the Supreme Court held that "the presumption against implied tax exemptions [is] too powerful to be overcome" even by the express exemption from "all taxation." This holding is not entirely surprising for two reasons. First, *no* court had upheld a challenge to the estate taxation of Project Notes until 1984. See Haffner v. United States, 585 F. Supp. 354 (N.D. Ill. 1984), aff'd,

757 F.2d 920 (7th Cir. 1985). Second, a contrary holding would have created a gaping hole in the estate tax (the Supreme Court in *Wells Fargo Bank* noted that a " 'rush to market' for Project Notes" had followed the *Haffner* decision).

It is unlikely that the Supreme Court will be called upon to decide additional questions of Congressional intent in this area. Congress reacted to *Haffner* by stating that no "law exempting any property (or interest therein) from taxation shall exempt the transfer of such property (or interest therein) from Federal estate, gift, and generation-skipping transfer taxes" unless Congress does so by specific reference to an appropriate provision of the Internal Revenue Code. See Deficit Reduction Act of 1984, P.L. 98–369, § 641.

Thus, as a general rule, it might be said that the transfer taxes apply to state or municipal bonds even when the interest paid on such bonds is exempt from federal income taxation in the hands of the bondholder by reason of I.R.C. § 103.

Even in the absence of an explicit statutory exclusion, the compass of § 2033 is by no means unlimited. In particular, the "substantial ownership" rule which plays such an important role in the income tax, sometimes known as the "*Clifford* doctrine," has been curtailed under the estate tax with respect to the reach of § 2033. See Helvering v. Safe Deposit & Trust Co., 316 U.S. 56 (1942). In that case, the Supreme Court held that § 2033 does not require inclusion in the gross estate of property subject to an unexercised general power of appointment. Subsequently, Congress enacted § 2041, which clearly reaches property subject to an unexercised general power. The remaining impact of the *Safe Deposit & Trust Co.* case lies mainly in its conclusion that Congress did not intend the general rule of § 2033 to cover every form of economic power or resource available to the decedent before or at death. Other, specifically targeted provisions, of course, will be applied according to their terms.

Nevertheless, some questions about the application of § 2033 to items of value and economic worth that may not seem clearly to constitute "property owned by decedent" or property "in which he had an interest at his death," continue to arise despite the enactment of other provisions dealing with more specific problems of inclusion in the gross estate.

By way of illustration, the scope of § 2033 has been questioned in its application to employee death benefits and rights to payment after death. Section 2039 covers much of this area, but there is room for the Service to assert the application of § 2033 as well. For example, § 2033 has been held to require inclusion in the gross estate of post-death partnership profits which were payable to a deceased partner's estate pursuant to a partnership agreement. The estate was found to possess an enforceable chose in action which passed from the decedent to the estate. Estate of Riegelman v. Commissioner, 253 F.2d 315 (2d Cir. 1958); Rev. Rul. 66–20, 1966–1 C.B. 214.

If the employer retains an unfettered power to revoke or terminate the death benefit plan, the employee has no property interest, but merely an expectancy. Thus, the Tax Court has held that § 2033 does *not* require inclusion of *discretionary* death benefits paid by the employer to a deceased employee's widow—neither the employee nor his widow had any enforceable right to payment nor did either of them own any property in this form. See Estate of Salt v. Commissioner, 17 T.C. 92 (1951); see also Estate of Barr v. Commissioner, 40 T.C. 227 (1963) (so-called wage-dividend death benefit paid by Eastman Kodak Company to widow of deceased employee did not amount at the time of his death to a property interest includable under § 2033).

It seems clear that where employee death benefits are payable only to those beneficiaries whom the employer designates, § 2033 does not apply. Where an employee had an enforceable lifetime right to amounts that became payable at death to his estate, § 2033 is applicable. If the employee did not own an interest in the benefits at death, but did have a contractual right to receive payments during life or a power to designate beneficiaries, the benefits may fall outside the scope of § 2033, but will likely be includable under other provisions such as §§ 2038, 2039, or 2041. For a case examining § 2033 and § 2039 as to employee death benefits, see Estate of Wadewitz v. Commissioner, 39 T.C. 925 (1963), aff'd, 339 F.2d 980 (7th Cir. 1964).

The Service has ruled that § 2033 does not bring a lump-sum payment received by the decedent's surviving spouse under the Social Security Act into the gross estate. The decedent had no control over the designation of the beneficiary or the amount of payment, both of which are fixed by statute; furthermore, the decedent had no property interest in the funds from which the payment was made. Rev. Rul. 67–277, 1967–2 C.B. 322. Similarly, damages payable to close relatives for wrongful death under the Federal Death on the High Seas Act are not includable. Rev. Rul. 69–8, 1969–1 C.B. 219.

Recoveries for wrongful death under statutes that create a new cause of action for the benefit of the surviving spouse or children are not includable under § 2033. It has also been held that a recovery or settlement for wrongful death under a survival statute is not includable either under § 2033 or § 2041, even if the proceeds are distributed under the decedent's will and are subject to claims against the estate. See Connecticut Bank & Trust Co. v. United States, 465 F.2d 760 (2d Cir. 1972). The Service has acquiesced in this line of cases, while continuing to include any such proceeds to the extent they represent damages to which the decedent became entitled during life, e.g., for medical expenses or for pain and suffering. Rev. Rul. 75–127, 1975–1 C.B. 297.

In general, whether a decedent had any interest or ownership right in property is to be determined under state law. However, whether the rights and interests held by the decedent amount to ownership of property or an interest in property sufficient to require inclusion under § 2033 is a question of federal tax law. Accordingly, the courts and federal tax authorities must look to state law to determine the decedent's interest in property.

State court litigation on the rights of the particular decedent will be exceedingly pertinent, of course. The question then arises whether such a state court decision is binding upon the federal court for federal estate tax purposes. The problem can be difficult because in some cases the state court litigation is not actively contested and is decided, perhaps, with some implicit consideration of the tax consequences that will follow. The Supreme Court has attempted to provide some guidance for federal courts in connection with this problem. In Commissioner v. Estate of Bosch, 387 U.S. 456 (1967), the Court said that decisions of the lower state courts are not controlling for federal tax purposes. "Proper regard," not absolute finality, should be given to such decisions of the lower state courts. The state's highest court, however, is regarded as the best authority on the state law. If no decision in the highest court of the state bears on the point, the federal authority must apply what it finds to be the state law after giving "proper regard" to pertinent rulings by other courts of the state. As an example of this problem, see Warda v. Commissioner, 15 F.3d 533 (6th Cir.), cert. den., 513 U.S. 808 (1994) (disregarding probate court order obtained by taxpayer who sought to disavow ownership of property previously awarded to her in settlement of will contest).

*Income in Respect of a Decedent—§ 691.** If a decedent earned income that was not properly includable in gross income before death, such income is known—for federal income tax purposes—as "income in respect of a decedent" (IRD). For example, if the decedent earned fees or salary or wages for work done before death but not payable until later, and if decedent was a cash-method taxpayer (rather than an accrual-method taxpayer), the earned but unpaid income would not be includable on the decedent's final income tax return, for that taxable period ends on the date of death. Rather it is IRD which becomes taxable to the recipient. See I.R.C. § 691(a). (If the income had been earned and was payable before the date of death, but simply had not been collected by the decedent, it would be treated as constructively received by the decedent and includable on his or her final income tax return.) Other examples of IRD include deferred payments from sales of property, deferred compensation, accrued rent or interest, and other contingent or delayed receipts. See Reg. § 1.691(a)–1. IRD retains the same character for the recipient that it would have had if received by the decedent. I.R.C. § 691(a)(3).

Paralleling IRD are certain expenditures that were incurred but not paid before death. They would not be deductible on the decedent's final income tax

---

* For a more detailed discussion of income in respect of a decedent, see Lathrope, Yamamoto & McNulty, Federal Income Taxation of Individuals § 84 (9th ed. 2023), and McCouch, Federal Income Taxation of Estates, Trusts, and Beneficiaries ch. 3 (4th ed. 2026).

return. If otherwise deductible, such expenses may be claimed on the payer's income tax return as "deductions in respect of a decedent" (DRD). See I.R.C. § 691(b).

IRD is taxed to the actual recipient of the income (the estate, a legatee or devisee, or other person entitled to receive it), in the year of receipt. I.R.C. § 691(a)(1). DRD may be taken by the person who is obligated to pay the expense and who actually does so.

Unlike other property acquired from a decedent, IRD does not receive a fresh-start basis for income tax purposes at the death of the owner. I.R.C. § 1014(c). Consequently, the recipient takes IRD with a carryover basis (which in many cases will be zero). In effect, the recipient steps into the decedent's shoes for income tax purposes, and each item of IRD has the same character in the recipient's hands as it would have had in the decedent's hands if paid before death.

Nevertheless, for estate tax purposes, IRD generally is includable in the decedent's gross estate, as something of value passing at death.

Section 691(c) allows an *income tax* deduction for the amount of *estate tax* attributable to items of IRD that are included in the decedent's gross estate. This deduction mitigates the burden of the combined estate and income taxes on items of IRD and produces roughly the same net tax burden as if those items had been subject to income tax during the decedent's lifetime.

§ 17 FUTURE INTERESTS AND CONTINGENT INTERESTS UNDER § 2033

Future interests in property often must be included in the gross estate under I.R.C. § 2033. Because such inclusion will increase the estate tax payable even though the interest is still suspended and the economic value it represents is not available to pay the tax, § 6163 permits the executor to elect to postpone payment of the portion of the estate tax attributable to "a reversionary or remainder interest" until six months after the termination of the preceding interest. The Service has authority to extend the date for payment for an additional three years upon a showing of reasonable cause. See I.R.C. § 6163(b).

To include some future interests in property in the gross estate seems logical enough with respect to remainder and reversionary interests that are *indefeasibly vested* at the time of the decedent's death. However, some question has arisen about including a future interest that is *contingent or defeasible*. Such an interest is one that will not come into possession and enjoyment unless a certain contingency or condition is met, or one that may be defeated by the occurrence or non-occurrence of some future event such as the death of a certain person without issue or without surviving for a specified period of time. Should such contingent or defeasible interests be subject to estate taxation and thus included in the gross estate of the decedent? The problem seems to be particularly difficult when it ultimately appears that the interest will not come into possession or enjoyment of the decedent or his successors at all because the required conditions are not met.

At one time, it was thought that the answer depended on whether the remainder or other future interest held by the decedent at death was vested or contingent. If the interest was contingent, some courts held that the interest would not be included if the decedent's death made it impossible for the interest to vest in possession. See, e.g., Commissioner v. Rosser, 64 F.2d 631 (3d Cir. 1933) (remainder contingent on decedent's survival until time for possession). However, it is now apparent that the pertinent question is *not* whether the interest of the decedent is classified as vested or contingent. The relevant question is whether the decedent's interest expired at death, in which case it will not be included in the gross estate under § 2033, or whether it survived (despite the decedent's death) and passed to someone else at death, in which case inclusion under § 2033 will and should follow. See In re Hill's Estate, 193 F.2d 724 (2d Cir. 1952).

For example, suppose that a grantor conveys Blackacre to A for life, remainder to B, but if B should die before A, then to C. If B predeceases A, then nothing is included in B's gross estate because his death terminates his interest. However, if C predeceases both A and B, his interest is not terminated because B could still predecease A and Blackacre would go to C's estate at A's death. Thus, if the death of the decedent is itself the contingency or if it prevents the required contingency from happening, so that the decedent's interest ceases to exist at death (as in the case of B predeceasing A in the example), there will be no inclusion in the gross estate even though the future possession and enjoyment of the property shifts to a substitute taker following and as a result of the decedent's death. In such a case, the substitute taker receives nothing from the decedent but rather takes and enjoys an interest created in him by the original transferor. In other words, a shifting of future possession and enjoyment from the decedent to the substitute taker is not the same as the taxable transfer of an interest *from the decedent* to the substitute taker. On the other hand, if the decedent's death fails to terminate his interest (as in the case of C predeceasing A and B, above), the value of the interest is includable in the gross estate under § 2033.

As a more general rule, any property interest that expires upon the death of the decedent is not included in the gross estate under § 2033. For example, if grandparent devises property to her child for life with remainder at the child's death to a grandchild, there will be no inclusion in the child's gross estate at his death even though possession of the property shifts from the child to the grandchild. What has happened conceptually is that the child's life estate has terminated and the grandchild's vested remainder has fallen in at the child's death. (Such an arrangement may, however, be subject to GST tax at the child's death, when his interest in the property terminates.)

In general, then, § 2033 *includes* in the gross estate not only all property owned by the decedent but also all property in which the decedent has an interest, to the extent of that interest, if it passes from the decedent at death. The interest must be a beneficial one, not mere legal title. Section 2033 does not reach interests that expire at the death of the decedent, whether contingent or not. A remainder interest or other future interest in property, if it survives in the hands of the decedent's successor, falls within § 2033. (The *valuation* of such interests presents a separate and potentially difficult problem.)

§ 18 APPLICATION OF THE GIFT TAX TO INTER VIVOS TRANSFERS OF PROPERTY

I.R.C. § 2501 imposes a gift tax on "the transfer of property by gift . . . by any individual, resident or nonresident." Section 2511(a) goes on to say that "the tax imposed by section 2501 shall apply whether the transfer is in trust or otherwise, whether the gift is direct or indirect, and whether the property is real or personal, tangible or intangible; but in the case of a non-resident not a citizen of the United States, shall apply to a transfer only if the property is situated within the United States." Under § 2512(a), the value of a gift made in property is the value of the property at the date of the gift. If property is transferred for less than an adequate and full consideration in money or money's worth, the amount by which the value of the property exceeds the value of the consideration received is treated as a gift. I.R.C. § 2512(b).

Section 2503(a) defines *taxable gifts* as the total amount of gifts made during the calendar year minus the *deductions* provided in §§ 2522 and 2523. Section 2503(b) grants an *exclusion* in the amount of $10,000 (indexed for inflation, $19,000 in 2026) per year per donee. This exclusion applies only in the case of a present interest in property; a gift of a *future interest* in property does *not* qualify for the annual exclusion. Section 2503(e) provides a separate exclusion, unlimited in amount, for payments made on behalf of a donee directly to an educational institution for tuition or to a health care provider for medical care.

Under § 2513, a married couple may elect to treat gifts made by either spouse to a third person as made half by each spouse. This gift-splitting treatment enables both spouses to share their § 2503(b) exclusions and unified credits.

These provisions comprise the basic statutory framework of the gift tax. Some more specialized provisions, such as §§ 2514 through 2519, will be considered later, as will the provisions for deductions in §§ 2522 and 2523 and, most importantly, the *unified credit* set forth in § 2505.

These deceptively simple statutory rules give rise to difficult questions about what is a "gift" for federal gift tax purposes. In the absence of more detailed statutory assistance, regulations, rulings and cases are important aids in construing the statutory rules. The regulations under § 2511 prove especially helpful in explaining the appropriate treatment of several commonly encountered gift situations. See Reg. §§ 25.2511–1 and 25.2511–2. One of the first questions encountered in applying the basic statutory rules is what will be regarded as "property" for purposes of the gift tax. (A "gift" of services is not taxed as a gift by the federal gift tax—which raises serious questions of equity, efficiency and transfer tax (and income tax) policy.)

§ 19 WHAT IS "PROPERTY" FOR FEDERAL GIFT TAX PURPOSES?

As implied by the valuation provision, I.R.C. § 2512, the question of whether "property" was transferred is to be viewed as of the time of the transfer. Thus, even though later facts reveal that neither the donor nor the donee ever received present possession or enjoyment of the underlying property, there still may have been a taxable gift of an interest in the property. This general rule is illustrated in the case of a transfer of a contingent or defeasible future interest which ultimately does not come into possession and enjoyment by either the donor or the donee.

For example, suppose that Muriel establishes a trust that provides a life income interest to Dorothy, with remainder to Dorothy's children who survive her, but goes on to provide that if Dorothy outlives all her children then the property shall go to Dorothy's estate in fee simple. If one month before her death Dorothy transfers all of her remainder interest in the trust to Roger and then dies survived by two children,

Dorothy has made a taxable gift. This is true even though at Dorothy's death her life interest in the trust ended and the contingent remainder she transferred to Roger never vested because she was survived by her two children. Still, at the time of the transfer one month before her death, she did transfer to Roger an interest in "property"—a contingent remainder. In other words, she gave Roger the chance of enjoying the property and taking a fee simple interest at her death if she outlived all her children. The *valuation* of that interest is a separate question; all that is asserted at this point is that there was a taxable *gift*. See Goodwin v. McGowan, 47 F. Supp. 798 (W.D.N.Y. 1942). For this purpose, the interest of the decedent or donor in the case of an inter vivos gift must be distinguished from the physical property itself or the economic value embodied by that property.

It has been said more generally that "property" as used in the gift tax law is to be given a broad meaning and should include every species of right or interest protected by law and having exchangeable value. Thus, the assignment of a judgment or an insurance policy or even the forgiveness of a debt may be treated as a gift for gift tax purposes. Similarly, a promissory note is property for purposes of the gift tax (although if the note transferred is the donor's own obligation the gift may remain incomplete until the note is either paid or negotiated for value). If the donor owns less than a complete interest in the property in question, the gift will be limited to the interest that he or she in fact owns and does in fact transfer. If the donor transfers less than his or her entire interest in the property, the donor is deemed to make a gift only of the portion actually transferred.

§ 20 WHAT IS A "TRANSFER" FOR FEDERAL GIFT TAX PURPOSES?

Taxable Transfers. I.R.C. § 2511 broadly states that the gift tax shall apply whether the transfer is in trust or otherwise and whether the gift is direct or indirect. Therefore, a gift may occur not only by an outright transfer from one person to another of some property interest, but also by such other techniques as, for example, the gratuitous discharge of the donee's obligation by the creditor or by a third party.

As to non-taxable transfers, it has been held that a wife who substituted her own promissory note to a bank for her husband's notes did *not* make a taxable gift, where all of the parties understood and expected that the obligation would be satisfied from the husband's assets, which remained pledged as security for the wife's note, and the wife had no significant assets of her own. Bradford v. Commissioner, 34 T.C. 1059 (1960). To be sure, a transfer that is not complete for income tax purposes, such that the donor remains taxable on the income from the property as its constructive owner, may nevertheless constitute a completed gift for gift tax purposes. See, e.g., Lockard v. Commissioner, 166 F.2d 409 (1st Cir. 1948). Furthermore, the gift and estate taxes are not perfectly correlated. For example, a transfer may be complete and taxable for gift tax purposes even though it is deemed incomplete for estate tax purposes, and hence subject to estate tax at the donor's death. See., e.g., Commissioner v. Beck's Estate, 129 F.2d 243 (2d Cir. 1942).

Rendering *services* for someone without compensation will not be taxed as a gift, even if those services produce definite, ascertainable financial gain for the recipient. See Commissioner v. Hogle, 165 F.2d 352 (10th Cir. 1947) (father's uncompensated investment services produced profits for children). But interest-free demand loans do give rise to taxable gifts of the value of the use of the money lent. See Dickman v. Commissioner, 465 U.S. 330 (1984) (interest-free demand loan has two components: an arm's-length loan from lender to borrower, with "constructive" interest, and a "constructive" gift from the lender to the borrower in the amount of the foregone interest).

Disclaimers. A disclaimer or renunciation of an interest in property may constitute an indirect transfer, as when a beneficiary refuses to accept his or her share in an estate or a trust and thereby enlarges the share of the other beneficiaries. Nevertheless, if the requisite formalities are observed, a disclaimer may escape being treated as a transfer for purposes of state property law: The disclaimed interest will be deemed to pass directly from the original owner to the ultimate recipient, without ever passing through the hands of the disclaimant. In some early cases, the courts looked solely to state law in deciding whether to afford similar treatment to disclaimers for federal gift tax purposes. If the disclaimer prevented any interest from vesting in the disclaimant under state law, there was no taxable gift; but if the interest was deemed to reach the ultimate recipient as the result of a transfer by the disclaimant, the gift tax was applicable. See Brown v. Routzahn, 63 F.2d 914 (6th Cir. 1933), cert. den., 290 U.S. 641 (1933); Hardenbergh v. Commissioner, 198 F.2d 63 (8th Cir. 1952), cert. den., 344 U.S. 836 (1952). The regulations now provide that, if the disclaimed interest was created by a transfer before 1977, the disclaimer escapes gift tax only if it is effective under state law *and* is made "within a reasonable time after knowledge of the existence of the transfer." Reg. § 25.2511–1(c). Thus, for example, a trust beneficiary's disclaimer of his contingent remainder interest, made shortly before the death of the life beneficiary and 33 years after the creation of the trust, though valid under state law, was held to be a taxable gift. Jewett v. Commissioner, 455 U.S. 305 (1982).

I.R.C. § 2518 was enacted in 1976 to provide definitive and uniform federal transfer tax rules concerning disclaimers. This provision applies to any disclaimer of an interest created by a transfer after 1976. If a person makes a "qualified disclaimer" (as defined in § 2518(b)) of an interest in property, the gift tax applies "as if the interest had never been transferred to such person." I.R.C. § 2518(a). Accordingly, for gift tax purposes the disclaimed interest is deemed to pass directly from the original transferor to the ultimate recipient. The effects of a qualified disclaimer extend also to the estate tax and the GST tax. I.R.C. §§ 2046 and 2654(c). Section 2518(b) defines a qualified disclaimer as "an irrevocable and unqualified refusal by a person to accept an interest in property," made in writing. The refusal must be made within nine months from the date of the "transfer" creating the interest, or from the date on which the disclaimant reaches the age of 21, whichever is later. See I.R.C. § 2518(b)(2); Reg. § 25.2518–2(c).

Two additional conditions must be met, and they introduce considerable complexity into the operation of the disclaimer provisions. First, § 2518(b)(3) states that the disclaimant must not have accepted the interest or "any of its benefits." In general, acceptance of one interest does not preclude a disclaimer of another separate interest created by the original transferor in the same property, but acceptance of any consideration for making a disclaimer is treated as an acceptance of the entire interest disclaimed. Reg. § 25.2518–2(d). Partial disclaimers are allowed with respect to an "undivided portion" of an interest, including a portion consisting of severable property or a pecuniary amount, if all the other statutory requirements are met. I.R.C. § 2518(c)(1); Reg. § 25.2518–3. Second, § 2518(b)(4) requires that the disclaimed interest must pass to the original transferor's spouse or to some person other than the disclaimant, "without any direction" on the part of the disclaimant. This means that the disclaimer must also be valid under state law. Thus, § 2518 does not operate as a uniform federal disclaimer rule pure and simple, but rather as a set of federal requirements superimposed on the disparate rules already in existence under state law.

Section 2518(c)(3) was enacted in 1981 to provide a purely federal disclaimer rule. This provision dispenses with the "pass without direction" requirement of § 2518(b)(4) in the case of a "transfer disclaimer," if all the other requirements of a qualified disclaimer are met. Thus, if a person makes a timely written *transfer* of his or her entire interest to the person who would have received it pursuant to a valid disclaimer under applicable state law, the transfer will be treated as a qualified disclaimer. Some uncertainty remains, however, because § 2518(c)(3) applies only to disclaimers of interests created *after* 1981. Thus there are three different sets of disclaimer rules governing interests created before 1977, after 1976 but before 1982, and after 1981, respectively. Note also that § 2518(c)(3) covers only disclaimers of "the transferor's entire interest in the property," so that partial disclaimers are still governed by § 2518(b).

Indirect Transfers. A gift may take the form of an indirect transfer, as when one person discharges another person's obligation by payment to a third party. A gratuitous transfer of property by an individual to a corporation is generally regarded as a gift by the transferor to the other shareholders, to the extent of their proportionate interests in the corporation. Similarly, a gratuitous transfer by a corporation to an individual will be treated as a gift to the transferee from the other shareholders. Reg. § 25.2511–1(h)(1). If one person transfers property to another person on condition that the transferee make a further payment to a third party, the whole transaction will be regarded as a gift from the original transferor to the third party, to the extent of the property received by the third party from the intermediary. Reg. § 25.2511–1(h)(2) and (h)(3). Such a determination will affect, among other things, the number of available annual per-donee exclusions. See Estate of Bartman v. Commissioner, 10 T.C. 1073 (1948).

Net Gifts. If a person makes a gift of cash or other property and conditions the gift on the donee's agreement to pay the resulting gift tax liability, the amount of the gift is less than the full value of the transferred property. Since the gift tax is primarily a liability of the donor, the donee's payment may be viewed as consideration received by the donor. In effect, the donor has made a "net gift" of the value of the transferred property less the amount of the gift tax. See Harrison v. Commissioner, 17 T.C. 1350 (1952). The gift tax computation is complicated by the fact that the amount of the taxable gift depends on the amount of the gift tax, which in turn depends on the amount of the taxable gift, giving rise to a problem of interdependent variables. The net gift rule and a formula to determine the amount of gift tax due on the net gift are set out in Rev. Rul. 75–72, 1975–1 C.B. 310.

A net gift transaction may also result in income tax consequences to the donor. In Diedrich v. Commissioner, 457 U.S. 191 (1982), the Supreme Court analyzed the transaction as a part-gift, part-sale in which the donor sold the property in exchange for the donee's payment of the donor's gift tax obligation. As a result, the donor had taxable gain to the extent the amount realized (i.e., the gift tax paid by the donee) exceeded the donor's basis in the transferred property.

Interest-Free Loans. For many years it was possible to make interest-free loans without incurring gift tax liability. Interest-free loans were an effective and simple technique for the tax-free transfer of wealth. Suppose a borrower needed a loan of $300,000 to start a business. A bank would charge 10% simple annual interest on the loan, requiring an interest payment of $30,000 per year. If the borrower could obtain an interest-free loan from a wealthy parent, there would be an implicit wealth transfer of $30,000 per year (assuming the parent could have loaned the money at a 10% rate), without gift tax. If, on the other hand, the parent transferred $30,000 to the borrower to pay the borrower's interest expense, the $30,000 would be subject to the gift tax (though a portion of this amount would be eligible for a § 2503(b) exclusion).

As early as 1953, the Tax Court ruled that a transfer of property in exchange for a below-market-interest note constituted a taxable gift to the extent the value of the property exceeded the present value of the note at the time of the transfer. See Blackburn v. Commissioner, 20 T.C. 204 (1953).

Subsequently, however, a distinction was made between interest-free (or below-market-interest) *term* loans and interest-free *demand* loans. In theory (though not often in practice), a demand note could be called by the lender for full repayment at any time.

In one 1966 case a federal district court, without citing *Blackburn,* found it significant that the lending parents had no duty to invest their money. Since the lenders (parents) could have kept their money in cash (perhaps under a mattress?), the court saw no reason to imply a gift of interest on a loan to the children. Johnson v. United States, 254 F. Supp. 73 (N.D. Tex. 1966).

It was not until 1973 that the Service announced its intention to ignore the *Johnson* ruling and to apply the logic of *Blackburn* to interest-free demand loans. See Rev. Rul. 73–61, 1973–1 C.B. 408.

The Service's position was challenged in the courts. By 1984, there was a conflict in the federal courts of appeal. One circuit followed the reasoning of *Johnson* (Crown v. Commissioner, 585 F.2d 234 (7th Cir. 1978)), while another upheld the Service's position (Dickman v. Commissioner, 690 F.2d 812 (11th Cir. 1982)).

In Dickman v. Commissioner, 465 U.S. 330 (1984), the Supreme Court resolved the conflict in favor of the Service's position—an interest-free demand loan gives rise to annual gifts of (uncharged) interest to the borrower, much as if the lender charged and collected interest each year and then immediately gave the interest back to the borrower.

Dickman did not end the controversy surrounding the use of interest-free loans as tax avoidance devices. Such loans remained popular because the $10,000 annual exclusion sheltered some fairly large loans from the gift tax. Even at a 10% implied rate, for example, spouses electing the § 2513 gift-splitting provision could make a $200,000 loan to a child without incurring gift tax on the uncharged $20,000 interest. In addition, any *income* generated from investment of the loan proceeds (e.g., bank account interest) would be attributed to the child and taxed at the child's (probably lower) marginal income tax rate. This income tax avoidance technique is called *income shifting*.

After standing on the sidelines of the interest-free loan controversy for a decade, Congress resolved most of the interest-free loan questions when it enacted I.R.C. § 7872 in 1984.

In the event of any below-market-rate (or interest-free) loan, the foregone interest is treated as a gift from the lender to the borrower. In order to eliminate income-shifting opportunities, the foregone interest is considered also to be *interest income to the lender*. I.R.C. § 7872(a)(1). In other words, § 7872 creates an imaginary world in which the recipient of an interest-free loan pays "interest" to the lender and the lender transfers this "interest" back to the recipient as a gift. Section 7872 applies to both term and demand loans. Interest is imputed at an "applicable Federal rate" determined under § 1274(d). I.R.C. § 7872(f)(2).

Section 7872 provides a general de minimis exception, from both its gift and income tax provisions, for gift loans between individuals not exceeding $10,000 outstanding at any one time. However, this exception does not apply if the borrower invests the loan proceeds in income-producing assets. I.R.C. § 7872(c)(2).

Time of Gift. As to the *time* of a transfer by gift, there is some authority that a taxable transfer takes place upon the making of a contract or promise to transfer in the future, rather than at the later time when property is transferred in satisfaction of the contractual promise. A transfer of property after the wedding pursuant to an antenuptial contract exemplifies this problem. See Commissioner v. Estate of Copley, 194 F.2d 364 (7th Cir. 1952).

In an attempt to clarify the treatment of a promise to make future payments, the Service has ruled that the effective date for gift tax purposes is the date on which the promise becomes enforceable under state law, not the later date on which the payment is actually made, at least if the gift is susceptible of valuation at the time the agreement becomes enforceable. See Rev. Rul. 69–347, 1969–1 C.B. 227 (future payments under antenuptial agreement, effective at time of marriage). If the value of the gift depends on the donor's future income or wealth, the Service may take the position that there is no completed transfer until the value of the gift becomes ascertainable. See Rev. Rul. 69–346, 1969–1 C.B. 227 (promise to allow community property to pass under will of living spouse, effective at spouse's death). The Tax Court, however, has rejected the Service's "open transaction" approach, reasoning that a gift becomes complete when the donor relinquishes dominion and control over the transferred property, without regard to whether the value of the property is readily ascertainable at that time. See Estate of DiMarco v. Commissioner, 87 T.C. 653 (1986) (death benefit payable to deceased employee's widow not included in decedent's adjusted taxable gifts).

In general, a transfer is deemed to be complete when the donor has fully relinquished dominion and control over the property that is the subject of the gift. Some special rules have been established to govern particular problems such as the gift of a note or check. For example, the gift of a donor's own promissory note is not complete until the note is paid or transferred for value. Similarly, the gift of a donor's own check generally is complete when the check is paid or negotiated for value to a third person; prior to payment or negotiation for value, the gift can be revoked at any time by stopping payment or by the donor's death. See Rev. Rul. 67–396, 1967–2 C.B. 351; Rev. Rul. 84–25, 1984–1 C.B. 191. Nevertheless, the Service concedes that a completed gift of the donor's own check may be deemed to occur at an earlier date when the check is deposited or cashed by the donee, if the check is paid upon presentation and the donor is still alive at the time of payment. See Rev. Rul. 96–56, 1996–2 C.B. 161. The gift of a note or check of a third party is complete at the time of transfer of the note or check.

Of course, a gift is not complete if it is revocable. Since the donor can get the property back at any time by exercising the power to revoke the gift, the occasion for imposing a gift tax has not arisen. See Burnet v. Guggenheim, 288 U.S. 280 (1933). Even if the donor cannot exercise the power to revoke, but retains a right to change beneficial interests—even in a way that will not benefit the donor—the gift will be regarded as incomplete. See Sanford's Estate v. Commissioner, 308 U.S. 39 (1939). So, if a donor establishes a trust and retains a power to alter the beneficial interests in the trust (though not in favor of the donor), the creation of the trust does not constitute a completed gift. As amounts are paid over to beneficiaries from the trust, the donor will be deemed to have made completed gifts, since those amounts are then no longer under the donor's dominion and control.

So, a transfer generally becomes complete for gift tax purposes when the donor relinquishes dominion and control over the property; it is not sufficient that the donor give up the power to take back the property for himself, nor is it necessary that a specific donee be assured of possession or enjoyment. See Reg. § 25.2511–2. If a gift causa mortis is revocable, it is not a completed gift for gift tax purposes. A gift made in connection with a separation or divorce is deemed to occur when the obligation to transfer the property first becomes enforceable. A transfer of property subject to a life interest in the transferor will be deemed to be a completed gift of the whole property minus the interest retained by him—in other words, a gift of the remainder interest—for gift tax purposes. If the transferor later were to make a separate transfer of the retained life interest, there would be another completed gift at that time.

If the donor does retain some interest in the property given away, that interest must be susceptible of valuation or else the value of the gift will be determined without any allowance for the retained interest. If a gift is regarded as incomplete because the donor has retained dominion and control, a completed gift for gift tax purposes will occur upon relinquishment or termination of the donor's dominion and control during his or her lifetime. In general, the degree of control that the donor must retain in order to render a gift incomplete for gift tax purposes is somewhat greater than what must be retained to render a transfer incomplete until death for estate tax purposes.

In general, the rules about when a transfer is complete for gift tax purposes do not coincide exactly with the rules about when a transfer is complete for estate tax purposes. Therefore, a transfer that is complete and thus incurs a gift tax may nevertheless be regarded as incomplete for estate tax purposes, with the result that estate tax is payable on the same property or interest at the time of the donor's death (with a credit for the gift tax incurred during life). See Chapter 5, especially § 39, *infra.*

§ 21 LIABILITY FOR GIFT TAX

Primary liability for the gift tax rests with the donor, but the donee is secondarily liable for the tax, to the extent of the value of the gift. In fact, the donee may be liable even if it has not been proven impossible to collect from the donor. The tax may be assessed against the donee at any time within one year after the expiration of the period of limitation for assessment against the donor. Also, the gift tax forms a lien against the gift property for a period of ten years from the date of the gift. Moreover, the recipient of a tax-free gift can be held liable (though only to the extent of the value of the gift) for any unpaid tax on other gifts made by the donor in the same year. See I.R.C. §§ 6324(b), 6901(a)(1)(A)(iii), 6901(c)(1), and related sections.

§ 22 APPLICATION OF THE GST TAX TO "TRANSFERS" AT DEATH AND DURING LIFE

It is important not to lose sight of the fact that the GST tax constitutes a separate tax on the transfer of wealth and may be imposed upon certain events that constitute direct skips, taxable terminations, or taxable distributions. The application of this tax was outlined in considerable detail in § 15, *supra*, and will not be further recapitulated here.

CHAPTER 4

DONATIVE INTENT AND CONSIDERATION

§ 23 GIFT TAX: DONATIVE INTENT AND CONSIDERATION

Donative intent (on the part of the transferor) is not an essential element in the application of the gift tax. Application of the tax is based on the objective facts of the transfer and the circumstances under which it is made rather than on the subjective intent or motives of the donor. Reg. § 25.2511–1(g)(1). Therefore, it will not avail the taxpayer to claim that a transfer otherwise constituting a gift was not a gift because he or she did not have the requisite intent; by the same token, it is not necessary for the Service to prove that the taxpayer did have donative intent in making the transfer in order to impose the tax.

A leading case standing for the proposition that donative intent is not necessary is Commissioner v. Wemyss, 324 U.S. 303 (1945). There, the taxpayer transferred shares of stock to his fiancée in performance of his obligations under an antenuptial agreement. The court of appeals had held that the marriage agreement was an arms-length bargain, that the transfer was not made with donative intent, and that in the absence of donative intent the transfer was not subject to gift tax. In reversing, the Supreme Court said that Congress intended to use the term "gift" in its broadest and most comprehensive sense (not in the common-law or colloquial sense) and chose not to require an ascertainment of an elusive state of mind. The transfer was taxable whether or not accompanied by "donative intent."

The Supreme Court went on to hold that for purposes of the gift tax Congress not only dispensed with the test of "donative intent" but also formulated an external or objective test: if property is transferred for less than an adequate and full consideration in money or money's worth, the excess value shall be deemed a gift for purposes of the gift tax. The adequate and full consideration rule is now embodied in I.R.C. § 2512(b). Whether the transferor receives something in return and the consideration received is worth less than the property transferred, or the transferor of property receives nothing in return, the excess value of the property transferred is deemed to be a gift.

In the *Wemyss* case, the Supreme Court further elaborated the consideration rule in holding that the transferor received no consideration, for gift tax purposes, in the promise of his betrothed to marry him or, evidently, in the marriage itself. Thus the Court emphasized that consideration for contract law or other purposes is not the same as consideration that is "full and adequate in money or money's worth" for gift tax purposes.

The gift tax regulations state that consideration that is not reducible to a value in money or money's worth (e.g., love and affection, or a promise of marriage) is wholly disregarded and the entire value of the property transferred constitutes the amount of the gift. The regulations go on to say that relinquishment or promised relinquishment of dower or curtesy, or of a statutory estate created in lieu thereof, or of other marital rights in the spouse's property or estate, shall not be considered to any extent a consideration "in money or money's worth." Reg. § 25.2512–8. (Special rules are provided in I.R.C. § 2516 with respect to some transfers made in connection with divorce. See § 25, *infra.*)

In point of fact, not every transfer or unequal exchange will be treated as a taxable gift. To illustrate, the regulations state that the gift tax is not applicable to ordinary business transactions and that a sale, exchange or other transfer made in the ordinary course of business will be considered as made for an adequate and full consideration in money or money's worth. A transfer made in the ordinary course of business is defined as a transaction which is "bona fide, at arm's length, and free from any donative intent." Reg. § 25.2512–8. Thus, many transactions in which an unequal transfer or exchange is made do not give rise to gift tax liability. Further, donative intent, which was held not to be an essential element of a taxable gift, is introduced as relevant to the question whether the transfer is a non-taxable transfer or exchange rather than a gift. Therefore, if a purchase or other exchange is made in the ordinary course of business and in a transaction where the parties deal at arm's length, if there is no attempt to disguise a gift in the form of a business transaction, and if there is no evidence of an intent on the part of one party to confer an unreciprocated benefit on the other, the transfer will not be taxable.

Many cases have demonstrated the principle that a transaction made in the ordinary course of business and at arm's length will not be taxed under the gift tax, even though the transferor does not receive consideration in money or money's worth equal to the value of the property transferred. See, e.g., Estate of Anderson v. Commissioner, 8 T.C. 706 (1947), involving senior executives who transferred some of their common stock in a corporation to junior executives at a bargain price. The transaction was conceded by the Service to be bona fide and at arm's length, and was part of a business plan to adjust the proportionate share ownership among the management group as responsibilities were shifted from senior executives to their junior colleagues. The court, concluding that no gift had been made, relied heavily on the business context of the transaction and distinguished it from the kind of marital or family transaction involved in the *Wemyss* case and other leading gift tax cases.

The exception for business or arm's-length transactions makes eminent good sense, of course. Otherwise, every purchase or exchange would have to be examined to determine whether in fact there was an inequality in actual value in the exchange for purposes of gift tax liability. Any time a taxpayer made an ill-advised sale or found a bargain, there would be a serious question of potential transfer tax liability. Such a state of affairs certainly would prove unworkable. Even under present law, however, difficult problems arise when a so-called business transaction arises in a family context, where one may suspect that the parties may not be dealing at arm's length, or when in a business context a transfer takes place involving a considerable difference in values exchanged that cannot be explained simply on the ground that someone drove a hard bargain or found a good deal.

Under the broad definition of "gift" as used in the Internal Revenue Code and interpreted by the Supreme Court in the *Wemyss* case, and under the so-called "external test" of when a gift is present, a great variety of transactions have been deemed to constitute gifts. For example, a wife who paid the annual premiums on policies of insurance on her husband's life was held to make annual gifts to the extent the premium payments exceeded the value of her rights therein under the trust in which the policies were held. (Under the terms of that trust, the proceeds of the life insurance policies would be held for the benefit of several beneficiaries including the wife. Thus, the wife's annual premium payments conferred benefits not only on herself but also on the other beneficiaries.) Commissioner v. Berger, 201 F.2d 171 (2d Cir. 1953). The court went on to say that the absence of donative intent is especially unimportant in family transactions where the lifetime transfer reduces the donor's potential estate tax liability.

In another case, a taxable gift was found when a guardian, with the approval of a court, made payments from the estate of the taxpayer, a well-to-do minor, to the taxpayer's mother. Evidently the taxpayer had no legal obligation to support her mother, but the payments were made for the mother's personal support. So, the court said, since neither the taxpayer nor her estate received any benefit from any of the payments made that could be recognized as consideration, the payments were taxable as gifts. Stokowski v. Pedrick, 52–2 USTC ¶ 10,861 (S.D.N.Y. 1952); see also Commissioner v. Greene, 119 F.2d 383 (9th Cir. 1941), cert. den., 314 U.S. 641 (1941).

In some other cases, transfers between family members have been found to have been made at arm's length and thus to fall beyond the reach of the gift tax under the doctrine noted earlier that a transaction which is bona fide, at arm's length and free from any donative intent will be considered as made for an adequate and full consideration in money or money's worth. See, e.g., Beveridge v. Commissioner, 10 T.C. 915 (1948). The transaction need not take place in the business world or in a commercial context to escape tax. However, a heavy burden rests on the taxpayer to demonstrate an absence of donative intent in a family transaction and to prove that the parties dealt with each other "bona fide" and at arm's length. In some situations, a taxable gift has been found even though there were many indications of rationally calculated, self-interested behavior by the taxpayer. See, e.g., Commissioner v. Siegel, 250 F.2d 339 (9th Cir. 1957) (widow's election to let community property pass under deceased husband's will, discussed more fully in § 38, *infra.*) (In other instances, the widow's election will not result in gift tax liability because she receives more than she gives up. See, e.g., Turman v. Commissioner, 35 T.C. 1123 (1961).)

The "external test" has also led some courts to honor installment sales between relatives, with the subsequent forgiveness of the debt at the rate of $10,000 per year qualifying for the annual gift tax exclusion. The original transaction is treated as a bona fide sale, despite the avowed intent of the "seller" to forgive each installment as it comes due, and thus, in the course of time, to forgive the entire debt. For example, suppose a parent sells property worth $100,000 to her child in exchange for $10,000 cash down and a $90,000 mortgage note payable in $10,000 annual installments over the next nine years. Under Haygood v. Commissioner, 42 T.C. 936 (1964), and Estate of Kelley v. Commissioner, 63 T.C. 321 (1974), the sale is deemed to be for adequate consideration, i.e., the down payment plus the note. The parent's forgiveness of each annual installment as it comes due constitutes a gift of $10,000 to the child, but the gifts are excludable under § 2503, with the result that the entire transaction escapes gift tax. The Service has indicated strong dissatisfaction with this result, and will not follow the decisions in *Haygood* and *Kelley*. Rev. Rul. 77–299, 1977–2 C.B. 343. Note, however, that under I.R.C. § 453B, any disposition of an installment obligation, even by gift or cancellation, will cause recognition of any gain inherent in the note. This limits the utility of the *Haygood* plan in many situations. Instead of forgiving annual installments under a note, a better plan might be for the transferor to make annual gifts of specified portions of the property equal in value to the available per-donee annual exclusion. See Rev. Rul. 83–180, 1983–2 C.B. 169 (distinguishing Rev. Rul. 77–299).

Notwithstanding the objective test of whether a gift has been made, the motive or state of mind of the donor has been examined in some instances to determine whether or not a particular transfer is subject to gift tax. See, e.g., Pascarelli v. Commissioner, 55 T.C. 1082 (1971), aff'd, 485 F.2d 681 (3d Cir. 1973), involving the liability of a donee for gift tax. A man lived with the donee as husband and wife, although they were unmarried. The man gave cash to the donee, opened a brokerage account in her name, and made improvements in her home. She rendered services in entertaining the man's business customers, but these were disregarded by the court. The court found that the transfers were motivated by affection, respect and admiration and held the donee liable for the tax as transferee of the property. These transfers would clearly have been taxable as gifts if a purely mechanical formula such as that suggested by I.R.C. § 2512(b) had been employed; the reason for inquiring into the donor's state of mind was to determine that the transfers were not made in the ordinary course of business, bona fide, at arm's length, and without donative intent. To use the motivations of affection, respect and admiration as affirmative evidence of a gift seems inconsistent with the Supreme Court's approach in the *Wemyss* case and with many other authorities, unless—perhaps—such evidence merely serves to negate a suggestion that the transfer was a business transaction at arm's length.

Some situations involve a mixed family and business context. For example, a gift may be found upon formation of a family business if some members of the family (usually children) receive disproportionately large shares in the business compared to other members of the family (usually parents) in exchange for their respective contributions of property or services. See Gross v. Commissioner, 7 T.C. 837 (1946) (family partnership); Heringer v. Commissioner, 235 F.2d 149 (9th Cir. 1956), cert. den., 352 U.S. 927 (1956) (family corporation). However, if all of the family members receive interests in proportion to their contributions, so that no member's contribution enhances the value of another member's interest, the formation of the business does not result in a taxable gift. See Estate of Strangi v. Commissioner, 115 T.C. 478 (2000), aff'd on this issue and rev'd on another issue sub nom. Gulig v. Commissioner, 293 F.3d 279 (5th Cir. 2002) (family partnership). (See §§ 2701–2704, discussed at § 49, *infra,* and the regulations thereunder for special valuation rules applicable to certain transfers of interests in family-owned business entities, transfers in trust, and transfers of property subject to rights and restrictions.)

For many years the status of political contributions or similar payments, made in either a business or a private context, was somewhat unclear. In an important early case, DuPont v. United States, 97 F. Supp. 944 (D. Del. 1951), a contribution by the taxpayer to the National Economic Council, an organization formed for economic, political and lobbying purposes, was held taxable as a gift. In Rev. Rul. 59–57, 1959–1 C.B. 626, the Service ruled that a contribution to a political party or to a candidate for public office was a taxable gift. However, the Service has also ruled that a transfer of property by local citizens to a manufacturing company in order to induce it to operate a manufacturing plant constituted a transfer in the ordinary course of business and not a gift. Rev. Rul. 68–558, 1968–2 C.B. 415. In Stern v. United States, 436 F.2d 1327 (5th Cir. 1971), political contributions to citizens' groups were held not to be taxable gifts. The court somehow concluded that the transfers were made in the ordinary course of business because they were bona fide, at arm's length, and free from donative intent. The Service then announced that it would not follow the *Stern* case outside the Fifth Circuit.

In 1975, Congress rendered the issue largely moot by enacting an unlimited exemption from gift tax for transfers of money or other property to "political organizations" (as defined in § 527(e)). I.R.C. § 2501(a)(4). A further unlimited exemption for transfers of money or other property to tax-exempt social welfare organizations, labor organizations, and trade associations was added in 2015. I.R.C. § 2501(a)(6). There are, it should be noted, no parallel provisions for testamentary transfers under the estate tax.

In summary, the Supreme Court has taken the partial consideration rule of I.R.C. § 2512(b) as part of the basic definition of the term "gift," even though the language and structure of that provision might suggest the more modest function of measuring the value of property transferred in a transaction otherwise determined to be a gift. The Supreme Court has therefore refused to import the common law concept of consideration and the requirement of donative intent into the gift tax law. Thus, the concept of a gift, for gift tax purposes, is given very wide scope, although a sale, exchange, or other transfer of property made in the ordinary course of business (a transaction which is bona fide, at arm's length and free from donative intent) falls outside the reach of the gift tax. The presence or absence of donative intent may be relevant in determining whether a transaction is a gift, although donative intent is generally not required for a transfer to be subject to gift tax.

By defining a gift largely in terms of the adequacy of consideration in money or money's worth, the Service and the courts have placed heavy pressure on the determination of what amounts to "consideration" for gift tax purposes. Clearly, the descriptive phrase "in money or money's worth" indicates that consideration will be determined by economic value rather than by concepts drawn from the law of contracts, where a peppercorn may still suffice. A loss of wealth or income or some other detriment incurred by the transferee is not counted as consideration, since it does not benefit the transferor.

Underlying the definition of a gift for gift tax purposes are considerations related to the role of the gift tax as a backstop for the estate tax. Thus, a transfer which depletes the estate of the transferor is likely to be regarded as a taxable gift. However, that notion cannot safely be translated into a rule, for many consumption expenditures and other disbursements that do in fact deplete the wealth and hence the gross estate of a person are not transfers subject to gift tax. Support given to a family member whom the taxpayer is obligated to support, such as a minor child or spouse, is not a taxable gift. A transfer by an elderly parent to a child will be scrutinized very carefully, even if it is cast in the form of a purchase or other business transaction, to determine whether it is a gift in disguise. While not every estate-depleting expenditure will be taxed as a gift, a transfer of property that confers a net benefit upon the recipient and is not offset by a benefit flowing to the transferor of the kind that will show up in his gross estate at death ("money or money's worth") is likely to be taxable as a gift unless it falls within the exemption for transfers in the ordinary course of business, the consumption expenditure area, or some other exception from the broad, "external" test laid down by the Supreme Court in determining whether a gift has been made.

Special problems with the concept of consideration in "money or money's worth" arise when one spouse transfers property to the other spouse in return for the recipient's relinquishment of marital property or support rights. The treatment of such transfers for gift and estate tax purposes is discussed in the following section.

§ 24 MARITAL PROPERTY AND SUPPORT RIGHTS AS CONSIDERATION: ESTATE TAX AND GIFT TAX

When a married person dies, leaving a surviving spouse, the gross estate includes the value of all property to the extent of the decedent's interest at the time of death. The gross estate is not reduced to the extent of any interest in such property accruing to the surviving spouse at the decedent's death as *dower* or *curtesy,* or by virtue of a statute creating an estate in lieu of dower or curtesy. I.R.C. § 2034. The full value of the property is included in the decedent's gross estate, without any deduction for the surviving spouse's interest and without regard to when the right to such an interest arose. Reg. § 20.2034–1.

Consider, then, the situation of a married decedent who dies in a separate property state with an estate worth $30 million. Suppose the decedent disinherited his wife and left the entire estate by will to his own relatives. The widow, however, exercises her right to claim a dower interest (or, more commonly, a statutory elective share in lieu of dower) equal to one-half of the estate, notwithstanding the terms of the decedent's will. For tax purposes, the decedent's gross estate will consist of $30 million, with no reduction for the value of the widow's dower interest that ripens into possession at the decedent's death. In other words, the gross estate will be $30 million, not $15 million.

This rule (and the result shown in the foregoing example) seems to make perfectly good sense. It treats equally the decedent involved in that example and a decedent who leaves an equivalent amount of property to his wife by will or whose wife takes an equivalent share of the estate under the laws of intestacy. In each case, the gross estate consists of the property owned by the decedent at death, not reduced by the inchoate dower or curtesy or statutory substitute interest held by the surviving spouse.

To evaluate § 2034 further, however, compare the preceding example with the situation of a similar married couple in a *community property* state. If the husband is the first to die and if the couple owns $30 million of community property, the husband's gross estate will consist of only $15 million, not $30 million. This follows because each spouse has an equal undivided interest in the community property owned at the husband's death. One half of the community property passes from the husband by will or intestacy and is includable in his gross estate under § 2033; the other half is already owned by the widow, and is not subject to the husband's testamentary control. Thus the widow's interest in the community property, which serves as a counterpart of the dower interest (or statutory substitute) held by a surviving spouse in a separate property state, is excluded from the husband's gross estate. It would seem, therefore, that very different tax treatment of the two decedents in the two states would result, although economically their positions are very similar.

Most disparity in treatment—between the community property decedent and the separate property decedent—is relieved by the unlimited estate tax *marital deduction* provided in I.R.C. § 2056 for property passing from the decedent to a surviving spouse. Although the *gross* estates of the two decedents are unequal, the marital deduction reduces the *taxable* estate of the separate property decedent from $30 million to $15 million if the widow is entitled to and does in fact receive $15 million worth of property. The result is the same whether she takes her share of the estate under the decedent's will, by intestate succession, or as an outright payment of an elective share; in each case, the property is deemed to pass from the decedent to the widow, as required by the statute. I.R.C. § 2056(c). Thus, assuming the widow receives half of the marital property, the taxable estate of the separate property decedent is no greater than that of the community property decedent. (The marital deduction does not apply to the widow's one-half share of the community property, since there was no transfer at death from the decedent to her).

Therefore, the rule of I.R.C. § 2034 (denying any reduction for dower or curtesy) makes sense when one compares the tax treatment of two decedents in separate property states, one of whom leaves property by will to his surviving spouse and the other who does not do so but whose spouse claims a dower interest or elective share. To the extent that § 2034 puts decedents in separate property states at a disadvantage relative to decedents in community property states, the disparity is ameliorated by the unlimited estate tax marital deduction under § 2056.

For estate tax purposes, a relinquishment (or promised relinquishment) of dower or curtesy or a statutory substitute, or of "other marital rights in the decedent's property or estate," shall not be considered to any extent a consideration in money or money's worth. I.R.C. § 2043(b)(1). This rule is intended to prevent a payment in satisfaction of marital rights—in substance, a donative transfer to a spouse—from being recast as a deductible claim against the estate. For example, if a wife releases her marital rights in her husband's estate in exchange for a specified sum payable from the husband's estate at his death, the payment to the wife cannot be deducted under § 2053. Even though the husband's promise is enforceable and binding on his estate under state law, he did not receive any consideration in money or money's worth (as defined in § 2043(b)) in exchange for the promised payment. See I.R.C. § 2053(c)(1)(A), discussed in § 59, *infra.* (Although the payment cannot be deducted as a claim under § 2053, it may still qualify for a marital deduction under § 2056, discussed in Chapter 13, *infra.*)

The rule of I.R.C. § 2043(b), defining "consideration in money or money's worth" to exclude a relinquishment of dower, curtesy, or similar marital rights in a spouse's property or estate, applies with equal force for purposes of the gift tax. See Reg. § 25.2512–8. Thus, if a husband transfers property to his wife, pursuant to an antenuptial agreement, in exchange for the wife's release of dower or other marital rights in the husband's estate, the amount of the husband's gift cannot be offset to any extent by the value of the rights relinquished by the wife. This is the holding of Merrill v. Fahs, 324 U.S. 308 (1945), which arose before the enactment of the marital deduction. (Today, a similar transfer under an antenuptial agreement would probably be sheltered from gift tax by the marital deduction of § 2523, discussed in Chapter 13, *infra.*)

To be distinguished from the marital rights that § 2043(b) decrees shall not be regarded as consideration in money or money's worth are rights to support and vested community property rights. For purposes of the gift tax, a relinquishment of support rights is regarded as consideration in money or money's worth. Rev. Rul. 68–379, 1968–2 C.B. 414. Consequently, an inter vivos transfer of property made in return for a release of support rights will not be a taxable gift to the extent of the value of the relinquished support rights. For estate tax purposes also, support rights fall outside the exclusionary rule of § 2043(b) and are therefore treated as consideration in money or money's worth. Accordingly, a deduction will be allowed under § 2053 for a claim founded on a promise or agreement given in return for a release of support rights.

Also, a spouse's vested rights in community property are not the kind of marital rights that are excluded from the definition of consideration in money or money's worth in § 2043(b) or the corresponding rule in the gift tax area. Such vested community property rights or interests amount to "property" which will be recognized as consideration in money or money's worth for estate and gift tax purposes. Hence, if one spouse makes or promises to make a transfer of property in return for the other spouse's release of such vested community property rights, the transfer will be deemed to be made for a consideration in money or money's worth up to the value of the community property rights released by the other spouse.

To regard the release of support rights as consideration and hence to refrain from applying the gift tax to a transfer made for equivalent value in the form of a release of support rights makes perfectly good sense. The transfer of property in exchange for the release of support rights can be viewed as an anticipatory lump-sum substitute for the provision of support during the joint lifetime of the two spouses. For example, expenditures actually made by one spouse to provide support for the other spouse during marriage would not be taxable as gifts, even in the absence of a marital deduction. Such outlays are not taxed as gifts because they are made in discharge of a legal obligation. Although expenditures for support do reduce the gross estate and hence the taxable estate of the person who makes them, they are not the kind of gratuitous transfers at which the federal transfer taxes are aimed. Similarly, if one spouse dies without having fulfilled his or her support obligations during life and the surviving spouse pursues a claim against the estate for delinquent support payments, that claim would give rise to a deduction under § 2053; even if founded on a promise or agreement, the claim would be deemed to have been contracted for consideration in money or money's worth. Since the lifetime provision of support would not be taxed as a gift and since the claim against the estate for support wrongfully withheld would give rise to a deduction from the estate tax, a transfer made in return for a surrender or release of the support obligation during life should not be taxable as a gift.

Similarly, the rule that a spouse's vested interest in community property is consideration in money or money's worth (rather than the kind of marital right which § 2043(b) excludes from the definition of consideration for tax purposes) produces correct results. To be sure, a transfer during life by a husband to his wife in exchange for the wife's conveyance of her interest in community property (or a release of her community property rights) does reduce the husband's wealth which will be included in his gross estate at death. However, in return the husband gains the property conveyed to him by his wife. Thus, the transfer does not result in an artificial depletion of the husband's gross estate.

In other words, this entire area of the law reflects a general policy of protecting the estate and gift tax base from being eroded by marital property settlements that result in artificial estate depletion. Against this policy lies a determination to allow expenditures or transfers that do not result in wrongful estate depletion to be made tax-free. Thus a concept of "artificial" or "wrongful" estate depletion may help to explain the gift and estate tax rules. Another way of viewing the matter is to ask whether the promisee or recipient of an inter vivos transfer either gave something in return that augmented the transferor's wealth (and presumably will augment his or her gross estate at death) or relinquished some right or claim that the transferor otherwise could have been compelled to pay without incurring gift or estate tax. This understanding of the underlying policy, however, is not a legal standard or a way in which the Service or the courts generally frame the matter. At best it can serve as a rationale and framework for thinking about these tax issues.

§ 25 TRANSFERS PURSUANT TO DIVORCE, SEPARATION OR ANNULMENT: APPLICATION OF THE GIFT TAX

Under the general rules governing consideration in money or money's worth, a transfer by one spouse to another (for example, by a husband to his wife) pursuant to a property settlement agreement in connection with divorce would be taxable to the extent the property transferred by the husband exceeded the value, in money or money's worth, of anything he received from his wife in return. Marital rights (i.e., dower, curtesy or a statutory substitute therefor) in property would not constitute consideration in money or money's worth, and thus there would be a gift by the husband except to the extent that the wife gave to him an outright interest in property or released him from a legal obligation of support.

I.R.C. § 2516 provides a special rule that is considerably broader in application and more advantageous for taxpayers than the general principles discussed above. Under this provision, if a husband and wife enter into a written agreement relative to their marital and property rights and if divorce occurs within two years thereafter (or within one year before), any transfers of property or interests in property made pursuant to the agreement to either spouse in settlement of his or her marital or property rights or to provide a reasonable allowance for the support of children of the marriage during minority are deemed to be made for a full and adequate consideration in money or money's worth. This is true regardless of whether the agreement is approved by the divorce decree. Thus, for example, if the husband transfers property to his wife and otherwise complies with the terms of § 2516, it is not necessary for him to show that he received a discharge of support obligations equal in value to what he transferred, in order to escape gift tax. The transfer is exempt from gift tax, so long as it meets the terms of § 2516.

One may well ask why a transfer of property by a husband to his wife in connection with divorce should be exempted from gift tax even though the value of the property he transfers exceeds the value of the rights surrendered by the wife. One answer may lie in a view that the transfer is not a voluntary, gratuitous transfer of the kind the gift tax was designed to reach. The husband's transfer is much like the transfer that he would make if no agreement were reached and the divorce court ordered him to transfer property to his wife. In other words, the transfer has very substantial aspects of involuntariness about it. However, the involuntary, compelled nature of the transfer would not suffice to distinguish it from other transfers that are taxable as gifts under the general principles of the gift tax, in the absence of § 2516.

An additional justification for § 2516 lies in the *marital deduction*. To illustrate: If a man in a separate property state remains married to his wife until death and at that time transfers all or part of his wealth to her, the estate tax marital deduction of § 2056 would enable him to make that transfer without incurring any estate tax liability. In a community property state, by remaining married until death the husband and wife would each have equal undivided one-half interests in their community property; thus, at the husband's death, the wife would have at least her one-half interest, which she received free of gift tax during the marriage.

When a marriage ends in divorce, it may be seen in some sense to suffer an early "death," and transfers made at that time pursuant to a property settlement may be viewed as anticipatory substitutes for the deathtime transfers which would otherwise be eligible for the estate tax marital deduction or which could be accomplished tax-free under a community property system to the extent of the wife's vested one-half interest in the community property.

Thus, a property transfer in connection with divorce, whether made under compulsion of the divorce decree or under a property settlement agreement reached within two years before (or one year after) the divorce, may typically be viewed as an arm's-length bargain by which a spouse makes a transfer as a substitute for later transfers that, if the marriage had survived, would have discharged the lifetime obligation of support and, if made at death to a surviving spouse, would have been wholly tax-free. Accordingly, transfers in connection with divorce are the functional equivalents of transfers which are permitted to be made without tax. They do not seem to be substitutes for a taxable testamentary disposition; they do not (prospectively) deplete the estate tax base.

Before the enactment of § 2516, the Supreme Court held (in a case that remains important for situations not covered by that provision) that the gift tax did not apply to a transfer made pursuant to a property settlement agreement that was conditioned on the entry of a divorce decree and was actually incorporated in the divorce decree. Harris v. Commissioner, 340 U.S. 106 (1950). The Court held that the transfer was founded not so much on a promise or agreement as on the divorce decree itself. The Court pointed out that if the transfer were effected by court decree, it would not be founded on a promise or agreement. Hence, it reasoned, the transfer made pursuant to a property settlement agreement that was incorporated in the divorce decree similarly was free of any promise or agreement. It is not immediately apparent why the freedom from promise or agreement should be the basis for exempting the transfer from gift tax, since the gift tax statute does not require a "promise or agreement." The Court, however, took the "promise or agreement" language from the estate tax provision that authorizes a deduction for claims against the estate, imported that language into the gift tax area, and then concluded that the language did not apply to the facts before it. Whatever the strength of the reasoning, the result was clear—the transfer was not subject to gift tax. The Court reached that result even though the covenants in the agreement were expressly made to survive any divorce decree that might be entered. Broadly speaking, the core of the *Harris* case was the idea that the transfer was made pursuant to a court decree rather than a promise or agreement.

I.R.C. § 2516 goes further than the *Harris* case and makes it unnecessary to show that the transfer was made for consideration, that it was in discharge of a legal obligation, that it was effected by a judicial decree, or even that the agreement was incorporated in or approved by the divorce decree. Under § 2516 it is not necessary to allocate any part of the transfer to the discharge of support rights or to dower or curtesy rights or to show actual consideration for any part of the transfer. And, the provision shelters not only transfers made to a spouse in settlement of marital or property rights but also transfers made to provide a reasonable allowance for the support of children during minority.

If the facts of a given situation do not fit § 2516, for example because the divorce does not occur within the three-year period (one year before or two years after the date of the written agreement), there is still some possibility for avoiding gift tax because § 2516 is not exclusive. If § 2516 does not apply, a transfer incident to divorce may still be sheltered from gift tax by the *Harris* case, which continues to have vitality in the area beyond the reach of § 2516.

If the safe harbor of § 2516 is unavailable, a transfer to a spouse may still escape gift taxation under the *Harris* case as long as the property settlement agreement is incorporated in a divorce decree granted by a court having jurisdiction to approve, disapprove or modify the terms of the agreement. Apparently the agreement need not be expressly conditioned on entry of the divorce decree, and the agreement may be made to survive the decree. See, e.g., McMurtry v. Commissioner, 203 F.2d 659 (1st Cir. 1953).

Another factor affecting the structure and planning of marital property settlement agreements is the unlimited marital deduction, which offers an alternative avenue to avoid gift taxation on interspousal transfers made during marriage.

Interspousal Sales or Gifts and the Income Tax. The income tax treatment of interspousal transfers is governed by I.R.C. § 1041, which must be mentioned in connection with the gift tax. Under § 1041, if an individual transfers property to (or in trust for the benefit of) a spouse, or a former spouse (if the transfer is incident to the divorce), then for income tax purposes the transferee is treated as acquiring the property by gift and the transferee's basis in the property is the same as the transferor's adjusted basis. This provision was designed to overrule the doctrine of United States v. Davis, 370 U.S. 65 (1962), in which the Supreme Court held that a husband's transfer of appreciated property to his former wife in a divorce settlement was a realization event for income tax purposes. Under *Davis,* the husband had to realize gain as if he had sold the property for cash, or exchanged it for property of equal value in a taxable exchange. The wife surrendered marital rights which were presumed to be equal in value to the property she received, and she took the property with a basis equal to its fair market value (even though she realized no gain on the receipt of property in exchange for the surrender of her marital rights). See Rev. Rul. 67–221, 1967–2 C.B. 63.

Under the broad rule of § 1041, the transferor is deemed to be making a gift even if he actually sells the property to his (or her) spouse for cash, and the transferee takes the transferor's basis even though she (or he) paid the purchase price in cash (or other property). These income tax non-recognition and basis rules flow from the § 1041(b) characterization of the transfer as a gift. But that characterization certainly does not make the transferor taxable under the gift tax, at least if he (or she) receives fair and adequate consideration in return. The transferor then is not making a gift, for gift tax purposes, in the sense of a gratuitous transfer. For gift tax purposes, § 2516 deems qualified transfers pursuant to marital property settlement agreements to be made for a full and adequate consideration in money or money's worth. For similar rules in the estate tax, see I.R.C. §§ 2053 and 2043, discussed in § 26, *infra.* Section § 2043(b)(2) incorporates the § 2516 exemption into the estate tax. Moreover, the "gift" characterization of § 1041(b) applies only for purposes of "this subtitle," meaning Subtitle A (I.R.C. §§ 1–1563), which includes only the income tax, and not Subtitle B, which contains the estate and gift taxes. Treating the property settlement transfer as a "gift" in § 1041 is a shorthand way of producing the specified income tax consequences (non-recognition of gain or loss and carryover of basis) for interspousal transfers, not a conclusive legal label with automatic gift tax consequences. Whether a taxable gift *is* involved when one spouse transfers property to the other must be analyzed under normal gift tax principles, not under § 1041.

§ 26 TRANSFERS PURSUANT TO DIVORCE, SEPARATION OR ANNULMENT: APPLICATION OF THE ESTATE TAX

Transfers or agreements to transfer property in connection with divorce sometimes give rise to estate tax questions. For example, suppose that a husband during his life signs a property settlement agreement with his wife, and that divorce occurs within the three-year statutory period beginning one year before the date of the agreement, so that I.R.C. § 2516 would shelter a transfer under that agreement from gift tax if the husband made the transfer during his lifetime. The husband dies, however, before making the transfer. As a result, his estate will still include the property to be transferred, even though the agreement is binding on his estate, which will then have to make the promised payment. Will any relief from the estate tax be available under these circumstances?

Some relief is provided by I.R.C. § 2053(a)(3), which declares that the value of the taxable estate shall be determined by deducting from the value of the gross estate such amounts for "claims against the estate" as are allowable by the laws of the jurisdiction under which the estate is being administered. The former wife's claim under the property settlement agreement qualifies and thus can be deducted in arriving at the taxable estate.

However, § 2053(c)(1)(A) raises an additional barrier. As noted earlier, in the case of a claim "founded on a promise or agreement," this provision requires that the allowable deduction be limited to the extent that the claim was contracted bona fide and for an adequate and full consideration in money or money's worth. This qualification blocks a potential avenue of estate tax avoidance for taxpayers who enter into collusive agreements to transfer property and do not make the transfer before death but attempt to obtain an estate tax deduction for what amounts to a disguised testamentary transfer. The difficulty with this limitation results from § 2043(b)(1), also noted earlier, which bars marital rights in the decedent's property or estate from being treated as consideration in money or money's worth. The question then arises whether the husband's promise to transfer property to his wife in connection with divorce was contracted bona fide and for an adequate and full consideration in money or money's worth, if the consideration involved is the surrender by the wife of rights of support and marital rights in the husband's property.

This question is resolved by § 2043(b)(2), which provides that for purposes of § 2053, a transfer of property that meets the requirements of § 2516(1) shall be considered to be made for an adequate and full consideration in money or money's worth. Even if the facts of a given situation do not come within the safe harbor of § 2043(b)(2), a deduction may still be allowable under § 2053.

It has been held that a deduction from the decedent's gross estate will be allowed for a claim against the estate arising out of a contractual promise incorporated in a divorce decree. Estate of Watson v. Commissioner, 216 F.2d 941 (2d Cir. 1954). The *Watson* case allowed the deduction even though the contractual promise was not contingent on divorce and was made to survive the divorce. In a sense, then, the rule of the *Harris* case (see § 25, *supra*) governs in this area just as it governs in the gift tax area when the conditions of § 2516 are not met. The claim is deemed to be founded not on a promise or agreement, but rather on the divorce decree, for purposes of § 2053.

The Service has accepted the rule of the *Watson* case, with the qualification that the estate tax deduction will be allowable only if the divorce court has the power to decree a settlement of all property rights or to vary the terms of a prior settlement agreement. If the divorce court does not have such power, as a matter of local law, then the indebtedness is considered to be founded on a promise or agreement rather than on the divorce decree, in which event the estate tax deduction will be allowable only to the extent of the reasonable value of support rights or other consideration in money or money's worth given in return by the transferee spouse. Rev. Rul. 60–160, 1960–1 C.B. 374; see also Estate of Barrett v. Commissioner, 56 T.C. 1312 (1971).

Once again, the unlimited marital deduction may affect the planning and structure of marital property settlements.

CHAPTER 5

TRANSFERS DURING LIFE: APPLICATION OF THE ESTATE AND GIFT TAXES

§ 27 INTRODUCTION

Some transfers made during life produce not only gift tax consequences, but estate tax consequences as well. More specifically, the gross estate of the decedent sometimes includes property actually transferred by the decedent during life and not owned by him or her at death. Loosely speaking, a lifetime transfer may be included if the decedent retained too much beneficial interest or control or if the transfer was made shortly before death to avoid the estate tax or to substitute for a testamentary transfer.

The gift tax will apply to an inter vivos transfer that is complete for gift tax purposes. But even though gift tax rates are nominally the same as those of the estate tax, the estate tax may also apply to a transfer made during life if that transfer is the functional equivalent of a testamentary transfer and offers an easy means of avoiding the estate tax. This potential avoidance results from the gift tax annual exclusion, from the different valuation dates under the two taxes, and from the fact that the estate tax base, but not the gift tax base, includes the assets used to pay the tax. These continuing advantages (even after the 1976 "unification" of the gift and estate taxes) of making a gift that is not included in the gross estate are discussed and criticized in § 79, *infra.*

The estate tax contains several provisions which may cause a decedent's gross estate to include property transferred by him during life. One example is the rule applicable to certain transfers made within three years of death (formerly called gifts "in contemplation of death"). Separate provisions apply to a transfer with a retained life estate, as well as a transfer that is revocable or over which the transferor retains a power to alter or amend the disposition or to designate the persons who shall possess or enjoy the property or its income. Also, certain transfers that take effect at death, even though made during life, will cause the transferred property to be included in the decedent's gross estate.

§ 28 TRANSFERS WITHIN THREE YEARS OF DEATH: APPLICATION OF THE ESTATE TAX

Since a transfer tax solely on property owned at death is easily avoided by making gifts shortly before dying, the federal estate tax, ever since its enactment in 1916, has contained a provision to bring some such gifts into the estate tax base. The federal gift tax, enacted in 1932, while limiting the scope of potential avoidance, did not entirely remove the need for special treatment of deathbed gifts, because of its lower rates, separate deductions and its fresh start up the rate schedule. Although the 1976 "unification" of the gift and estate taxes eliminated the most glaring disparities in the tax burden on inter vivos and testamentary gifts, still, enough differences remain (see § 79, *infra*) to warrant inclusion of certain deathbed gifts in the gross estate.

Prior Law: Gifts in Contemplation of Death. From 1916 to 1976, the statutory test for drawing an inter vivos gift back into the donor's gross estate at death was based on the donor's subjective intent, i.e., whether the gift was made "in contemplation of death." This was, of course, very difficult to ascertain, and the statutory presumptions under prior law did not greatly alleviate the difficulty.

As long ago as 1926, Congress experimented with a statute that provided a *conclusive presumption* that gifts made within two years before death were made "in contemplation of death." That statute was held unconstitutional on due process grounds. Heiner v. Donnan, 285 U.S. 312 (1932). Later, Congress adopted a *rebuttable* presumption that gifts within three years of death were made "in contemplation of death," but this approach gave rise to new problems. Since the burden of proof was on the taxpayer, and since the factual question was so hard to prove, it was very costly to fight the three-year presumption. As a result, most small gifts made within three years of death were included in the gross estate, while many large gifts escaped inclusion after a costly trial.

Even apart from difficulties in ascertaining the exact meaning of the statutory phrase "in contemplation of death," the Service encountered problems in administering the statute and in obtaining results that were fair, reliable, and evenhanded. A number of cases involved optimistic octogenarians who made transfers within three years of death and yet escaped the contemplation-of-death rule because of evidence that, though elderly and perhaps even not in the best of health, the transferors were vigorous and life-motivated in their thinking and did not have imminent death on their minds as a controlling reason for their transfers. A leading example of this judicial phenomenon is the case involving Frank L. Felix, who made gifts at the age of 99 and died within three years, when over 100 years old. Nevertheless, the court held that his transfers were not made in contemplation of death and were not includable in his gross estate. Kniskern v. United States, 232 F. Supp. 7 (S.D. Fla. 1964).

Evolution of the Three-Year Rule. The difficulties in administering the "contemplation of death" rule of prior law caused much dissatisfaction. In 1976, therefore, Congress amended § 2035(a) to provide for *automatic inclusion* in the gross estate of gifts made within three years of death, thus eliminating the old three-year rebuttable presumption (as well as the old irrebuttable presumption that gifts made more than three years before death were *not* made "in contemplation of death"). Under the 1976 amendment, *all* gratuitous transfers made within three years of death were automatically drawn back into the gross estate at death. Since there was no conclusive presumption, nor any presumption at all, the three-year rule appeared not even to raise any due process question.

Like other property included in the gross estate, the valuation of property drawn back under the three-year rule was to be determined as of the applicable valuation date. See § 48, *infra.* But it was only the transferred property itself which would be includable at such value. Therefore, if the transferee made improvements or additions to the property, any resulting enhancement in value would not be included in the gross estate. Also, income received from the property after its transfer (or property purchased with such income) would not be drawn back into the gross estate.

The 1976 Act also added a new "gross-up" rule which now appears in § 2035(b). This provision requires that the gross estate be increased by the amount of any *gift tax* paid by the decedent (or his estate) on any gift made by the decedent or his spouse within three years of death. Thus, if the decedent made taxable gifts within three years of death, not only the transferred property but also the amount of gift tax paid or payable thereon would be included in the gross estate. The import of this gross-up rule is discussed in § 79, *infra.* Prior law had provided for no such gross-up, and therefore never completely eliminated the tax advantages of making deathbed gifts, since the amount of gift tax paid by the donor escaped both gift and estate taxation, even if the gift itself were drawn back into the gross estate under the old contemplation-of-death rule.

After the gift tax became more fully integrated with the estate tax in 1976, the need to draw deathbed transfers back into the gross estate waned in importance. Since all post-1976 transfers in principle affect the cumulative estate tax computation, whether they were made during the full flower of life, near death, or at death, Congress came to accept the idea that the three-year rule of § 2035(a) could largely be declawed without a serious loss to the transfer tax system. As the Senate Finance Committee explained, it may not be "appropriate to tax appreciation that accrues after a gift has been made under the unified estate and gift taxes merely because the donor died within 3 years of the gift." S. Rep. No. 97–144, at 138.

In 1981, therefore, Congress drastically curtailed the scope of § 2035(a). The 1981 amendments repealed the three-year rule for all but a few specified types of transfers. As a result, the vast majority of ordinary, outright gifts of property involving no retained interests or powers are no longer subject to inclusion in the gross estate, even if made within three years of death. The current version of § 2035(a) applies only if a person dies within three years after transferring an interest in property (or relinquishing a power) which, had it been retained until death, would have caused the underlying property to be included in the gross estate under §§ 2036, 2037, 2038, or 2042. In such a case, § 2035(a) requires that the value of the property be included just as if the decedent had actually retained the interest (or power) until death.

For example, if a person transfers property and retains a life estate such that the underlying property would be includable in his gross estate under § 2036, and if within three years of death he releases or otherwise transfers the life estate earlier retained, § 2035(a) will result in inclusion of the entire property in the gross estate. Inclusion will follow even though at the time of death the transferor owns neither the property itself nor the life estate retained in the initial transfer. Because the retained life estate was transferred or released within three years of death, without consideration in money or money's worth, the transferor will be treated for estate tax purposes as if he had retained the life estate until death.

As a practical matter, perhaps the most important application of § 2035(a) involves deathbed gifts of life insurance. Under § 2042(2), the proceeds of a policy on the decedent's own life are includable in the gross estate if the decedent held any "incidents of ownership" at death. See § 41, *infra*. Since the value of a life insurance policy on a living person is often considerably less than the proceeds payable at death, the owner of a policy may seek to avoid estate taxation on the full amount of the proceeds by making a gift of the policy shortly before death. By including § 2042 in its list of enumerated sections, § 2035(a) blocks this gambit and ensures that the proceeds will be included in the gross estate if the insured person transferred any incidents of ownership within three years before death.

The scope of the revised three-year rule bears further analysis. As an example, assume that D owns two pieces of real estate, Blackacre and Whiteacre. In 2026 D gives away Blackacre subject to a retained life estate. In 2030 D unconditionally gives away Whiteacre, and also gives away the life estate he had retained in Blackacre. When D dies in 2031, the value of Blackacre, but not Whiteacre, will be included in his gross estate under § 2035(a), because the value of Blackacre would have been included in his gross estate under § 2036 had he retained the life estate until death.

One may be inclined to wonder just what difference between the two transactions justifies the disparity in treatment. One answer would appear to lie in the fact that the valuation date for gifts is the date of the gift, while property drawn back into the estate will be valued for transfer tax purposes as of the date of death (or alternate valuation date). Assume now that D had given away Blackacre, retaining a life estate, not in 2026, but in 2000. In the absence of a special inclusionary rule, i.e., if the property were not drawn back into his gross estate, D would have succeeded in enjoying the property for many years, until shortly before his death, and yet a transfer tax would have been paid on only the property's 2000 value, and not on the possibly much larger deathtime value. It is this type of abuse which is prevented by the three-year rule of § 2035(a).

An alternative explanation of the disparate treatment between the two-step transfer of Blackacre (which is drawn back into D's gross estate by § 2035(a)) and the outright gift of Whiteacre (which is subject to gift tax but not estate tax) may lie in a Congressional view that a two-step transfer involving §§ 2036–2038 or 2042 is "inherently" testamentary, even if made many years before death. Under this view, it might seem especially important to prevent escape from these other provisions by a "last minute" disposition (within three years before death) of the testamentary "string." In contrast, an outright gift of the property itself, with no strings attached, even if made within three years of death, might seem less "testamentary" than a staggered disposition in two steps.

A potential ambiguity in the scope of § 2035(a) involves transfers made from a revocable trust within three years before the grantor's death. If a gift of property from the trust was made directly to the donee at the grantor's direction, the grantor may be viewed as having relinquished a power of revocation which, if retained until death, would have caused inclusion under § 2038; accordingly, the gift may be drawn back into the grantor's gross estate under § 2035(a). On the other hand, if the gift is viewed as an outright transfer made by the decedent following a constructive distribution from the trust, § 2035(a) does not apply. Section 2035(e), enacted in 1997, reflects the latter view and treats a transfer made from a revocable trust as if it were made directly by the decedent for purposes of § 2035(a).

Current Law: Overview of § 2035. When all is said and done, § 2035—after being substantially restricted in 1981 (so that it no longer includes in the gross estate all property simply transferred within three years of death)—serves two principal functions. First, as noted above, § 2035(a) ensures that if a taxable "string" under §§ 2036–2038 or 2042 is released within three years before death, presumably to avoid inclusion under one or more of those sections, the decedent will be treated as if the string had been retained until death. In addition, § 2035(b) increases the gross estate by the amount of any gift tax paid by the decedent (or his estate) on a transfer made by the decedent or his spouse within three years of death. This "gross-up" provision is designed to erase the benefit of making large deathbed gifts so as to remove the resulting gift tax from the estate tax base.

It bears emphasizing that the three-year rule of § 2035(a) and the gross-up rule of § 2035(b) operate independently of each other. For example, suppose that D makes an outright gift of property with no retained interests or powers, and then dies one day later. The gift itself will *not* be drawn back into the gross estate under § 2035(a), because the transferred property would not have been included under §§ 2036–2038 or 2042 even if D had retained it until death. (The property, if actually owned at death, would have been included under § 2033, which is not one of the enumerated provisions referred to in § 2035(a).) Nevertheless, any gift tax imposed on the gift, whether paid by D during life or by D's estate after death, *will* be included in the gross estate under § 2035(b).

Even when otherwise applicable, the inclusionary rule of § 2035(a) does not apply to a transfer that is a bona fide sale for adequate and full consideration. I.R.C. § 2035(d).

For income tax purposes, property transferred within three years of death, but no longer drawn back into the estate by § 2035(a), will not get a fresh start basis under § 1014. And the income tax basis rule of

§ 1014(e), denying a fresh start basis for property transferred *to* a decedent within one year of death and bequeathed back to the transferor, might be said to be a "contemplation of death" rule of its own.

Despite the restricted scope of the inclusionary rule of § 2035(a), the broad pre-1981 version of the three-year rule still has relevance for certain collateral tax provisions. Under § 2035(c), transfers made within three years of death are treated as if they were includable in the gross estate for the limited purpose of determining eligibility for the following relief provisions which are dependent on the size and composition of the gross estate: § 303(b), allowing favorable income tax treatment for certain redemptions of stock to pay death taxes; § 2032A, providing special estate tax valuation rules for qualified real property; and § 6166, granting an extension of time for the payment of the estate tax attributable to a closely held business. Also, § 2035(c)(1)(C) makes property transferred within three years of death subject to the tax liens created by §§ 6321–6327.

§ 29 INCOMPLETE TRANSFERS: APPLICATION OF THE GIFT TAX AND THE GIFT TAX CREDIT

If a donor makes a completed transfer of property during life, the gift tax will apply pursuant to its own rules, even though the same transfer may also give rise to an estate tax at death by virtue of I.R.C. § 2035 or some other provision pertaining to transfers not complete for estate tax purposes. To mitigate the burden of overlapping taxes, a credit or equivalent offset is allowed against the estate tax for gift taxes previously imposed on such transfers. For pre-1977 transfers, the basic rules of the credit for gift tax paid are spelled out in I.R.C. § 2012 and the regulations under that section. The amount of the credit is limited so that it cannot exceed the amount of the gift tax paid on the transfer or, if less, the amount of estate tax attributable to the same transfer when it is later included in the gross estate. The statute and regulations should be consulted for more detailed rules pertaining to the credit.

For gifts made after 1976, the gift tax credit of § 2012 is unavailable. I.R.C. § 2012(e). This is because the method for calculating the estate tax under the unified transfer tax system automatically provides an offset (equivalent to a credit) for any gift tax payable on post-1976 gifts. See I.R.C. § 2001(b)(2); see also § 2001(d) and (e), providing special rules for split gifts that are drawn back into the donor's gross estate.

§ 30 INCOMPLETE TRANSFERS—ESTATE TAX: INTRODUCTION

The current statutory provisions calling for inclusion in the gross estate of property transferred during life, but not deemed completely transferred until death for estate tax purposes, are found in I.R.C. §§ 2036, 2037, and 2038. These sections have their roots in a more general statutory rule which, as originally enacted in 1916, asked simply whether a transfer was one "intended to take effect in possession or enjoyment" at or after the transferor's death. This general section later was broken out into more specific rules which cover several kinds of inter vivos transfers that are treated as substitutes for testamentary transfers because of a retained interest or power which makes the transfer not complete until death. The present statutory rules cause inclusion in the gross estate of property transferred during life where the transferor retained the economic benefit of the property, in the form of possession or enjoyment or a right to the income, for his life and until his death. I.R.C. § 2036(a)(1). Also included is property transferred during life with possession or enjoyment by the transferee postponed until the death of the transferor and contingent in some way on his death. I.R.C. § 2037. The gross estate also includes property transferred during life if the transferor reserved significant powers over the possession or enjoyment of the property. Such a power might consist of a power to revoke the transfer, a power to alter or amend it in significant ways, or a power to designate who would possess or enjoy the property or the income therefrom. I.R.C. §§ 2036(a)(2) and 2038.

Sections 2036–2038 are in some ways not coherently drafted, with the result that they sometimes overlap or conflict. A particular disposition of property may be governed by more than one section and, still more troublesome, the different sections may yield disparate tax results. Dependably, the Service will assert all applicable sections and will strive to include the largest possible amount in the decedent's gross estate. The representative of the estate, in contrast, will urge the application of only that section which produces the smallest inclusion. If it is unmistakable that two or more sections apply, the one that produces the larger includable amount will prevail. However, if it is uncertain whether more than one section applies, there may be room for real controversy about the amount to be included in the decedent's gross estate.

Sections 2036–2038 have in common the effect of including in the gross estate some property not actually owned by the decedent at death. In this respect, they resemble § 2035 and other statutory rules to be encountered. In another respect, they share a more unique characteristic.

Sections 2036–2038 are sometimes called the "grantor sections" because they apply to decedents who earlier transferred property (in trust or otherwise) and *retained* or *reacquired* the powers or interests specified in the statutory provisions. In other words, §§ 2036–2038 will apply only if a decedent, at death, holds an interest in or a power over property that he or she previously transferred during life. They will not apply, however, to an interest or power given to the decedent by someone else with respect to property that the decedent never owned or transferred.

In considering these statutory provisions more particularly, it is important to identify the kinds of dispositions described in each separate provision, to understand the policy and logic behind the inclusionary rule and its limitations, to ask whether some other provision would also cover the disposition presented, and finally to think about whether some or all of these statutory provisions could be repealed without significantly changing the law because § 2033 could cover the same ground. (Also, it may be useful to ask whether a single general rule, encompassing "transfers taking effect in possession or enjoyment" at or after the grantor's death, could be substituted for the present complexities of §§ 2036–2038.)

Sections 2036–2038 present many questions as to the scope and meaning of their terms. These provisions will be examined in greater detail in the following sections of this book. While examining the statutes and regulations, it is helpful to keep in mind the general thrust of the rules. They are designed to tax inter vivos transfers having the character of will substitutes. They apply to transfers *other than* a bona fide sale for an adequate and full consideration in money or money's worth. They cause inclusion in the gross estate of property *not owned* by the decedent at death. They may cause *inclusion* of all the property transferred or of some lesser amount, namely the amount subject to the described power or the amount in which the decedent had the described interest. As "grantor sections," they apply only to interests or powers in *property transferred* by the decedent. In some instances they apply only to interests or powers *retained* by him, but in others they may apply to powers *reacquired* or obtained in some other way. They apply to powers held at death, even if not actually exercised. Also, some of the provisions contain different rules for transfers made at different times, geared to changes in the law and to prevent unfair surprise by a retroactive application of new legal rules.

All in all, they apply to inter vivos transfers that are regarded as incomplete for estate tax purposes, whether or not deemed complete for gift tax purposes.

§ 31 TRANSFERS WITH A RETAINED LIFE ESTATE: § 2036(a)(1)

If a person transfers property and retains a life estate in that property, either by a transfer in trust or by retaining a legal life estate, the full value of the transferred property will be included in the gross estate at the transferor's death. I.R.C. § 2036(a)(1) provides, in somewhat cumbersome language, that the value of the gross estate "shall include the value of all property to the extent of any interest therein of which the decedent has at any time made a transfer (except in case of a bona fide sale for an adequate and full consideration in money or money's worth) by trust or otherwise, under which he has retained for his life, or for any period not ascertainable without reference to his death, or for any period which does not in fact end before his death, the possession or enjoyment of, or the right to the income from, the property." By its terms, this section is a "grantor section" and thus will apply only when the decedent's life estate is held in property which he himself formerly owned and transferred. Therefore, if a grandmother transfers property in trust with income to her son for life and remainder at the son's death to a grandchild, there will not be any inclusion in the gross estate of the son at his death under § 2036(a)(1) because the son (the decedent for present purposes) was not the transferor or grantor. He did not make a transfer within the terms of § 2036. (Of course, the termination of the son's interest may well incur a GST tax.)

Section 2036 applies when there has been a *retention* of a life estate or similar interest, but not when there has been an acquisition or reacquisition of such an interest. Therefore, if the transferor of property disposes of all his interests in the property and then reacquires a life estate in the property which remains in effect until his death, there will not be any inclusion under § 2036(a)(1), because the life estate was acquired or reacquired, not retained.

Although the language of § 2036 requires a retention of a life estate "under" the transfer, the life estate need not be expressly reserved in the instrument of transfer. For example, if the retention of the life estate occurs by simultaneous agreement on the part of the transferee, or if such an agreement can be inferred from objective evidence, § 2036(a)(1) will apply.

If the transferor of property retains a life estate in only a portion of the property transferred, then only a corresponding portion of the property will be included in his or her gross estate under § 2036(a)(1). Similarly, if a decedent transfers community property into a trust and retains a life estate in the transferred property, only the decedent's one-half share of the property will be includable under § 2036. See Katz v. United States, 382 F.2d 723 (9th Cir. 1967).

Under § 2036, the transferor is considered to retain the equivalent of the use, possession or right to the income or other enjoyment of the transferred property to the extent that the income is to be applied toward the discharge of his or her legal obligations, including, of course, a legal obligation to support a dependent family member during the transferor's lifetime. See Reg. § 20.2036–1(b)(2).

Under the language of the statute, the period for which the possession or enjoyment or right to income must be retained is defined as the transferor's life, or "any period not ascertainable without reference to his death" or "any period which does not in fact end before his death." Consequently, § 2036(a) covers more ground than that occupied solely by dispositions with a retained life estate, strictly defined. To illustrate, if a grantor transfers property in trust and retains a right to the income from that property for his life but provides that no installment of the annual income shall be paid for the calendar quarter preceding his death, § 2036(a) will apply even though the grantor does not receive all the income earned during his lifetime. Since the period for which he has a right to the income cannot be ascertained without reference to his death, the transfer comes within the terms of the statute.

Suppose a grantor transfers property in trust and provides that the income shall be received by her for ten years with the remainder to be distributed to a named beneficiary. If the grantor dies before the expiration of the ten-year period, § 2036(a)(1) will cause the property to be included in her gross estate because she retained the right to income for a period which did not in fact end before her death. However, if she lived longer than the ten year period, there would be no inclusion because the statutory requirement would not be met.

Section 2036(a)(1) also applies to a retained *secondary* life estate in the grantor. Thus, if the grantor transfers property in trust and provides that the income is to be paid first to his wife for her life and then to the grantor for his life, with remainder at his death to their children, and if the grantor survives his wife, at his death the value of the remainder, i.e., the transferred property, will be included in his gross estate.

Suppose, however, that the grantor in the preceding example dies before his wife, the primary income beneficiary. In that event, although the grantor retained a right to trust income, that right would not yet have taken effect in enjoyment at the time of his death. Moreover, since it was contingent on the grantor surviving his wife, that interest would never take effect in possession or enjoyment. Nevertheless, § 2036(a)(1) does require inclusion as a result of such a transfer. See Marks v. Higgins, 213 F.2d 884 (2d Cir. 1954); Commissioner v. Nathan's Estate, 159 F.2d 546 (7th Cir. 1947), cert. den., 334 U.S. 843 (1948). However, the value of the transferred property to be included in the grantor's gross estate will be reduced by the value of the wife's outstanding life income interest at the grantor's death, since that interest precedes and is, therefore, unaffected by the grantor's retained interest in the property. See Reg. § 20.2036–1(a). In other words, the interest that shifts at the grantor's death is not the entire property, because the wife received a life income interest in the property under a completed inter vivos transfer. The interest that shifts at the grantor's death is the remainder which will take effect in possession or enjoyment only after the wife's death. Thus, the amount to be included is the present value of that remainder interest, which is determined by taking the value of the property at the grantor's death and subtracting the present value of the wife's outstanding life income interest.

If a grantor who has retained a life estate or other interest which will produce inclusion under § 2036(a)(1) gives away that retained interest within three years of death, the entire amount of the trust property will be includable in the grantor's gross estate under § 2035(a). See § 28, *supra.* Thus, the grantor cannot escape the impact of § 2036(a)(1), which is designed to reach property given in a way that amounts to a substitute for a testamentary transfer, by making a deathbed gift—another substitute for a testamentary transfer—of the life estate retained in the original transaction.

Section 2036 contains an exception for a transfer that would otherwise fit the terms of the section but which is a bona fide sale for an adequate and full consideration in money or money's worth. As a result of this provision, a transfer of property by a grantor who in return receives cash or other property of equal value will not result in inclusion under § 2036. This result makes sense if the property received is equally likely to be included in the transferor's gross estate at death. In that event, there has been no depletion of the prospective estate tax base.

The measure of adequate consideration can prove tricky in the case of lifetime transfers to which the estate tax may apply. See § 37, *infra.*

A few specific applications of § 2036(a)(1) in the family context have presented problems resulting in important court decisions. One is the problem that arises when a person transfers the family residence to his or her spouse and then continues living in the house, with the spouse, until death. In this situation, the Service has argued that the decedent transferred the house with a retained life estate in the form of retained possession or enjoyment. This argument did not prevail in Estate of Gutchess v. Commissioner, 46 T.C. 554 (1966), where the Tax Court stated that the spouses' joint occupancy of the house after an interspousal transfer was not sufficient in and of itself to indicate the existence of an agreement for retained enjoyment.

After announcing its acquiescence in the *Gutchess* decision, the Service has taken the position, in cases involving a transferor and transferee who are not husband and wife, that continued exclusive occupancy of the house by the transferor after the transfer *will* be evidence of an agreement for retained enjoyment for purposes of § 2036(a)(1). (Since the advent of the unlimited marital deduction, these are the only cases that matter.) See Rev. Rul. 70–155, 1970–1 C.B. 189. The Service's position was upheld in Estate of Maxwell v. Commissioner, 3 F.3d 591 (2d

Cir. 1993). In *Maxwell,* a parent sold her house to her son and his wife, forgiving $20,000 of the purchase price and accepting a $250,000 mortgage note for the balance. The parent rented the home back from the son and his wife and continued to live there until her death, paying a monthly rental that was close to the amount of interest due on the note. Each year during her life, the parent forgave another $20,000 on the note, and the outstanding balance at her death was forgiven in her will. The court held that there was an implied agreement that the parent would continue to live in the house until her death. Furthermore, the exchange was not made for adequate consideration because of an implied agreement that the note would never be enforced. Therefore, the transaction was a transfer with a retained life estate, not a sale, and the full value of the house at the parent's death was includable in her gross estate. See also Guynn v. United States, 437 F.2d 1148 (4th Cir. 1971), and Estate of Linderme v. Commissioner, 52 T.C. 305 (1969).

For a brief period, some tax planning enthusiasts believed, or sought to persuade others, that the estate tax could be circumvented by an arrangement called a "family estate trust." This concoction called for the grantor to contribute all of his property (including the family residence) and to assign his "lifetime services" to an irrevocable inter vivos trust, while continuing to occupy the residence and enjoy the benefits of the paychecks and investment income held "in trust." To the surprise of few, the Service ruled that the property was fully taxable in the gross estate of the grantor at death under §§ 2036, 2038, and 2033. See Rev. Rul. 75–259, 1975–2 C.B. 361.

Another important application of § 2036(a)(1) lies in the so-called private or family annuity transaction. Such a transaction involves a transfer of property by one person to a family member or other transferee in return for a promise to make periodic payments to the transferor for his or her lifetime. If properly structured, the transaction will be treated as a bona fide sale of property in exchange for an adequate and full consideration (i.e., the promised payments); the transferor's right to receive payments will not be viewed as a retained life estate; and the transferred property will accordingly not be includable in the transferor's gross estate under § 2036. See, e.g., Estate of Bergan v. Commissioner, 1 T.C. 543 (1943); Estate of Costanza v. Commissioner, 320 F.3d 595 (6th Cir. 2003). There is a risk of inclusion, however, if the promised payments are secured by an interest in the transferred property or are geared to the income from the transferred property. In such cases, the transaction may be recast as a transfer with a retained right to income, causing the transferred property to be included in the gross estate under § 2036(a)(1). See, e.g., Estate of Fry v. Commissioner, 9 T.C. 503 (1947); Tips v. Bass, 21 F.2d 460 (W.D. Tex. 1927). See also §§ 43 and 44, *infra*.

One more annuity problem involving § 2036 remains to be mentioned. Suppose that a person purchases a single-premium life insurance policy together with a separate, single-premium life annuity policy from a commercial issuer. The package is designed to neutralize the mortality risk to the issuer, so that if the insured person dies prematurely, the proceeds to be paid out under the life insurance policy will be covered by the combined premium payments, less the annuity payments already made, plus interest. The insured person then irrevocably assigns all incidents of ownership in the life insurance policy, but retains the annuity policy and continues to receive annuity payments until her death. Are the life insurance proceeds payable to named beneficiaries includable in the gross estate, on the theory that the insured person, by receiving annuity payments for life, in effect retained a right to the income derived from the combined life insurance-annuity package? In Fidelity-Philadelphia Trust Co. v. Smith, 356 U.S. 274 (1958), the Supreme Court rejected the Service's attempt to draw the life insurance proceeds into the decedent's gross estate under § 2036. The Court noted that the life insurance policy and the annuity policy were separate items of property which could be assigned or retained independently of one another; the annuity policy was in no way conditioned on the continued existence of the life insurance policy. Therefore, the Service could not aggregate the two policies in one investment for purposes of § 2036.

A final area in which § 2036 plays an important and controversial role involves the estate tax treatment of family limited partnerships. To illustrate the problem, suppose that a parent and her child form a partnership with the parent as a limited partner and the child as a general partner. As long as the partners' interests in the partnership are proportionate to their respective capital contributions and capital accounts are properly maintained, the courts, relying on the absence of any capital shift from one partner to the other, have held that the formation of the partnership does not give rise to any taxable gift. See Estate of Strangi v. Commissioner, 115 T.C. 478 (2000), aff'd on this issue and rev'd on another issue sub nom. Gulig v. Commissioner, 293 F.3d 279 (5th Cir. 2002). When the parent dies, the question for estate tax purposes is whether the property to be included in her gross estate consists only of the *partnership interest* that she actually owned at death under § 2033, or whether her proportionate share of the *partnership assets* can be drawn back into the gross estate under § 2036 on the ground that she retained lifetime enjoyment of the assets that she contributed to the partnership. As a practical matter, the most serious consequence of applying § 2036 is that the partnership assets will be included at fair market value, without any of the valuation discounts for lack of marketability and lack of control that routinely apply in valuing a limited partnership interest (see § 48, *infra*).

The Service has met with some success in applying § 2036 to family limited partnerships, especially where a partnership appears to have been created solely to reduce estate taxes rather than to conduct business operations or manage assets. In Estate of Thompson v. Commissioner, 382 F.3d 367 (3d Cir. 2004), the decedent at age 95 contributed most of his assets, consisting largely of marketable securities, to newly-formed limited partnerships. The decedent did not retain sufficient assets outside the partnership for his own support, but the partnership distributed cash as needed to meet his personal expenses (including gifts to family members) until his death two years later. Noting the "general testamentary character" of the arrangement, the court held that the decedent had retained enjoyment of the transferred assets for life, pursuant to an implied agreement with his children, and that the transfer did not come within the statutory exception for a bona fide sale. Consequently, the decedent's ratable share of the partnership assets was includable in his gross estate under § 2036. The result might have been different, however, if the decedent had retained sufficient assets for his own needs and if the partnership had been formed for legitimate business reasons. See Kimbell v. United States, 371 F.3d 257 (5th Cir. 2004). Quite apart from the level of the decedent's retained enjoyment and control, § 2036 will not apply if the decedent's lifetime transfer to the partnership comes within the statutory exception for a bona sale for adequate and full consideration in money or money's worth. (See § 37, *infra*).

Former § 2036(c) and "Estate Freezes." Often, in planning the estate of a wealthy taxpayer, a central objective is to minimize the growth in value of assets retained by the client until death, while passing substantial appreciation to the next generation free of transfer taxes. Sometimes this principle simply suggests that an elderly parent retain income producing bonds while making lifetime gifts of growth stock to children, to "get the growth out of the estate."

A well-known estate freezing technique for a person who owns all, or a large portion, of the stock of a corporation is to divide the equity ownership into voting preferred stock (representing most of the corporation's net or equity value) and non-voting common stock (having little present value but standing in a position to appreciate rapidly if the corporation enjoys future success). This is sometimes termed an "old-to-young recapitalization" when coupled with the next step, a gift of the common stock to the children or grandchildren. Thus, the senior generation would keep the voting control (at least for a while) and the preferred dividend and liquidation rights, while giving away the chance for future capital appreciation in the value of the common stock.

This and other related "estate freezing" techniques were the target of former I.R.C. § 2036(c), which was enacted in 1987, amended in 1988, and then repealed in 1990. Former § 2036(c) provided that if a person who held a substantial interest in an enterprise transferred property having a disproportionately large share of the potential appreciation in such person's interest while retaining an interest in the income of, or rights in, the enterprise, the retention of the retained interest would be considered to be a retention of the enjoyment of the transferred property within the meaning of § 2036(a). Consequently, the transferred property (i.e., the common stock, in the above example) would be drawn back into the gross estate of the transferor at death. The perceived complexity, breadth and vagueness of former § 2036(c) provoked widespread complaints and ultimately led to the repeal of the provision in 1990. In its place, Congress enacted the special rules of I.R.C. §§ 2701–2704, which govern valuation of the transferred and retained interests for gift tax purposes at the time of the lifetime transfer. Those rules are discussed in § 49, *infra*.

§ 32 REVOCABLE TRANSFERS AND POWERS TO ALTER, AMEND, TERMINATE OR AFFECT ENJOYMENT: § 2038

If a decedent made a lifetime transfer of an interest in property and if at the time of death the enjoyment of the interest remains subject to a change through the exercise of a power held by him to alter, amend, revoke, or terminate the transfer (or where any such power is relinquished within three years of his death), the interest subject to such power will be included in the decedent's gross estate. I.R.C. § 2038(a). Here too, the decedent has kept too many "strings attached" to be allowed to avoid the estate tax. Section 2038(b) goes on to provide that the described power shall be considered to exist on the date of the decedent's death even if the exercise of that power is subject to some precedent giving of notice or even though the revocation or amendment will take effect only after the expiration of a stated period after the exercise of the power, whether or not notice has been given or the power has in fact been exercised on or before the date of death.

Section 2038, like § 2036(a)(1), is a "grantor section" and applies only where the property whose enjoyment is subject to the power was at some point owned and transferred by the decedent. (Unlike the language of other grantor sections, however, § 2038 does not require that the power over the enjoyment be *retained* by the decedent; it is enough that the power be *held* by the decedent at the time of death.) The purpose and policy of this rule are evident. If the transferor can get the property back by revoking or terminating the transfer, he is for all practical purposes the owner of the property until his power disappears at death. Section 2038 goes further than that, however, and includes any power to alter or amend the transfer in such a way as to affect the enjoyment of the property. Again the theory seems to be that such power is an important attribute of ownership and for tax purposes should be treated as tantamount to ownership of the property at death. The estate tax should not be subject to avoidance by a lifetime transfer when substantial ownership rights have been retained or reacquired by the decedent.

Reservation of a power to alter or amend a transfer of property will result in inclusion of the property in the gross estate even though the power could not be exercised in favor of the decedent or his estate. See Porter v. Commissioner, 288 U.S. 436 (1933). Therefore, under § 2038, a power to name new beneficiaries of a trust or to rearrange the beneficial interests among a limited class of beneficiaries will produce inclusion in the gross estate.

Section 2038 applies if the enjoyment of transferred property was subject to "any change" through the exercise of a described power. Even a power that affects only the time or manner of enjoyment of property, but not the identity of the beneficiary, falls within the broad terms of the statute. Thus, for example, if the decedent created a trust for her child and reserved a power to accumulate the trust income or distribute it to the child, and to distribute corpus to the child, the decedent's power would give rise to inclusion under § 2038, even though the remainder interest was indefeasibly vested in the child (or the child's estate) and no other person had a beneficial interest in the trust. See Lober v. United States, 346 U.S. 335 (1953).

If, however, the power is governed by some objective, ascertainable external standard, such as a power to invade trust corpus for the benefit of an income beneficiary only in the event of prolonged illness, the estate tax can be avoided. The standard limits the scope of the power and makes the holder of the power less than substantially the owner of the property.

For example, in the leading case of Jennings v. Smith, 161 F.2d 74 (2d Cir. 1947), the court held that a decedent's retained powers did not give rise to inclusion under § 2038 because the power was restricted by an external standard. In that case, decedent created identical irrevocable inter vivos trusts for each of his two sons. By the terms of each trust, the trustees (of whom the decedent was one) were given power in their absolute discretion to use any or all of the trust income as they determined to be reasonably necessary for the maintenance of the son and his family in comfort and in accordance with the son's station in life. In addition, the trustees had power to invade trust corpus in the event of prolonged illness or extraordinary financial misfortune. The court found that the trustees were not free to exercise untrammeled discretion but instead were governed by determinable standards which were enforceable by a court of equity. Accordingly, the court concluded that the decedent's powers over income and corpus fell outside the reach of § 2038.

So, in general it can be said that when the power is held in a fiduciary capacity and is limited by an external standard which restricts the power to definite amounts or uses which a court could enforce, the power is not deemed to be one which requires inclusion of the property in the decedent's gross estate under § 2038. (Courts have adopted the same reasoning, with identical results, under § 2036(a)(2), discussed in § 33, *infra.*) Many cases have dealt with the question whether a particular standard is sufficiently specific and enforceable to satisfy this test.

Section 2038 requires inclusion in the gross estate if the enjoyment of transferred property was subject to change through the exercise of a power by the decedent "at the date of his death." Section 2038 does not apply, however, to a power the exercise of which was subject to a contingency beyond the decedent's control which did not occur before his death. Reg. § 20.2038–1(b). Thus, for example, if the decedent created an inter vivos trust and retained a power of revocation which was exercisable only if the decedent outlived his brother, and the decedent in fact died before his brother, the trust property would not be includable in the decedent's gross estate under § 2038.

Under § 2038, inclusion will result whether the decedent held the forbidden power alone or with another person, whether adverse, friendly, or independent. One exception is specified by Reg. § 20.2038–1(a)(2), which provides that § 2038 does not apply if the decedent's power could be exercised only with the consent of all parties having an interest (vested or contingent) in the transferred property and if the power adds nothing to the rights of the parties under local law. (In Helvering v. Helmholz, 296 U.S. 93 (1935), the Supreme Court decided that a power to terminate a trust exercisable by the grantor only with the consent of all persons having a beneficial interest in the trust was exempt from the reach of the federal estate tax. This decision accounts for the provision in the regulations to the same effect, but is hard to reconcile with the statutory language which applies to powers held by the decedent "in conjunction with any other person.")

A power to amend or alter enjoyment, if held by a third person alone, generally will not result in any inclusion in the decedent's gross estate under § 2038. Thus, if a decedent created an inter vivos trust and named another person as sole trustee with broad power to invade corpus for one or more beneficiaries (other than the decedent), the trustee's power of invasion is not attributed to the decedent in applying § 2038. However, if at the time of his death the decedent held an unrestricted power to remove the trustee at any time and appoint himself as successor trustee, the decedent is considered as having all the powers of the trustee, even if the power of removal and replacement remains unexercised. Reg. § 20.2038–1(a)(3).

Section 2038 applies if the decedent at the time of death held a power affecting the enjoyment of property that the decedent transferred during life. The provision applies whether the power was exercisable by the decedent during life or at death by will, and regardless of whether the power was actually exercised. Thus, for example, suppose the decedent created an irrevocable inter vivos trust to pay income to his wife for life, with remainder at her death to their children, and named himself as trustee. Section 2038 will require inclusion in the decedent's gross estate if he retained, as trustee, a discretionary power, not limited by any ascertainable standard, to invade the corpus of the trust for the benefit of the wife. Similarly, § 2038 will apply if the decedent retained a power to terminate the trust during his lifetime or to appoint the remainder interest by will to one or more of the children. In each case, the amount includable in the gross estate will be the value of the interest that was subject to change through exercise of the decedent's power. See Reg. § 20.2038–1(a).

§ 33 POWERS TO DESIGNATE THE PERSONS WHO SHALL ENJOY OR POSSESS PROPERTY OR INCOME: § 2036(a)(2)

I.R.C. § 2036(a)(2) contains rules that much resemble and often overlap with the rules of § 2038. Under § 2036(a)(2), the gross estate includes the value of all property to the extent of any interest of which the decedent has made a transfer under which he has retained for his life or a related period the right, either alone or in conjunction with any person, to designate the persons who shall possess or enjoy the property or the income therefrom. This power, to determine who will actually possess or enjoy property earlier transferred or the income from it, is much like a § 2038 power to affect the enjoyment of the property through an exercise of a power to alter, amend, revoke, or terminate.

Thus it may generally be said that these two statutory provisions draw into the gross estate the value of any interest in property which the decedent has transferred during his life if the enjoyment of that property or its income is subject to a substantial measure of control by him at the time of his death. In State Street Trust Co. v. United States, 263 F.2d 635 (1st Cir. 1959), § 2036(a)(2) was held to include property transferred in trust based on the decedent's retention, as one of the trustees, of very broad investment and management powers. The First Circuit found that these broad powers, considered together, allowed the trustees to shift enjoyment between the income beneficiaries and the remainder beneficiaries through their choice of investments yielding high current income or no income at all. The *State Street Trust Co.* decision drew heavy criticism, and was repudiated several years later in Old Colony Trust Co. v. United States, 423 F.2d 601 (1st Cir. 1970). In *Old Colony Trust Co.*, the First Circuit said that no aggregation of purely administrative powers could rise to the level of sufficient dominion and control to be equated with ownership for estate tax purposes. (Nevertheless, because the decedent had also retained a power, not limited by an ascertainable standard, to withhold income from the primary beneficiary, the court went on to hold that the trust property was includable in the decedent's gross estate.)

In United States v. Byrum, 408 U.S. 125 (1972), the Supreme Court held that a decedent's retained voting and other control over a corporation did not cause stock of the corporation which he had transferred during life to be drawn back into his gross estate under § 2036. The decedent had transferred stock of three closely held corporations to a bank as trustee of an inter vivos trust for the benefit of his children. In his individual capacity, the decedent retained the rights to vote the transferred stock, to approve or disapprove any disposition or investment of trust assets, and to remove and replace the corporate trustee. By virtue of his voting rights in the transferred stock and in other stock owned by him, the decedent retained voting control of the corporations until his death. The Service argued that this voting control, combined with the powers over the trust administration, gave the decedent de facto power to regulate the flow of dividends from the corporations and thus indirectly to affect the enjoyment of the trust income. The Court rejected this argument, however, noting that the decedent's rights as a controlling shareholder did not amount to an "ascertainable and legally enforceable power" over the enjoyment of the trust income.

Congress responded to the *Byrum* decision in 1976 by enacting § 2036(b), which requires inclusion in the decedent's gross estate of the value of transferred stock of a "controlled corporation," if the decedent retains the right to vote such stock. For the purpose of § 2036(b), a corporation is controlled only if, after the transfer and within three years of his death, the decedent had the right (alone or in conjunction with any other person) to vote at least 20% of the total voting stock in the corporation, or the decedent and his family (i.e., using the constructive ownership rules of I.R.C. § 318) owned at least 20% of the total voting stock. In addition, the cessation or relinquishment of the right to vote the transferred stock is treated as a "transfer" of property for purposes of § 2035(a). Thus, if the decedent gives up the voting rights within three years of death, the transferred stock may nonetheless be included in his gross estate. See I.R.C. § 2036(b). Section 2036(b) is effective for transfers after June 22, 1976. It should be noted that § 2036(b) does not fully adopt the position taken by the Service in *Byrum*. By its terms, the provision applies only if the decedent retained voting rights in the *transferred* stock. If a decedent transferred voting stock in a closely held corporation and retained no voting rights in the transferred stock but retained full ownership of other stock with voting control, only the stock owned at death will be includable in his gross estate (under § 2033); the transferred stock will not be drawn back under § 2036(b). Similarly, if the decedent transferred *nonvoting* stock, § 2036(b) will not apply. See Rev. Rul. 81–15, 1981–1 C.B. 457.

Another "strings attached" transfer consists of a "preferred stock estate freeze" (or similar technique) in which a parent who owns a controlling interest in a family corporation makes a lifetime gift to his children of common stock (representing potential future growth) while retaining preferred stock (representing fixed income rights). By doing so, the parent may seek to remove most of the future appreciation in the value of the corporation from his gross estate and pass it to his children at a relatively low current value for gift tax purposes, while keeping a disproportionately large share of income or rights and control for himself. Former § 2036(c) attempted to reach such transactions by an estate tax inclusion rule, but the experience with this approach was not satisfactory. See § 31, *supra*. Estate freezing techniques are now dealt with by the special valuation rules of I.R.C. §§ 2701–2704, which discourage or counteract such transfers by minimizing the value of certain retained interests and attributing an artificially high (taxable) value to the transferred interests, for gift tax purposes. These provisions are discussed in § 49, *infra*.

Neither § 2036 nor § 2038 will require inclusion in the case of a transfer made for an adequate and full consideration in money or money's worth. Section 2036(a)(2), like § 2038, is a "grantor section" which applies only when the described power relates to property or income transferred by the decedent. Unlike § 2038, § 2036(a)(2) does not apply to an acquired or reacquired power; it applies only if the decedent transferred property during life and *retained* the described power under the transfer. Under the regulations, however, an interest or right is treated as having been retained or reserved if at the time of the transfer there was an understanding, express or implied, that the interest or right would later be conferred. Reg. § 20.2036–1(a).

Section 2036, like § 2038, generally does not apply to a power held solely by a person other than the decedent. However, if the decedent reserved an unrestricted power to remove a trustee at any time and appoint himself as successor trustee, the decedent is considered as having all the powers of the trustee. Reg. § 20.2036–1(b)(3). At one time the Service took the position that the trustee's powers would be attributed to the decedent under §§ 2036 and 2038 if the decedent had an unrestricted power to remove a corporate trustee and substitute another corporate trustee, even though the decedent could not name himself as trustee. Rev. Rul. 79–353, 1979–2 C.B. 325. This position was implicitly at odds with the Supreme Court's holding in *Byrum* and was explicitly rejected by lower courts in subsequent cases. See Estate of Wall v. Commissioner, 101 T.C. 300 (1993). The Service eventually revoked its earlier ruling and announced that a decedent's retained power to remove a trustee and appoint a successor trustee who is not "related or subordinate" to the decedent (within the meaning of I.R.C. § 672(c)) will not cause the trustee's powers to be attributed to the decedent. Rev. Rul. 95–58, 1995–2 C.B. 191.

§ 34 §§ 2038 AND 2036(a)(2): OVERLAPS, CONFLICTS AND CONGRUENCE

Much the same kinds of power that fall under § 2038 will also be taxable under § 2036(a)(2). A power to accumulate income for remainder beneficiaries or to invade corpus for an income beneficiary constitutes a power to "designate the person who will possess or enjoy the property or the income therefrom" under § 2036(a)(2). A power to revoke a trust set up for the grantor's spouse for life with remainder to their child, would produce inclusion to the same extent under § 2038 or § 2036(a)(2).

It is not clear, however, whether a power to affect only the timing of possession or enjoyment, for example by accumulating income for distribution to the income beneficiary at a later time, or a power to invade corpus for the benefit of those who ultimately will enjoy it if it is not invaded, will be treated as a taxable power over some or all of the property for purposes of § 2036(a)(2). Since those powers will be regarded as taxable powers under § 2038, it may seem to make little difference whether they also are regarded as powers fitting the description of § 2036(a)(2). The additional application of a second statutory rule can make a difference, however, if the interest or amount of property to be included under the second rule is greater than the amount to be included under the first rule. This problem leads us into difficult intricacies of §§ 2038 and 2036(a)(2).

Under the terms of § 2038, the decedent's gross estate includes the value of all property to the extent of any interest of which he has made a transfer where the enjoyment "thereof" was subject at his death to one of the described powers. This statutory language suggests that only the interest whose enjoyment was subject to the described power will be included in the gross estate. The regulations support this interpretation, in saying that "only the value of an interest in property subject to a power to which section 2038 applies is included in the decedent's gross estate under section 2038." Reg. § 20.2038–1(a). Thus, if the transferor retains a power to affect the enjoyment only of the life estate but not the remainder, it would seem that only the value of the life estate will be included in his gross estate, not the remainder. Similarly, if his power extends only to the remainder interest or interests, it would seem that under § 2038 only those interests will be included since only they are subject to the § 2038 power.

The language of § 2036 appears to be somewhat broader. It requires inclusion of all property to the extent of any interest therein of which the decedent has made a transfer under which he has retained a described power. This language suggests that it is not just the interest subject to the described power but rather the entire property transferred that will be included in the gross estate.

The regulations under § 2036 say that if a decedent retained an interest or right with respect to all of the property transferred by him, the amount to be included in his gross estate under § 2036 is the value of the entire property, less the value of any outstanding income interest which is not subject to the decedent's interest or right and which is actually being enjoyed by another person at the time of the decedent's death. Reg. § 20.2036–1(c). The regulations then go on to specify that if the decedent retained an interest or right with respect to only a *part* of the property transferred by him, the amount to be included under § 2036 is only a corresponding proportion of the amount described in the preceding sentence. Reg. § 20.2036–1(c). To illustrate, suppose that a grantor conveys both Blackacre and Whiteacre in trust to pay income to his wife for life with remainder at the wife's death to the grantor's children, and that the grantor retains until his death a power to accumulate the income from Blackacre (not from Whiteacre) and add it to corpus, such that the accumulated income will be paid over to the remainder beneficiaries (the children) at the wife's death. The statutory language is generally interpreted to mean that the grantor's retained power to designate who shall possess or enjoy the income will cause the entire value of Blackacre (not Whiteacre) to be included in his gross estate under § 2036 but that under § 2038 only the value of the wife's outstanding income interest in Blackacre would be includable, because the interest of the remainder beneficiaries cannot be diminished and therefore is fixed as to time and amount of enjoyment.

The Service has given some indication of its position concerning the application of § 2038. Rev. Rul. 70–513, 1970–2 C.B. 194, involved the following situation. The decedent created an inter vivos trust to pay income to his son for life and to distribute the corpus at the son's death to the beneficiaries of the son's estate. The trustees were given a discretionary power to terminate the trust at any time and pay the corpus over to the income beneficiary, but they could not exercise that power without the decedent's consent. (Therefore, the decedent was viewed as holding the power of termination for purposes of § 2038.) The Service ruled that only the value of the remainder interest would be included in the decedent's gross estate under § 2038 because inclusion under that section is limited to the value of the property interest that was subject to the decedent's power. Therefore, since the enjoyment of the son's life estate was not subject to change through the exercise of the decedent's power, only the value of the remainder interest was required to be included. One might say, however, that the enjoyment of the life estate was subject to change because it would be ended if the power to terminate the trust were exercised. To be sure, the same person who was the life beneficiary would then enjoy the property as its outright owner, rather than as a life tenant, but he would then enjoy the property through a different interest.

It is not possible at this time finally to state a single broad principle to settle the questions concerning possible differences in the amounts includable under §§ 2038 and 2036(a)(2). One Supreme Court case, Lober v. United States, 346 U.S. 335 (1953), suggests, without specifically discussing the point, that the inclusion would be the same. See also Leopold v. United States, 510 F.2d 617 (9th Cir. 1975). However, there is not a sufficient supply of authoritative decisions squarely on point to provide a definitive answer. In light of the fact that the amounts required to be included by §§ 2038 and 2036 may not be identical and that the Service will seek to apply both sections in order to make sure to include the larger amount, the taxpayer should be prepared to argue or negotiate with respect to both statutory sections and to fight the claim that the larger amount should be included.

One very important limitation on the reach of § 2036(a)(2), compared to § 2038, is a statement in the regulations to the effect that the phrase "right to designate the person or persons who shall possess or enjoy the transferred property or the income therefrom" does *not* include a power over the transferred property itself which does not affect the enjoyment of the income received or earned during the decedent's life. But, the regulations note that such a power may cause the property to be included in the gross estate under § 2038. Reg. § 20.2036–1(b)(3).

An important application of §§ 2036(a)(2) and 2038 is in the area of gifts to minors under the Uniform

Transfers to Minors Act (or its predecessor, the Uniform Gifts to Minors Act). In Rev. Rul. 59–357, 1959–2 C.B. 212, the Service ruled that the value of property transferred under the Act will be included in the donor's gross estate for federal estate tax purposes if the donor appoints himself custodian and dies while serving in that capacity. Citing Reg. § 20.2038–1(a), the Service reasoned that the Act gives the custodian discretion to apply the custodial property for the minor's benefit and hence to withhold or alter enjoyment of the property. The statutory language of §§ 2036(a)(2) and 2038 makes clear that a grantor cannot escape from the far-reaching inclusionary rules of those provisions by retaining prohibited powers in a fiduciary capacity (e.g., as a trustee or custodian). This is important to remember, when deciding whether to name the grantor or a third person as a fiduciary for gifts made in trust or in custodianship form and in deciding which powers should be retained by a grantor who acts as a fiduciary. The authorities agree that purely administrative powers or powers limited by an ascertainable standard will not trigger the inclusionary rules, while broad discretionary powers to accumulate or expend trust property for the beneficiaries will constitute a "right" under § 2036(a)(2) or a "power" under § 2038.

When property or an interest in property is includable in the gross estate under § 2036(a)(2) or § 2038, the property or interest is valued at the date of the decedent's death under § 2031, unless the executor makes an election under § 2032 to use the alternate valuation date (usually a date six months after the decedent's death).

Problems of valuation may arise if the property transferred during life has been squandered, converted, depreciated, improved, or transferred by the donee between the time of the transfer and the date of the decedent's death, or if income earned in the interim has been accumulated. In general, the problem becomes whether to apply the statute literally so as to include in the gross estate only the value of the specific property actually transferred or whether accumulated income, proceeds of sales or exchanges, accretions, and improvements should also be included in the valuation. The answers to some of these questions remain uncertain; answers to others can be found in various rulings and cases too numerous and variegated to summarize here. See § 52, *infra.*

§ 35 TRANSFERS TAKING EFFECT AT DEATH: § 2037

I.R.C. § 2037 is captioned "Transfers Taking Effect at Death." Under this provision, property transferred during life by the decedent will be included in his or her gross estate if two conditions are met. The first condition is that possession or enjoyment of the property, through ownership of a transferred interest, can be obtained only by *surviving* the decedent. Secondly, the decedent must have retained some form of *reversionary interest* in the property which, immediately before the death of the decedent, exceeded 5% of the value of such property. A "reversionary interest" includes the possibility that the property will return to the decedent (or his estate) or may be subject to a power of disposition by the decedent. I.R.C. § 2037(b).

An example of a § 2037 transfer will help explain its rules. Alice makes a lifetime transfer of property in trust with income to be paid to Ben for as long as Alice lives, with the remainder to be paid at her death to Charles if he is then living; if Charles is not living, the property will revert to Alice (meaning Alice's estate). Another example would be: Alice transfers property in trust, income to be accumulated for Alice's life, with corpus and accumulated income to be paid at her death to Charles if he is then living; if not, all the property and income to revert to Alice. In each of these examples, the survivorship test of § 2037 is met with respect to Charles' interest. Charles can take possession and enjoyment of the property only if he survives Alice. If the value of her reversionary interest exceeds 5% of the transferred property, § 2037 will cause inclusion in her gross estate. To sum it up, her transfer to Charles will take effect only at her death; until then, it remains uncertain whether Charles will ever possess and enjoy his interest. Alice's heirs may "get it back," to the disappointment of Charles' heirs. Alice's transfer of the interest to Charles has not been completed during her life, for estate tax purposes, and remains incomplete until her death.

In contrast with the foregoing dispositions covered by § 2037, consider the following situation, which does not satisfy all the tests of § 2037. David creates a trust to pay the income to Emily for her life, with remainder at Emily's death to Frank if Frank is then living; if Frank fails to survive Emily, the property is to revert to David or his estate. Suppose also that David dies while Emily is still living. Even if David's reversionary interest is worth more than 5% of the property, § 2037 will not require inclusion of anything in David's gross estate. Frank need not survive David in order to come into possession of the property; all Frank has to do is survive Emily, in order to take possession or enjoyment of the property through his remainder interest.

Now consider the rules of § 2037 as applied to another example. George places property in trust, the income to be accumulated during George's life, with principal and accumulated income to be distributed to his children at his death, but if none of them survive him, then to his wife. Section 2037 will *not* require inclusion in George's gross estate because he has retained no reversionary interest. If none of George's children are alive at his death the property will pass to his wife or her estate, not to George's estate.

The purpose of § 2037, a purpose that can sometimes be lost in the intricacies of its rules, seems clear. When a transfer will take effect only at the death of the decedent because only at that time can another beneficiary be sure that he or she will possess or enjoy the property and if, all along, there existed a substantial possibility that the property would return to the decedent or his estate, the decedent has not fully parted with the property (to the extent of the interest transferred) until death, and the property should therefore be included in the gross estate. In other words, a transfer with a retained reversionary interest and a survivorship condition is not a completed lifetime transfer for estate tax purposes, but amounts to a substitute for a testamentary transfer. Historically, § 2037 is the residuum, after §§ 2036 and 2038 had been carved out, of the original, broad rule in the 1916 statute covering all transfers that were "intended to take effect in possession or enjoyment" at or after the death of the transferor.

If either the survivorship or the reversionary interest requirement is not met, § 2037 will not draw any interest in the transferred property into the decedent's gross estate. In that event, however, some other provision may require inclusion of the property or some interest in it. For example, if the decedent retained a reversionary interest but the survivorship requirement is not met, § 2037 will not apply, but § 2033 will cause inclusion of the decedent's reversionary interest, if that interest survives the death of the decedent and passes to another beneficiary. See Reg. § 20.2037–1(e) (Example 1), as well as the discussion of § 2033 in § 16, *supra*.

Section 2037 is a "grantor section" and applies only if the decedent made a lifetime transfer of the property subject to a *retained* reversionary interest.

Section 2037 can apply when the time for possession or enjoyment of the transferred interest is measured by reference to the life of the grantor. To detect the application of § 2037 when the grantor's life is the measuring life proves relatively easy. In that event, the grantor's death is the occasion for a shift of immediate possession or enjoyment of the property or a resolution of a contingency affecting future possession or enjoyment.

The survivorship requirement can also be met even if the grantor's life is not the measuring life. To illustrate, suppose Andrew makes a lifetime transfer of property in trust to pay income to Betty for her life; the trust will terminate at Betty's death, and the property is to be distributed to Andrew if he is then living; if not, the property is to be distributed to Charles or his heirs. To take possession and enjoyment of the property through ownership of his interest, Charles must survive Andrew; under no circumstances can the interest in Charles or his heirs become possessory while Andrew is still living. If Charles does not survive Andrew, Charles's heirs, rather than Charles himself, will take the property if Andrew does not outlive Betty. In this example, the grantor's life is not the measuring life and no immediate shift of possession or enjoyment occurs at his death. Nevertheless, § 2037 will apply since the survivorship test is met and the reversionary test too, if Andrew's reversion exceeds 5% of the property's value.

If a beneficiary whose interest is being tested under § 2037 could obtain possession or enjoyment of the property either by surviving the decedent or through the occurrence of some other event, there will be no inclusion under § 2037 (unless the other event is so unlikely as to be "unreal" and the decedent in fact dies before that other event occurs). See Reg. § 20.2037–1(b). A transferred interest will not be included in the decedent's gross estate under § 2037 if possession or enjoyment of the property could have been obtained by any beneficiary during the decedent's life through the exercise of a general power of appointment that was in fact exercisable immediately before the decedent's death. I.R.C. § 2037(b).

If possession under an interest commenced during the life of the decedent but might terminate and if that possibility of termination does not end until the death of the decedent, the survivorship test of § 2037 will be deemed to have been met. See Thacher v. Commissioner, 20 T.C. 474 (1953).

Like the other "incomplete transfer" sections of the estate tax, § 2037 contains an exception for a transfer that is a bona fide sale for an adequate and full consideration in money or money's worth.

Section 2037 also contains some special rules. Under § 2037(b), the term "reversionary interest" includes a possibility that property transferred by the decedent may return to him or his estate or may be subject to a power of disposition by him, but the term does not include a possibility that the income alone from such property may return to the decedent or become subject to a power of disposition by him. (Note, however, that such rights may give rise to inclusion under § 2036. Reg. § 20.2037–1(c)(2).) As stated in the regulations, the term "reversionary interest" is not used in a technical sense but refers to any reserved right under which the transferred property shall or may return to the grantor. Thus, it encompasses an interest arising either by the express terms of the transfer or by operation of law. The term "reversionary interest" does not include the possibility that the decedent during his lifetime might have received back an interest in transferred property by inheritance from the estate of another person or as a surviving spouse under a statutory right of election or a similar right. Reg. § 20.2037–1(c)(2).

Under § 2037, the important question is not whether an interest is classified as vested or contingent, but rather whether possession and enjoyment of property through the ownership of the interest remain deferred or uncertain until the decedent's death. The survivorship requirement of § 2037 is met if the beneficiary must survive the decedent in order to possess or enjoy the property; conversely, there is no inclusion under § 2037 if the beneficiary's interest could have become possessory during the decedent's lifetime.

The 5% rule of § 2037(a)(2) refers to the value of the decedent's reversionary interest, not to the amount that is to be included in the gross estate. Thus, if the survivorship test is met and if the decedent's reversionary interest (measured immediately before death) exceeds 5% of the value of the transferred property, the amount includable under § 2037 may be much greater than the value of the reversionary interest alone. As another example of the difference between the 5% rule and the rule of inclusion, the value of a preceding life estate would be taken into account in determining whether the reversionary interest exceeds 5% of the value of the transferred property, but the value of that preceding life estate would be excluded from the amount includable in the gross estate under § 2037. See Reg. § 20.2037–1(c)(4).

The question of what interest is to be included under § 2037 is not always easy, but can be outlined by several examples. Suppose, for example, that Danielle transfers property in trust to pay income to Edward for Danielle's life, and at her death to pay the corpus to Edward if he is then living and if not to Danielle's estate. Assume that Edward survives Danielle and that Danielle's reversion (immediately before her death) was worth more than 5% of the trust property. In that event, the entire value of the trust property will be includable, corresponding to the value of the remainder interest transferred by Danielle to take effect in possession or enjoyment at her death. No subtraction is made for Edward's outstanding income interest since that income interest terminates at Danielle's death. The includable interest must be ascertained and valued at the time of the decedent's death.

Now suppose that Danielle transfers property in trust to pay income to Edward for his life, and at Edward's death to pay the corpus to Danielle, the grantor, if she is then living and if not to Danielle's son Fred or his heirs. Assume that Edward and Fred survive Danielle. In that event Edward's interest is not dependent on Danielle's death; he got immediate enjoyment of the property for his life, and his life income interest is not affected by whether Danielle, the grantor, lives or dies. Therefore, the value of Edward's interest would not be included in Danielle's gross estate under § 2037. However, Fred or his heirs must survive Danielle in order to obtain possession or enjoyment of their respective interests. Therefore, the value of those interests will be fully includable in Danielle's gross estate.

Further examples demonstrating the application of § 2037 can be found in the regulations. See Reg. § 20.2037–1(e).

The value of the retained reversionary interest is to be determined immediately before the death of the decedent, without regard to the fact of death, by the usual methods of valuation, including the use of tables of mortality and actuarial principles. I.R.C. § 2037(a) and (b). Thus, for example, if the decedent's reversionary interest is subject to a condition of surviving a specified person, the interest will be valued under the mortality tables set forth in the estate tax regulations (see § 48, *infra*); but if the reversionary interest is not susceptible of valuation according to recognized actuarial rules (e.g., if it is conditioned on the death without surviving issue of a woman of childbearing age), then relevant facts will be taken into account under general valuation principles. See Reg. § 20.2037–1(c)(3). In Estate of Roy v. Commissioner, 54 T.C. 1317 (1970), the Tax Court held that the mortality tables were conclusive in valuing a reversionary interest conditioned on the grantor outliving his father, even though the grantor's actual life expectancy immediately before death was greatly reduced due to his deteriorating medical condition. The court noted that a valuation based on the grantor's actual life expectancy would limit the application of § 2037 to "cases of sudden death." In determining the value of a possibility that property may be subject to a power of disposition by the decedent, that possibility is to be valued as if it were a possibility that such property would return to the decedent or to his estate.

Because the logic of the operation of § 2037 is not always easy to grasp or keep in mind for someone who does not work with such material frequently, it may prove desirable to test the application of § 2037 in a somewhat mechanical fashion, under its own rules, whenever a lifetime disposition of property has been made and the question is raised whether any estate tax consequences are presented. In this connection, it is most important to remember that the section employs two principal tests, the *survivorship* condition and the *reversionary interest* requirement, both of which must be satisfied for § 2037 to cause some property or interest to be included in the gross estate.

§ 36 RECIPROCAL TRUSTS: WHO IS THE GRANTOR?

For purposes of I.R.C. §§ 2035–2038, the decedent must have been the grantor, donor, or transferor of the property which is to be included in his gross estate. In this regard, however, the substance of a transaction will prevail over its form, and some possibility exists that a person will be treated as the grantor of a trust or the transferor of property for purposes of §§ 2035–2038 even though he is not nominally or apparently the transferor. For example, if Arthur transfers property or pays money to Barbara under an agreement or understanding that Barbara will make a transfer in trust with income to be used for the benefit of Arthur for life, with remainder at death to other beneficiaries, Arthur will be viewed, quite properly, as the grantor or transferor of property with a retained life estate. Sections 2035–2038 cannot be so easily circumvented through the use of a "dummy" or a "straw man" or a "conduit."

A particular example of the attribution of transfers or trusts to someone other than the nominal transferor involves an estate planning technique known as "reciprocal trusts." A simple example of this technique would be the following. Husband and wife, each owning separate property, establish separate trusts for each other's benefit; the husband's trust gives the wife a life estate with remainder to their children, and the wife's trust gives the husband a life estate with remainder to their children. If the two trusts are of approximately equal value and are established pursuant to a common plan or agreement, each spouse will be treated as the grantor of the trust created by the other spouse, on the ground that he or she provided consideration for the other spouse's transfer by establishing an equivalent trust with reciprocal benefits. The husband will be treated as the grantor of the trust established by his wife for his benefit, and vice versa.

If cross attribution of reciprocal or crossed trusts is done, then it remains simply to determine what the tax consequences will be in view of the property that is deemed to have been transferred, the powers retained or held, and the statutory rules of inclusion and valuation in §§ 2035–2038.

Over the years, some cases found that the reciprocal trust doctrine was not applicable on the facts presented, either because there was no concerted action or because the transfers were independently motivated and were not made directly in consideration of each other. See, e.g., Estate of Ruxton v. Commissioner, 20 T.C. 487 (1953). It even proved possible for inconsistent decisions to be reached when the doctrine was applied to one spouse but not the other. See Estate of Guenzel v. Commissioner, 258 F.2d 248 (8th Cir. 1958). As a result, many well-to-do couples were able to escape the estate tax by creating separate trusts, even though the spouses granted to each other interests or powers that were economically indistinguishable from interests and powers that would have caused estate tax inclusion under §§ 2035–2038 if they were retained by the nominal grantor.

This problem was addressed by the Supreme Court in United States v. Estate of Grace, 395 U.S. 316 (1969). There the Court stated that the reciprocal trust doctrine does not depend on a finding that each trust was created in consideration of the other in the sense of *quid pro quo,* nor on the existence of a tax avoidance motive. The Court held that the reciprocal trust doctrine requires only that the trusts be "interrelated" and that the arrangement, to the extent of mutual value, leave the grantors in approximately the same economic position as if they had created trusts naming themselves as beneficiaries. In *Grace,* the trusts were interrelated in the sense that they were substantially identical in terms and were created at approximately the same time. Therefore, the trusts were uncrossed and the decedent was treated as the grantor of the trust (nominally created by his wife) for his benefit, causing the value of that trust to be included in his gross estate under § 2036. As a result of the broad statement of the reciprocal trust doctrine in *Grace,* reciprocal transfers have lost much of their viability as a tax planning technique. By treating each spouse as the grantor of the trust established for his or her own benefit, the reciprocal trust doctrine deters this technique for circumventing the application of §§ 2035–2038.

The reciprocal trust doctrine has also been applied in the gift and income tax areas, and presumably will carry over for purposes of identifying the transferor for purposes of the GST tax as well.

§ 37 ADEQUATE AND FULL CONSIDERATION UNDER §§ 2035–2038

Each of the statutory rules of inclusion in I.R.C. §§ 2035–2038 contains an exception, cast in identical terminology, for a transfer made as a "bona fide sale for an adequate and full consideration in money or money's worth." The meaning of this apparently simple phrase turns out, on closer examination, to be somewhat complicated.

Some of the most difficult problems in this area involve the questions of what constitutes "consideration in money or money's worth" and of whether any such consideration received by a transferor is "adequate and full" so as to block the application of §§ 2035–2038. Some light is shed on this problem by I.R.C. § 2043(a), which provides that if any of the transfers, interests or powers described in §§ 2035–2038 (or § 2041) are made, exercised or relinquished for a consideration in money or money's worth but in a transaction that is not a bona fide sale for an *adequate* and *full* consideration in money or money's worth, the amount includable in the gross estate shall be limited to the excess of the fair market value at the time of death of the property otherwise to be included on account of the transaction over the value of the consideration received by the decedent. The regulations amplify the statutory language slightly by saying that to constitute a bona fide sale for an adequate and full consideration in money or money's worth, the transfer must have been made in good faith and the price must have been an adequate and full equivalent reducible to a money value. See Reg. § 20.2043–1(a). Section 2043(b), examined earlier, goes on to provide that a relinquishment or promised relinquishment of dower or curtesy or of a statutory estate created in lieu of dower or curtesy or other marital rights in the decedent's property or estate shall not be considered to any extent a consideration in money or money's worth.

If a transaction constitutes a bona fide sale for an adequate and full consideration in money or money's worth, there will be no inclusion in the gross estate even though the other conditions of §§ 2035–2038 are met. This result is entirely appropriate, since there has been no estate depletion and no evasion of the estate tax by any incomplete inter vivos gift. If there has not been a sale or if it was not for an adequate and full consideration in money or money's worth, the language of § 2043(a) indicates that if any of §§ 2035–2038 would otherwise apply, there shall be included in the gross estate only the excess of the fair market value of the property or interest otherwise to be included over the value of the consideration received by the decedent. See § 52, *infra*.

If the interest transferred during life is an interest in property which, if retained by the decedent at death, would cause inclusion of some property different from or greater than the interest transferred, the question presented is whether the consideration received for the transfer must equal only the value of the interest transferred or must equal the value that would have been included in the gross estate had that interest been retained by the decedent, in order to satisfy the statutory language calling for "an adequate and full consideration in money or money's worth."

By way of illustration, suppose that a person makes a transfer of property subject to a retained life estate—in effect, a transfer of a remainder interest in the property—and receives in return cash or other property equal to the value of the transferred remainder interest. Assume that the transferor continues to possess or enjoy the property until his death several years later. Will the transferred property be drawn back into the transferor's gross estate, due to his retained life estate, under § 2036, or will the transaction come within the bona fide sale exception? More specifically, the question is whether the transferor received adequate and full consideration when he sold a remainder interest in the transferred property for its fair market value, which was obviously less than the full value of the underlying property.

This is the problem raised in the important case of Estate of D'Ambrosio v. Commissioner, 101 F.3d 309 (3d Cir. 1996), cert. den., 520 U.S. 1230 (1997). In that case, the decedent sold a remainder interest in shares of stock in a family corporation in return for an annuity equal in value to the remainder interest. She retained a life estate in the shares, and continued to receive dividends on the shares (as well as payments under the annuity) until her death a few years later. The Service sought to include the shares in the decedent's gross estate under § 2036, subject to an offset under § 2043 for the amount of consideration that she received at the time of the lifetime transfer. The Service argued that in order to put the transfer beyond the reach of § 2036, the decedent would have had to receive the full value of the shares (i.e., the property that would otherwise be includable in the gross estate), measured at the time of the lifetime transfer. The court rejected this argument, however, and held that the transfer was a bona fide sale for an adequate and full consideration.

The court noted that both the transferred remainder interest and the consideration received by the decedent in the exchange were to be valued as of the date of the lifetime transfer, and concluded that as long as those values were equivalent there was no risk of improper estate tax avoidance.

In the *D'Ambrosio* case, the court offered an example to show why a sale of a remainder interest for its fair market value should not be viewed as abusive. Suppose that a parent sells a remainder interest in land to her child, retaining a life estate. The value of absolute ownership of the land (i.e., a fee simple absolute) is $1 million; the values of the life estate and the remainder at the time of the sale are $800,000 and $200,000, respectively. If the child purchases the remainder from the parent for $200,000, the court pointed out that, in theory, the consideration in the parent's hands at death would be equal to the value of the transferred land, assuming that the rates of return for both assets were equal and that the decedent lived out her actuarial life expectancy. Therefore, the court reasoned, the consideration includable in the parent's gross estate would constitute an adequate replacement for the transferred land.

As the court noted, the theoretical equivalence between the transferred interest and the consideration received by the transferor is based on assumptions concerning rates of return and longevity. If those assumptions prove to be inaccurate, as they often do, the assets included in the transferor's gross estate may be worth far less than the transferred property. The problem is nicely illustrated by the facts of the *D'Ambrosio* case itself. There, the decedent's untimely death cut short both her retained life estate and the annuity that she received as consideration for the transferred remainder interest. As a result, the decedent actually received dividends and annuity payments with a combined value of less than $620,000 after the sale and before her death, while the transferred shares with a fair market value of $2,350,000 escaped gift and estate tax entirely. Despite the court's observation that any given transferor of a remainder would be equally likely to outlive his or her actuarial life expectancy and end up incurring a greater tax burden than if there had been no lifetime transfer, the fact remains that the transfer in *D'Ambrosio* produced substantial tax savings precisely because the decedent did *not* outlive her life expectancy. It is difficult to imagine that family members would enter into such a transaction without the inducement of potential tax savings, or that a transfer on similar terms would ever take place between unrelated parties acting at arm's length.

A similar problem arises when a person makes a transfer subject to a retained life estate and then, within three years of death, transfers the life estate in exchange for consideration equal to its fair market value. Clearly, if the transferor released or transferred the life estate for no consideration (or for inadequate consideration) within three years of death, the underlying property would be drawn back into the gross estate under § 2035(a), producing the same result that would have occurred under § 2036 if the transferor had actually retained the life estate until death. Here, the question is whether the sale of the life estate for its fair market value will put the entire transaction beyond the reach of §§ 2035 and 2036. The rationale of the *D'Ambrosio* case would seem to indicate an affirmative answer, but there is authority for a contrary view.

In United States v. Allen, 293 F.2d 916 (10th Cir. 1961), cert. den., 368 U.S. 944 (1961), the decedent created an irrevocable trust and reserved for herself an interest in three-fifths of the income for life, with remainder to her two children (who were also to receive the remaining two-fifths of the income). At the age of 78 and anticipating that her retained life estate would cause a corresponding portion of the trust corpus to be included in her gross estate, the decedent sought to avoid inclusion by selling her life estate to her son. At the time of the sale, the fair market value of her outstanding life estate, based on her actuarial life expectancy, was $135,000, and the corresponding portion of the corpus (i.e., three-fifths of the corpus) was valued at $900,000. The decedent's son paid her $140,000 for her life estate; shortly afterward, the decedent was discovered to have an incurable disease which resulted in her untimely death.

The decedent's executors argued that the sale of the life interest was for an adequate and full consideration and hence no part of the trust corpus was includable in the gross estate. The Service, however, argued that the contemplation-of-death rule then in force required inclusion in the gross estate of three-fifths of the trust corpus minus the $140,000 consideration received by the decedent on the sale of her life estate. So the question was presented whether the adequacy of the consideration must be measured by the value of the transferred interest or by the value of the interest that would have been included in the gross estate if the decedent had retained the taxable "string" until death. The court accepted the latter view, and concluded that Congress intended the gross estate to include the corresponding portion of corpus or, in its place, an amount equal in value. The court found it implausible that a transferor should be able to transfer property subject to a retained life estate and then, shortly before death, remove the underlying property from the reach of the estate tax by selling the life estate for its fair market value.

Although the *Allen* case, involving a deathbed sale of a life estate retained by the decedent in an earlier transfer, can be distinguished from the *D'Ambrosio* case, involving a sale of a remainder interest, the two decisions reflect fundamentally different approaches to the question of adequate and full consideration. The *Allen* approach has been applauded for its efficacy in deterring artificial estate-depleting techniques, even though it seems to read out of the statute the exception for bona fide sales for adequate and full consideration. (What rational purchaser of a life estate or a remainder interest would ever pay consideration equal to the full value of the underlying property?) In contrast, the *D'Ambrosio* approach adheres more closely to the statutory language, even though it produces results seemingly at odds with the purposes of §§ 2035–2038. As a practical matter, the *D'Ambrosio* approach appears to represent the prevailing trend of authority, at least in cases arising under § 2036. See Wheeler v. United States, 116 F.3d 749 (5th Cir. 1997); Estate of Magnin v. Commissioner, 184 F.3d 1074 (9th Cir. 1999).

The bona fide sale exception has figured prominently in cases involving family limited partnerships, where the question is whether § 2036 requires inclusion in the gross estate of a decedent's ratable share of partnership assets attributable to his lifetime capital contribution (see § 31, *supra*). Even if the decedent is found to have retained enjoyment of the contributed assets for life, the assets themselves will not be drawn back into the gross estate if the decedent's lifetime capital contribution in exchange for his partnership interest qualifies as a bona fide sale within the meaning of § 2036. In this context, notwithstanding the additional statutory language requiring "adequate and full consideration in money or money's worth," the courts have not insisted on strict parity between the amount of the decedent's capital contribution and the value of the partnership interest that he received in exchange. (Indeed, such a requirement would be impossible to satisfy because the decedent's partnership interest is invariably valued with discounts for lack of marketability and lack of control.) Instead, the courts have focused on the nature and purpose of the partnership. Specifically, the Tax Court has held that the statutory safe harbor is met if (1) there was "a legitimate and significant nontax reason for creating the family limited partnership," and (2) the partners received partnership interests proportionate to their respective contributions. Estate of Bongard v. Commissioner, 124 T.C. 95 (2005). This formulation, though logically consistent with the absence of a taxable gift on formation of the partnership, appears to ignore the statutory requirement of an adequate and full consideration in money or money's worth and makes the application of § 2036 turn on a heavily fact-dependent (and necessarily retrospective) inquiry into the purposes of the partnership and the circumstances surrounding its formation.

§ 38 THE WIDOW'S ELECTION AND ADEQUATE AND FULL CONSIDERATION

The widow's election is a much discussed estate planning technique, and one that depends in part on the meaning given to the concept of adequate and full consideration. Available both in community property states and in separate property states, the so-called widow's election actually can be used by any testator and beneficiary regardless of their relationship and regardless of the kind of property in question. In the typical case, the election is used by a married couple whose assets consist entirely of community property in which each spouse has an equal one-half vested interest, or by a couple in a separate property state if each spouse owns separate property.

In the usual community property situation, the husband (assumed to be the first spouse to die) by will purports to transfer both halves of the community property in trust, with income payable to the widow for life and the corpus at her death to be distributed to their children. The widow is then put to an election, either to accept a life estate in the entire community property by allowing her one-half share of the community property to pass under the husband's will or to assert her right to outright ownership of half of the community property, in which event the husband's half would pass directly to the children. The widow's consent is necessary for the disposition to take effect as planned, since the husband has testamentary power over the community property only to the extent of his one-half share. If the widow elects to take under the will, she gives up a remainder interest in her one-half share of the community property in exchange for a life estate in the husband's one-half share, leaving her with a life estate in both halves of the community property. (In a separate property state, a similar transaction occurs if the husband's will puts his separate property in trust for the wife for life, with remainder to their children, on condition that the wife transfer her separate property to the same trust.)

If the widow elects to accept the terms of the husband's will, the gift and estate tax consequences depend on whether the widow is treated as receiving adequate and full consideration in money or money's worth in return for the interest she gives up. Some cases have held that, for gift tax purposes, the widow's transfer is made for full consideration (and hence not taxable as a gift) if the value of the life estate she gets in her husband's share of the property is at least equal to the value of the relinquished remainder interest in her share of the property. (Since she retains a life interest in her share of the property, she has not "given" that interest to anyone.) If the consideration received is worth less than the interest given up, the difference would be a taxable gift. See Commissioner v. Siegel, 250 F.2d 339 (9th Cir. 1957).

For estate tax purposes, however, the life estate that the widow retains in her share of the property cannot be regarded as consideration received by her. (To do so would read § 2036(a)(1) out of the Code.) Therefore, some cases suggest that, in order to escape at least partial inclusion under § 2036(a)(1), the property she receives from her husband must be at least equal in value to the whole of the property she transferred (comprising both the life estate and the remainder interest in her share of the property). If the consideration received is worth less than the transferred property, § 2036(a)(1) will cause inclusion in her gross estate, since she has *retained* a life estate in the transferred property. See Gradow v. United States, 897 F.2d 516 (Fed. Cir. 1990). Arguably, however, this analysis carries the "estate depletion" notion of consideration too far. Under an alternative analysis, the transfer should come within the bona fide sale exception to § 2036(a)(1), and hence escape estate tax at the widow's death, if the life interest she received in her husband's share of the property was at least equal to the value of the relinquished remainder interest in her share of the property. This analysis is consistent with the approach of the *D'Ambrosio* case (discussed in § 38, *supra*).

If everything works according to plan, none of the trust property will be included in the widow's gross estate at her death. This result follows from the fact that she has only a life estate in the property contributed by her husband (which is not includable under § 2033), and she (arguably) received adequate and full consideration for her lifetime transfer of a remainder interest in the property she contributed (which therefore is not includable under § 2036(a)(1)).

An example will illustrate this technique. For purposes of comparison, first consider a husband and wife in a community property state who have $30 million in wealth, all of which is community property. At the husband's death he leaves his one-half share of the property to the wife, and at her death she leaves all of the property to their children. No estate tax will be imposed at the husband's death, due to the unlimited marital deduction; at the wife's death, her taxable estate will consist of the couple's combined assets of approximately $30 million. Alternatively, if the husband left his share of the property in trust to pay income to the wife for life with remainder to their children, and no marital deduction was claimed at his death, $15 million would be subject to estate tax at the husband's death and $15 million would be taxed at the wife's death. (These rough figures assume no depletion for support or consumption and no appreciation in value.)

Now consider the widow's election technique. If the wife elects to take under the husband's will and surrenders her one-half share of the community property, the husband in effect is allowed to put $30 million in trust with a life estate to the wife in return for her surrender of $15 million (or, more properly, a remainder interest in $15 million, since she has retained, rather than received back, the life estate in her one-half share of the property). The husband's gross estate will consist of his share of the community property, worth approximately $15 million. The wife's gift will consist only of the excess of what she transferred (a remainder interest in her $15 million share) over what she received (a life estate in the husband's $15 million share). With careful planning the two amounts could be equalized and no gift tax would be payable (assuming that the special valuation rules of § 2702, discussed in § 49, *infra,* do not apply). If the consideration she received is also deemed adequate and full for estate tax purposes, none of the property will be included in her gross estate under § 2036(a)(1). If any inclusion takes place, the includable amount would be the value (at the wife's death) of what she transferred minus the value (at the date of her election) of her life estate in the husband's share. As a result, the total amount subject to estate tax will have been based on gross estates totaling considerably less than the $30 million of the previous example. It may be possible to produce a similar result in a separate property state if the widow has separate property of her own.

A shadow has been cast over the widow's election technique by the *Gradow* case with its estate-depletion concept of adequate and full consideration. Possibly that shadow has been lengthened by the Supreme Court's decision in United States v. Estate of Grace, 395 U.S. 316 (1969), although *Grace* involved a different consideration issue. The *Grace* case suggests that the Supreme Court might view the transfers involved in the widow's election as not truly involving a transfer for consideration but rather mutual gifts by the widow and the decedent to the children. Certainly it is arguable that in the family context no arm's-length, bona fide sale for adequate and full consideration is likely to have taken place. The children are the natural objects of the bounty of both spouses and there usually is nothing to suggest a bargaining context.

As a practical matter, the utility of the widow's election as an estate planning technique is severely limited by the special valuation rules of § 2702 (discussed in § 49, *infra*). Those rules, if applicable, treat the widow as making a taxable gift of the full value of her one-half share of the community property, with no offset for her retained life estate, in computing the amount of her taxable gift for gift tax purposes. The transaction may also constitute a taxable exchange for income tax purposes. All in all, the widow's election must be regarded as a complex and delicate estate planning instrument not to be employed without careful study of all the federal (and state) tax and non-tax issues it involves.

§ 39 TRANSFERS INCOMPLETE UNTIL TRANSFEROR'S DEATH: GIFT TAX CONSEQUENCES

So far, this chapter has considered various types of lifetime transfers that are treated as incomplete until the transferor's death for estate tax purposes, thereby giving rise to inclusion in the gross estate at death. Such transfers, however, must also be viewed through the glass of the gift tax. In fact, many transfers that remain incomplete until death for estate tax purposes are viewed as complete, when first made, in part or as a whole, for gift tax purposes.

At this point, the particular focus is on those lifetime transfers that will be drawn back into the transferor's gross estate under I.R.C. §§ 2036–2038. Thus the present topic raises the question "what is a completed gift?" or "when is a gift complete for gift tax purposes?". The general problem of what constitutes a completed gift has been addressed earlier (see § 20, *supra*). The present issue is whether a transfer that will produce estate tax consequences under any of §§ 2036–2038, because viewed as not complete until death, will also produce gift tax consequences when made.

The starting point is I.R.C. § 2501. That section imposes a tax on "the transfer of property by gift" by any individual. Section 2511 goes on to provide that the tax imposed by § 2501 shall apply whether the transfer is in trust or otherwise, whether the gift is direct or indirect, and whether the property is real or personal, tangible or intangible. Section 2512 states that a gift shall be valued at the date thereof, and that in the case of a transfer for less than adequate and full consideration, only the excess of the value of the transferred property over the value of the consideration received shall be taxed as a gift.

These bare statutory provisions do not go far towards determining what transfers are "gifts" or "completed gifts" for purposes of the gift tax. Further elaboration must be found in the Treasury regulations, revenue rulings, and judicial decisions.

As the regulations make clear, the gift tax is not imposed on the receipt of the property by the donee but is imposed on the donor with respect to the act of transferring the property and is measured by the value of the property passing from the donor; the tax attaches regardless of the fact that the identity of the donee may not then be known or ascertainable. Reg. § 25.2511–2(a). Thus, the focus is on the release of dominion and control by the donor, not on the apparent receipt of some benefit by any particular donee. Furthermore, it should be kept in mind that a donor may make a completed gift of a partial interest in property, for example, by transferring a remainder interest while retaining a life estate or vice versa. In such cases, the valuation of the transferred interest may raise difficult questions, but these are separate from the threshold question of whether the gift of the interest is complete for gift tax purposes. The concepts of completion and valuation should be kept distinct.

Consider the gift tax consequences of a transfer of property, in trust or otherwise, if the transferor retains a power to *revoke* the transfer. Such a transfer will be viewed as incomplete until death under § 2038 for estate tax purposes. Will a gift tax be imposed, only to be somehow relieved if the transfer is revoked and thus the gift ultimately is not made? Or will the gift tax be payable in any event and no adjustment made if the transfer is later revoked? Or, will there be deemed to be a gift back if the power to revoke is exercised?

As one might expect, the law has clearly established that a revocable transfer is not a completed gift when made and only becomes a completed gift when the transferor gives up or loses his power to revoke. See Burnet v. Guggenheim, 288 U.S. 280 (1933). Thus the gift tax consequences coincide with the estate tax consequences. The result will be the same whether the gift is revocable due to a power retained by the donor or due to a rule of law, such as a rule that a gift made by a minor person is subject to disaffirmance. See Commissioner v. Allen, 108 F.2d 961 (3d Cir. 1939), cert. den., 309 U.S. 680 (1940). A revocable transfer will be regarded as incomplete for gift tax purposes whether the power to revoke is held by the donor alone or is exercisable by him only in conjunction with another person, so long as that other person does not have a substantial beneficial interest that would be adversely affected by an exercise of the power of revocation. See Camp v. Commissioner, 195 F.2d 999 (1st Cir. 1952). Thus, as the regulations put it, a gift is incomplete in every instance in which a donor reserves the power to revest the beneficial title to the property in himself. Reg. § 25.2511–2(c). If the transfer is not revoked and annual distributions of income or other payments are made from the trust or the transferred property, such distributions or payments will be treated as completed gifts by the donor, who is deemed to have made them by refraining from exercising the power to revoke. See Reg. § 25.2511–2(f).

Suppose a person makes a § 2036(a)(1) transfer, that is to say an irrevocable gift in trust or otherwise subject to a reserved life estate. What will be the gift tax consequences of this transfer which, we know, will be regarded as incomplete for estate tax purposes? More specifically, suppose a donor transfers property in trust and provides that the income shall be paid to him for his life and at his death the remainder shall be paid to his wife if she is living and if not to their children or the children's heirs. Will a gift tax be imposed at the time of the initial transfer? The donor has retained a life estate but has made a completed transfer of the remainder interest. It is uncertain whether his wife or his children or their heirs will actually come into possession or enjoyment of the remainder interest, but there is no possibility that the donor himself will get it back through a retained interest. By analogy to a gift of one of several pieces of property, the donor is treated as having transferred an interest less than his entire interest in the property; accordingly, the gift tax is imposed only on the completed gift of the transferred remainder interest. However, the value of the underlying property at the donor's death will be included in his gross estate under § 2036(a)(1) due to his retained life estate.

For gift tax purposes, the donor will be deemed to have made a completed transfer of the remainder interest. The value of the retained life estate, determined under actuarial principles (unless the transfer is governed by the special valuation rules of § 2702, discussed in § 49, *infra*), will be subtracted from the value of the property to determine the amount of the gift to which the gift tax will apply. If the donor retained not a simple life estate but rather a right to specified annual payments for life or for a period of years, the retained interest similarly could be valued and the gift reduced by the value of the retained interest. If a donor transfers property subject to a retained interest for life or for a term of years and later relinquishes that interest, he or she will be deemed to have made a gift of the retained interest at that later time. Thus, in the above example, it is not necessary to compute separately the values of the contingent remainders in the wife and the children, based upon the actuarial chances of survival, since the donor is taxed on the total value of all the interests he gave away.

A more complicated disposition, involving a life estate, a contingent remainder and a reversion, is illustrated by the leading case of Smith v. Shaughnessy, 318 U.S. 176 (1943). There the taxpayer made an irrevocable transfer of stock in trust with the income payable to his wife for life; at her death the stock was to be returned to the taxpayer if living; if he was not in fact living at that time, the stock was to go to the persons designated by his wife in her will or to her intestate successors. The Supreme Court held that the taxpayer had made a completed gift of the life estate and the contingent remainder, but not of the retained reversionary interest. In other words, the Court viewed the case as involving three interests, two of which had been transferred and one of which had been retained.

The taxpayer who seeks to reduce gift tax by showing that some interest in property has been retained must bear the burden of valuing that interest, as demonstrated by Robinette v. Helvering, 318 U.S. 184 (1943), decided the same day as the *Smith* case. There the taxpayer, a 30-year-old woman, contemplating marriage, transferred property with a reserved life estate for herself but also provided a secondary life estate for her mother and stepfather if she should predecease them. The remainder was to go to her issue upon reaching the age of 21, or in the absence of such issue the property was to go as directed by the will of the last surviving life tenant. Thus the taxpayer retained a reversionary interest subject to specified conditions. The taxpayer argued that the gift of the remainder was not complete because there was no donee then in existence who could accept the remainder. In any event, she argued, in computing the value of the gift an allowance for the value of her reversionary interest should be made. Since that reversionary interest depended not only on survivorship but also upon the death of the taxpayer without issue who should reach the age of 21 years, the Supreme Court concluded that there was no recognized method by which to determine the value of the reversionary interest. The burden was on the taxpayer to show that she had retained an interest with an ascertainable value. Since she failed to carry that burden, no reduction was allowable in determining the amount of the gift by reason of the retained reversionary interest.

The principles of the *Smith* and *Robinette* cases are reflected in the regulations governing the application of the gift tax to a transfer of less than the donor's entire interest in property, as well as the treatment of a retained interest that is not susceptible of measurement. See Reg. § 25.2511–1(e).

If a donor transfers property in trust and gives the trustee a power to invade the corpus of the trust for the benefit of the donor, the question arises whether the power of invasion will cause all or a portion of the transfer to be incomplete for gift tax purposes. In general, a discretionary power over transferred property exercisable solely by another person does not prevent a gift from being complete, at least if the donor has no enforceable right to compel an invasion of corpus. If the trustee's power of invasion is limited by a fixed or ascertainable standard that is enforceable by or on behalf of the donor, however, the gift is incomplete to the extent of the ascertainable value of any rights thus retained by the donor. Reg. § 25.2511–2(b). Moreover, if the trustee has very broad discretionary powers to invade the trust corpus for the donor's benefit and under the circumstances there appears to be no assurance that anything of value will ever be paid to other beneficiaries, the transfer is likely to be regarded as incomplete. See Commissioner v. Vander Weele, 254 F.2d 895 (6th Cir. 1958); Rev. Rul. 62–13, 1962–1 C.B. 180. The same result can be justified on the ground that the donor indirectly retained a power of revocation if the trust property is available under local law to satisfy claims of his or her creditors, since the donor could obtain the economic benefit and enjoyment of the trust property by incurring debt and then relegating creditors to the trust property for repayment. See Paolozzi v. Commissioner, 23 T.C. 182 (1954). Of course, as distributions of income or corpus are actually made to other beneficiaries, completed gifts would occur and would be subject to gift tax when made.

A somewhat different problem is presented if a person makes a transfer and retains a power, not exercisable for his or her own benefit, to alter or amend the transfer or otherwise to designate the beneficiaries who will actually enjoy the property. For example, suppose that a donor transfers property in trust and reserves a power to distribute income or corpus to his wife and child at such times and in such proportions as he determines in his sole discretion for a period of 20 years, at the end of which any remaining property is to be paid to the child or the child's heirs. Under a disposition such as this, the donor has not retained any power of revocation or any interest that will return the property to him. Barring the case where distributions of income to the wife or child would discharge the donor's obligation of support, there is no way under the terms of the trust that the property will come back to provide economic benefits to the donor. Therefore, one might think that the gift was complete because, in the language of the regulations mentioned earlier, the donor has reserved no power to revest the beneficial title to the property in himself. However, under the regulations and the case law, this transfer will not be regarded as a completed gift of any of the property transferred. Even though the power to designate new beneficiaries does not include the donor himself or, for that matter, anyone other than the beneficiaries named in the instrument, the gift will become complete and subject to the gift tax only at the time the donor relinquishes the power. (Of course, if the donor retains the power until death, the trust property will be includable in his gross estate under §§ 2036(a)(2) and 2038.) See Estate of Sanford v. Commissioner, 308 U.S. 39 (1939). The regulations put it as follows: "As to any property, or part thereof or interest therein, of which the donor has so parted with dominion and control as to leave in him no power to change its disposition, whether for his own benefit or for the benefit of another, the gift is complete. But if upon a transfer of property (whether in trust or otherwise) the donor reserves any power over its disposition, the gift may be wholly incomplete, or may be partially complete and partially incomplete, depending upon all the facts in the particular case." Reg. § 25.2511–2(b).

Thus for gift tax purposes the question is not so much whether the donor has transferred legal title or relinquished all beneficial interests in the property, but rather whether the donor has so parted with dominion and control over the property as to leave no power in himself to affect beneficial enjoyment of the property. To put it another way, the power to control the disposition of property that has been transferred is regarded as such an important aspect of ownership as to make the transfer of the property incomplete, for gift tax purposes, until that power disappears. This general principle is subject to a few qualifications. First, a gift is not considered incomplete merely because the donor reserves the power to change the manner or time of enjoyment. Reg. § 25.2511–2(d). Second, if the only retained power is a fiduciary power, the exercise or nonexercise of which is limited by a fixed or ascertainable standard, to change the beneficiaries of the transferred property, the donor will be treated as having made a completed gift and the entire value of the transferred property will be subject to gift tax. Reg. § 25.2511–2(g).

The relinquishment or termination of a power to change the beneficiaries of transferred property, occurring otherwise than by the death of the donor (the gift tax being confined to transfers by living donors), is regarded as the event which completes the gift and causes the gift tax to apply. Reg. § 25.2511–2(f).

Therefore, not only the power to revest the beneficial title to the property in himself, but also a power that gives the donor the ability to name new beneficiaries or to change the interests of the beneficiaries as between themselves (unless the power is a fiduciary power limited by a fixed or ascertainable standard), will render a gift incomplete. Reg. § 25.2511–2(c). A power affecting beneficial enjoyment of the transferred property will make the gift incomplete if it is exercisable by the donor either alone or in conjunction with any person not having a substantial adverse interest in the disposition of the transferred property or the income from it. A trustee, as such, is not a person having an adverse interest in the disposition of the trust property or its income. Reg. § 25.2511–2(e).

Another form of inter vivos transfer that is viewed by the estate tax as incomplete until death is a conditional or so-called § 2037 transfer. To illustrate, suppose that Carl irrevocably transfers property in trust to pay income to Diane for life, with remainder at Diane's death to Carl if he is then living; if he is not living, the property is to be distributed to Eric (or his heirs). Carl has retained a reversionary interest which will return possession and enjoyment of the property to him if he survives Diane. Also, the survivorship requirement of § 2037 is met because Eric (or his heirs) can obtain possession or enjoyment of the property only by surviving Carl. If Carl dies before Diane, and if his reversionary interest immediately before his death exceeds 5% of the value of the property, § 2037 will draw the remainder interest in the property back into Carl's gross estate on the ground that the transfer was incomplete until his death. See Reg. § 20.2037–1(e). If Carl survives Diane, the property will return to him and will be included in his gross estate under § 2033.

For purposes of the gift tax, Carl's retained reversionary interest will serve to reduce the amount of his taxable gift (assuming that the special valuation rules of § 2702, discussed in § 49, *infra,* do not apply). He will be deemed to have made completed gifts of the other interests, the life estate and the remainder interest. Even if Carl's retained reversionary interest fell below the 5% threshold, so that there would be no inclusion in his gross estate under § 2037, that small reversionary interest would nevertheless reduce the amount of the gift for gift tax purposes. (However, if the reversionary interest were subject to conditions that made its value impossible to determine, no reduction would be allowed in the amount of the taxable gift.)

Overall, it appears that a retained power or interest, of the kind the estate tax is concerned with in §§ 2036–2038, may render a gift incomplete for gift tax purposes as well, but will not necessarily do so in every case. In other words, the gift tax and the estate tax are not mutually exclusive or perfectly coordinated. Some transfers will be treated as complete when made for gift tax purposes even though they are incomplete until death for estate tax purposes.

In general, for gift tax purposes one must inquire not only whether the donor has retained a power to revest beneficial title or enjoyment in himself, but also whether he has parted with dominion and control over the property and its disposition. If the donor has retained no power—exercisable by himself alone or with someone who has no substantial adverse interest—either to revest the transferred property in himself or to affect beneficial enjoyment of the property by himself or others, a completed gift of the entire property will be deemed to have been made. Anything less than this may cause the gift to be treated as wholly or partially incomplete, depending on the extent of the power retained by the donor.

However, a gift will not be considered incomplete merely because the donor retains standard administrative or managerial powers. This is consistent with the treatment of administrative powers for estate tax purposes under §§ 2036(a)(2) and 2038.

For purposes of the gift tax, a power exercisable by the donor only in conjunction with someone else must be investigated further to determine whether the other person has a substantial beneficial interest that would be adversely affected by an exercise of the power in question. To the extent the other person has such an "adverse interest," the power in the donor's hands will be disregarded in determining whether there is a completed gift. The rationale is that the donor would be constrained in exercising the power, since the other person would have an incentive to block any exercise that would impair his or her interest. The adverse interest rule is applied even in the family context where one must recognize that a beneficiary whose interest is apparently adverse to the donor may in fact be likely to consent to a revocation or amendment desired by the donor due to personal and familial considerations. See Camp v. Commissioner, 195 F.2d 999 (1st Cir. 1952); Commissioner v. Prouty, 115 F.2d 331 (1st Cir. 1940). If the other person does not have an adverse interest, the gift will be incomplete to the same extent as if the power were exercisable by the donor alone, without the consent of any other person. (In contrast, for estate tax purposes, the retention of similar powers, whether exercisable by the transferor alone or in conjunction with any other person, will give rise to inclusion in the transferor's gross estate under §§ 2036(a)(2) and 2038, since those provisions contain no adverse interest exception.)

Thus, if the donor can exercise the retained power only with the consent of all persons having an interest in the trust, the power counts for nothing and the gift is complete. If a power to affect beneficial enjoyment of the transferred property is exercisable solely by a person other than the donor, with no requirement of consent or participation by the donor, and the power cannot be exercised for the benefit of the donor, the power will not render the gift incomplete.

Just as the gift and estate taxes are not perfectly correlated, differences may arise in the application of the gift tax and the income tax or the estate tax and the income tax. For example, in Lockard v. Commissioner, 166 F.2d 409 (1st Cir. 1948), the court held that a taxable gift had been made when a wife set up a short-term trust for her husband, even though for income tax purposes the transfer was regarded as incomplete and the wife was taxed on the trust income each year during the term of the trust.

CHAPTER 6

JOINTLY OWNED PROPERTY AND COMMUNITY PROPERTY

§ 40 JOINTLY OWNED PROPERTY AND COMMUNITY PROPERTY—ESTATE AND GIFT TAX: § 2040

Introduction. Property may be jointly owned by two or more people in one of several forms. One of these forms, called joint tenancy (or, in the case of a married couple as co-tenants, tenancy by the entirety) has the distinctive feature of a right of survivorship. At the death of one joint tenant, the surviving joint tenant is entitled to full ownership of the property by operation of law. In contrast, tenancy in common is a form of co-ownership of property in which each tenant has a separate, undivided interest in the property, an interest which he or she can transmit during life or at death. In a tenancy in common, there is no right of survivorship; at the death of one tenant, the decedent's interest passes by will or intestacy and will be included in the gross estate under I.R.C. § 2033, along with other property owned at death. If property is held by two people as tenants in common, an undivided one-half interest will be included at the death of each tenant in his or her gross estate.

By its nature, joint ownership with right of survivorship presents special gift and estate tax problems. When one of the co-owners of a joint tenancy or tenancy by the entirety dies, the surviving tenant becomes the outright owner of the entire property by virtue of the form of ownership in which the property was held. The right of survivorship takes effect automatically, by operation of law; the decedent's interest does not pass by will or intestacy and is not subject to probate administration as an asset of the probate estate. In other words, the decedent's interest in the property terminates at death. A joint tenancy also can be terminated before death, either by mutual agreement of the parties or by either of them acting alone (e.g., by partition or conveyance). If one joint tenant transfers his interest to a third person, the right of survivorship is destroyed and the result is a tenancy in common between the third person and the other original tenant. A tenancy by the entirety is essentially the same as a joint tenancy except that it can arise only when the co-owners are a married couple and can last only as long as their marriage endures. Furthermore, a tenancy by the entirety cannot be destroyed by the unilateral act of either tenant. The tenancy will come to an end if the spouses are divorced or if they both agree to end the tenancy or at the death of either spouse.

Each joint tenant is viewed as owning all of the property, subject to the rights of the other joint tenant or tenants. Each joint tenant has equal, undivided rights in the property and is entitled to an equal share of any income from the property.

Joint-and-survivor bank accounts are a form of ownership that resembles a plain joint tenancy in important respects. Each party has a right of survivorship and also has the right during his life to withdraw all the funds in the account, although he may be liable to account to the other party or parties for any amounts withdrawn in excess of his net contributions to the account.

Still another form of joint ownership is found in the community property systems of a number of states. Community property ownership differs from joint tenancies and tenancies by the entirety, varies somewhat from state to state, and has evolved over time within some states. Community property exists, of course, only between spouses. Under the most prevalent system, each spouse is viewed as having an equal, present, vested interest in each item of community property. As a result, at the death of either spouse, the decedent's one-half share of the community property will be includable at death in his or her gross estate under § 2033. In this respect, community property resembles a tenancy in common, for estate tax purposes.

Estate Tax. For estate tax purposes, property held in joint tenancy or tenancy by the entirety is governed by I.R.C. § 2040. In the absence of § 2040, the estate tax treatment of property held jointly by the decedent and another person with a right of survivorship would be difficult to determine. An argument could be made that all, or none, or only a portion of the jointly owned property should be included in the gross estate of the first joint owner to die.

In general, § 2040(a) provides that a decedent's gross estate shall include the value of property held jointly by the decedent and another person (or persons) with right of survivorship. One exception: if the property was acquired by the decedent and the other joint owner by gift, devise, bequest, or inheritance, only the decedent's fractional share of the property must be included in his gross estate. In all other events, the entire value of the jointly owned property is included in the estate of the first joint owner to die, *except* such part of the entire value as the taxpayer can show was attributable to consideration in money or money's worth furnished by the other joint owner (or owners).

In determining what consideration was furnished by the other joint owners, there is taken into account only that portion of such consideration which is shown not to have been acquired from the decedent for less than an adequate and full consideration in money or money's worth. Under this general rule, it is obvious that if A gives $10,000 to B, which B turns around and invests in joint tenancy property with A, and A then dies survived by B, the entire value of the property at A's death will be includable in his gross estate. Although B nominally furnished the consideration for the joint tenancy property, the funds used to acquire the property were acquired as a gift from A and will therefore be attributed to A under the tracing rules of § 2040(a). Reg. § 20.2040–1(c)(4). An important exception, however, involves income from property given by the decedent to the other joint owner. The income generated by such gift property in the hands of the other joint owner will not be traced back to the decedent; if such income is used to acquire joint tenancy property, it will be treated as consideration furnished by the other joint tenant and will reduce the amount includable in the decedent's gross estate. Reg. § 20.2040–1(c)(5). Moreover, the same rationale applies to income from the joint tenancy property itself, which belongs in equal shares to the joint tenants regardless of the source of the purchase price for the property. Therefore, each joint tenant is deemed to have furnished an equal share of consideration for any improvements on the joint tenancy property that are paid for out of income from the property. New joint tenancy property paid for with such income is treated similarly.

The treatment of income from gift property, e.g., rent, dividends and interest, must be distinguished from the treatment accorded appreciation in tracing the source of consideration under § 2040(a). If A gives Blackacre, worth $10,000, to B and B sells it for $15,000 and then uses the proceeds to purchase joint tenancy property with A, what result? There would seem to be little basis for reaching a different result than if income from Blackacre were used, and the cases agree that B should be treated as having contributed the $5,000 attributable to the appreciation in Blackacre. See Harvey v. United States, 185 F.2d 463 (7th Cir. 1950); Estate of Goldsborough v. Commissioner, 70 T.C. 1077 (1978), aff'd, 673 F.2d 1310 (4th Cir. 1982). This, however, is where the similarity of treatment ends. If instead of selling Blackacre, B contributed the appreciated property directly as his share of a joint tenancy with A, the regulations treat A as having contributed the entire consideration for the joint tenancy. Reg. § 20.2040–1(c)(4). Furthermore, at least one case has held that if one person provides all of the consideration for joint tenancy property, and that property is sold and the proceeds, including appreciation, are used to acquire other property held in joint tenancy by the same parties, none of the appreciation in the first property may be attributed to the non-contributing joint tenant. Endicott Trust Co. v. United States, 305 F. Supp. 943 (N.D.N.Y. 1969). The court in *Endicott Trust Co.* reasoned that the property was held in joint tenancy at all times and that a change in the character of the property, with no change in the character of the ownership, should not permit an escape from taxation as joint property under § 2040(a).

If it is determined that some of the joint property is attributable to consideration furnished by the other joint owner or owners, part of the value of the property will be excluded from the decedent's gross estate. The excludable portion is that portion of the entire value of the property at the decedent's death which the consideration in money or money's worth furnished by the other joint owner or owners bears to the total cost of acquisition and capital improvements of the property. Thus, the entire value of the jointly held property will be included in the decedent's gross estate unless the executor submits facts sufficient to show that the property was not acquired entirely with consideration furnished by the decedent or that the property was acquired by the decedent and the other joint owner or owners by gift, bequest, devise or inheritance. See I.R.C. § 2040(a); Reg. § 20.2040–1(a).

To illustrate the application of § 2040(a), consider the tax consequences if two people, A and B, *not* a married couple, purchase real property in joint tenancy and each pays a portion of the purchase price. (The special rules governing spousal joint tenancies will be considered below.) The portion of the purchase price furnished by the respective joint tenants will determine the proportional share of the value of the property to be included in the gross estate of the first to die. If the property is purchased entirely with A's separate property and A dies before B, the entire value of the property at A's death will be included in his gross estate because it cannot be shown that any part of the value at his death is attributable to consideration furnished by B, the other joint owner. If A had given B some funds which B then used to pay part of the purchase price, the entire value of the property at A's death would still be included in A's gross estate because the funds contributed by B would be attributable to money or other property received from A for less than an adequate and full consideration in money or money's worth. However, if B was the original source of the funds he contributed toward the purchase price, then the amount included in A's gross estate would be limited to the value of the property at A's death multiplied by the ratio of A's contributions to the total purchase price.

Obviously, the taxpayer may face difficult problems of proof; inadequacies in his records will work only to his disadvantage. Under § 2040(a), it is up to the taxpayer to show the extent to which contributions were made by someone other than the decedent, both as to the original purchase price of the property and as to any subsequent capital improvements. Tracing will be required in instances where property has been sold and the proceeds reinvested. If contributions have been made out of income from separate property or other jointly held property, precise calculations will be required.

Tracing may also be required when joint property is acquired with borrowed funds. In general, contributions are measured by actual payments toward the purchase price of the property, including principal payments on the debt, as well as a ratable share of the outstanding balance of the debt at the decedent's death. To illustrate, suppose that A and her child B purchase Blackacre as joint tenants with right of survivorship. A and B each pay $10,000 cash down toward the total purchase price of $100,000, and the balance of $80,000 is financed with proceeds of a mortgage loan on which A and B are jointly and severally liable. Prior to her death A pays $20,000 of principal on the mortgage, and B makes no further payments. A then dies survived by B, when the fair market value of Blackacre is $200,000 and the outstanding mortgage balance is $60,000. To determine the amount includable in A's gross estate under § 2040(a), the respective contributions of A and B are computed as follows: A is credited with her $10,000 cash payment and $20,000 of principal payments on the mortgage, as well as $30,000 representing half of the outstanding mortgage balance at her death; B is credited with a $10,000 cash payment and $30,000 representing the other half of the outstanding mortgage balance. Thus, A is treated as having contributed $60,000 of the original purchase price of $100,000, and B is treated as having contributed $40,000. Accordingly, 60% of the fair market value of Blackacre at A's death, or $120,000, is includable in A's gross estate. (A deduction of $30,000 for A's share of the outstanding mortgage will be allowed under § 2053, resulting in a net inclusion of $90,000 in her taxable estate.) The application of the tracing rules to debt-financed property is discussed in Rev. Rul. 79–302, 1979–2 C.B. 328.

Of course, § 2040 applies only to property held in joint tenancy or tenancy by the entirety that passes at the death of the decedent to one or more surviving joint owners. The last surviving joint owner receives absolute ownership of the property, which will be included, along with all other property owned at death, in his or her gross estate under § 2033. The order of deaths can therefore make a substantial difference in the overall tax burden. For example, assume that A contributed all of the consideration for property held by A and her son B as joint tenants with right of survivorship. If A dies first, the entire value of the property will be included in her gross estate under the tracing rule of § 2040, and then at B's death the property will be included in his gross estate under § 2033. If B dies first, however, nothing will be includable in his gross estate under § 2040, since all of the consideration was contributed by A, the surviving joint tenant; at A's subsequent death, of course, the entire value of the property will be includable in her gross estate under § 2033.

What if A and B die simultaneously, or in circumstances such that the order of deaths cannot be ascertained? In this situation, state law generally provides that half of the joint property shall pass as if one of the joint tenants survived and the other half shall pass as if the other joint tenant survived. Thus, one half of the property is treated *as if A died first,* so that it passes to B as surviving joint tenant and then, since B is also dead, to his testate or intestate successors. For estate tax purposes, this half will be included in A's gross estate under the tracing rule of § 2040, and it will also be included in B's gross estate under § 2033, along with all other property actually owned by B at his death. The other half of the property is treated *as if B died first,* and therefore passes to A as surviving joint tenant and then through A's estate to her testate or intestate successors. This half of the property will escape inclusion in B's gross estate under § 2040 because all of the consideration was contributed by A, who is deemed to be the surviving joint tenant; but it must be included in A's gross estate under § 2033. The end result is that the full value of the property will be included in A's gross estate (one half under § 2040, the other half under § 2033), and half the value of the property will be included in B's gross estate (under § 2033). See Rev. Rul. 76–303, 1976–2 C.B. 266. This sequential application of §§ 2040 and 2033 may at first seem counterintuitive. On further reflection, however, it can be viewed as "splitting the difference" between full inclusion in both estates (as if A died first) and full inclusion in only one estate (as if B died first), which seems perfectly sensible in a situation where it is impossible to determine which joint tenant actually survived the other.

The regulations under § 2040 provide additional examples illustrating the application of § 2040(a).

Spouses. The problem of tracing contributions under § 2040(a) proved very burdensome, particularly in light of the fact that joint tenancy is a favored form of property ownership for married couples. Partly in order to obviate these tracing difficulties, and also to recognize a spouse's services toward accumulating joint property, the 1976 Act added special rules for certain joint tenancies, *between spouses,* created after 1976. The treatment of spousal joint tenancies was greatly simplified by the 1981 Act, in conjunction with the advent of the unlimited marital deduction. The governing provision is now found in § 2040(b).

Section 2040(b)(1) provides that one half of any "qualified joint interest" is to be included in the gross estate of the first joint tenant to die, no matter which joint tenant actually furnished the consideration. A qualified joint interest is defined as any interest in property held *solely* by the decedent and his or her spouse as tenants by the entirety or as joint tenants with right of survivorship. I.R.C. § 2040(b)(2). (Accordingly, if there are any joint tenants other than the decedent and his or her spouse, the joint tenancy is not a qualified joint interest and will therefore be subject to the tracing rules of § 2040(a) rather than the 50–50 rule of § 2040(b)(1).)

When Congress amended the definition of "qualified joint interest" in § 2040(b)(2), as part of the 1981 Act, it may have intended to make the 50–50 rule of § 2040(b)(1) applicable to all spousal joint tenancies, whenever created, for decedents dying after 1981. The courts, however, have held that the 1981 amendment did not override the original effective date of § 2040(b)(1), with the result that the 50–50 rule applies only to joint tenancies created after 1976. Accordingly, the tracing rules of § 2040(a) continue to apply to spousal joint tenancies created before 1977. See Hahn v. Commissioner, 110 T.C. 140 (1998).

In fact, the 50–50 inclusionary rule for spousal joint tenancies will have only a negligible impact on the estate tax liability of a decedent's estate, since any interest passing to the surviving spouse by right of survivorship will automatically qualify for the unlimited estate tax marital deduction (unless the surviving spouse is not a U.S. citizen). See I.R.C. § 2056(a), (c)(5), and (d)(1). As a practical matter, the real significance of the 50–50 rule lies in its effect on the basis of the joint tenancy property in the hands of the surviving spouse for income tax purposes. Since only one half of a qualified joint interest is includable in the decedent's gross estate, only one half of the value of the property at the date of death is eligible for a stepped-up basis under § 1014(a). Thus, for example, if H and W acquired property for $100,000 in 2020 and the property appreciates in value to $200,000 at H's death in 2030, W will take the property with an income tax basis of $150,000—a stepped-up basis of $100,000 in the one-half share included in H's gross estate, plus a cost basis of $50,000 in the other half of the property.

Interaction with Lifetime Transfer Provisions. The tracing rules of § 2040(a), as well as the 50–50 rule of § 2040(b), apply to an interest in property held by the decedent and another person as joint tenants with right of survivorship. The relevant time is the date of the decedent's death. Thus, § 2040 does not apply if the joint tenancy is terminated before death, since the property is no longer "held" at death by the decedent and another person as joint tenants with right of survivorship. Nor will the underlying property be drawn back into the gross estate under § 2035, even if the joint tenancy is terminated within three years before death, since § 2040 is not among the sections enumerated in § 2035(a). (Of course, if the joint tenancy is terminated during life and the decedent receives a share of the property or its proceeds which he owns at death, such property will be includable in his gross estate under § 2033.)

Now suppose that A and B, holding property jointly so as to require inclusion in A's estate under § 2040(a) if the property were retained until his death, transfer the property in trust subject to a retained life estate. Under § 2036(a)(1) alone, the retained life estate should produce inclusion of the interest transferred. But that interest would apparently be limited to A's one-half share of the property, not the entire amount that would have been included in his gross estate under § 2040(a) if he had not made the transfer with a retained life estate. At one time the Service argued that the whole property should be included in the decedent's estate in a situation like this, explicitly relying on the "estate depletion" theory of the *Allen* case (see § 37, *supra*). The courts, however, rejected the Service's position. See United States v. Heasty, 370 F.2d 525 (10th Cir. 1966); Glaser v. United States, 306 F.2d 57 (7th Cir. 1962). Although the *Heasty* approach allows some joint tenants to escape the reach of the estate tax by severing the tenancy shortly before death, it fits the language of §§ 2036 and 2040. The Service has accepted the *Heasty* result. Rev. Rul. 69–577, 1969–2 C.B. 173.

The constitutionality of § 2040(a) was upheld in United States v. Jacobs, 306 U.S. 363 (1939). In that case it was held constitutional even as applied to joint tenancy property that had been acquired before the enactment of the estate tax. The Supreme Court said that the tax did not operate retroactively in an impermissible manner merely because some of the facts or conditions upon which the application of the tax depends came into being prior to the enactment of the tax.

Gift Tax. The gift tax consequences of the formation or termination of a joint tenancy are governed by general gift tax principles and not by specific statutory provisions. In general, if each of the joint tenants contributes a proportionate share of the consideration for the property and if the joint tenancy can be severed so as to defeat the survivorship rights of the other tenants, no gift has been made upon formation and no gift tax consequences will follow at that time. If one of the joint tenants contributes more than his or her proportionate share of the consideration, there is a gift to the extent of the surplus contribution. Reg. § 25.2511–1(h)(5). So, for example, if A and B purchase property for $100,000 and take title as joint owners, and if A contributes the entire purchase price, he will be deemed to have made a gift of $50,000 to B. If A contributed $80,000 and B contributed $20,000, A would be deemed to have made a gift to B of $30,000. The relative ages of the joint tenants do not matter, even though one joint tenant may be far more likely than the other to survive and receive full ownership of the property. This result follows from the fact that the joint tenancy could be severed at any time by either tenant acting alone, and thus either tenant could obtain his proportionate share of the property or the proceeds of selling the property.

The preceding example should be distinguished from a joint bank account in which each person can withdraw his or her net contributions without any obligation to account to the other party. In this situation, there is no completed gift until one party withdraws an amount in excess of his or her net contributions. Reg. § 25.2511–1(h)(4). Thus, if A and B are joint owners of a bank account which was funded entirely by A's contributions, there is no completed gift as long as the account remains subject to A's dominion and control. However, if B withdraws amounts from the account for his own benefit during A's lifetime, A will be treated as making completed gifts of the amounts withdrawn.

In the case of a spousal joint tenancy, any deemed transfer between the spouses upon formation or termination will automatically qualify for the unlimited marital deduction and will therefore not result in any gift tax (unless the donee spouse is not a U.S. citizen). See I.R.C. § 2523(a), (d), and (i). Special rules governing the gift tax treatment of spousal joint tenancies were formerly found in §§ 2515 and 2515A, but these rules were repealed by the 1981 Act, in conjunction with the advent of the unlimited marital deduction.

CHAPTER 7

LIFE INSURANCE: ESTATE TAX AND GIFT TAX

§ 41 PROCEEDS OF LIFE INSURANCE—ESTATE TAX TREATMENT: § 2042

Introduction. I.R.C. § 2042 sets forth two rules for the estate tax treatment of life insurance proceeds paid on a policy on the life of the decedent. The first rule, contained in § 2042(1), requires that the value of the gross estate shall include the value of all property to the extent of the amount receivable by the executor as insurance under policies on the life of the decedent. Therefore if the proceeds of a life insurance policy on the decedent's life are payable to the executor, the entire proceeds are includable in the decedent's gross estate. More usefully put, the rule is that insurance proceeds receivable *by or for the benefit of the estate* must be included. See Reg. § 20.2042–1(a). Thus, proceeds which are subject to administration, available to pay claims of creditors, and distributable as an asset of the estate are deemed receivable by the executor for purposes of this rule. Under applicable state law, policies that are nominally payable to the decedent's executor may actually be held for the exclusive benefit of the decedent's surviving spouse and children, for example, free of claims of the decedent's creditors. In that event, the proceeds will not be included in the gross estate under § 2042(1), although they may be includable under § 2042(2) if the decedent held incidents of ownership in the policy. Insurance proceeds payable to named beneficiaries other than the decedent's estate will be included in the gross estate to the extent that the proceeds are received by such a beneficiary subject to a legally binding obligation to pay taxes, debts or other charges, despite the fact that the decedent possessed no incidents of ownership in the policy. See Reg. § 20.2042–1(b). In other words, the determining test for inclusion under § 2042(1) is whether the insurance proceeds produce a benefit for the estate, not whether the proceeds are formally payable to the executor. Also, if the insurance had been made payable or assigned as collateral security for a loan to the decedent, it is considered to be receivable for the benefit of the estate. See Reg. § 20.2042–1(b). These results make perfectly good sense because the insurance serves to satisfy debts of the estate and thus to increase the net estate that will pass to the heirs just as if the insurance proceeds had been payable directly to the estate.

Under a second rule, set forth in § 2042(2), the gross estate will also include the value of all property to the extent of the amount receivable by all other beneficiaries (other than the executor) as insurance under policies on the life of the decedent with respect to which the decedent possessed at his death any of the incidents of ownership, "exercisable either alone or in conjunction with any other person." Thus, for example, it has been held that a decedent had an incident of ownership at his death because his consent was required for his wife to revoke or amend a trust, part of the corpus of which consisted of an insurance policy on the life of the decedent. See

Commissioner v. Estate of Karagheusian, 233 F.2d 197 (2d Cir. 1956).

Incidents of Ownership. The term "incidents of ownership" is not employed in a way that limits it to ownership of the policy in a technical sense. It refers more generally to the right of the insured or his estate to the economic benefits of the policy. Accordingly, it includes the power to change the beneficiary, to surrender or cancel the policy, to assign the policy, to revoke an assignment, to pledge the policy for a loan, or to obtain from the insurer a loan against the surrender value of the policy. Reg. § 20.2042–1(c)(2).

If the decedent was the sole or controlling shareholder of a corporation which owned an insurance policy on his life, the regulations provide that the corporation's incidents of ownership will not be attributed to the decedent to the extent the proceeds of the policy are payable either to the corporation itself or to a third party for a valid business purpose. However, to the extent the proceeds are not payable to or for the benefit of the corporation, and hence are not reflected in the value of the decedent's shares, any incidents of ownership held by the corporation will be attributed to the decedent through his controlling stock ownership. For this purpose, a decedent will not be deemed to be the controlling shareholder unless he owned stock with more than 50% of the total combined voting power of the corporation. Reg. § 20.2042–1(c)(6).

The statute specifies that the term "incident of ownership" includes a reversionary interest only if the value of that interest exceeded 5% of the value of the policy immediately before the death of the decedent. The term "reversionary interest" also includes the possibility that the policy or its proceeds may return to the decedent or his estate or may be subject to a power of disposition by him. I.R.C. § 2042(2). However, the terms "reversionary interest" and "incidents of ownership" do not include the possibility that the decedent might receive the policy or its proceeds by inheritance from the estate of another person or as a surviving spouse under a statutory right of election or a similar right. Reg. § 20.2042–1(c)(3).

The decedent will be deemed to possess incidents of ownership in a life insurance policy if, at the time of his death, he had the general, legal power to exercise ownership, without regard to his actual ability to exercise that power at a particular moment. See Commissioner v. Estate of Noel, 380 U.S. 678 (1965). In the *Noel* case, the decedent had purchased life insurance at the airport and handed the policies to his wife before he departed; he could not exercise his power to alter the beneficiary or assign the policies while he was in the airplane, where he remained until his death a few hours later when the airplane crashed. Nevertheless, the Supreme Court held that he did have the incidents of ownership at his death.

A similar question is whether the formal right to exercise the incidents of ownership or the practical power to do so is to be determinative for estate tax purposes. In United States v. Rhode Island Hospital

Trust Co., 355 F.2d 7 (1st Cir. 1966), the court held that proceeds of insurance policies on the decedent's life were includible in his gross estate because he held incidents of ownership at his death even though the policies had been taken out by the decedent's father who personally dominated him and was in a position to command or direct the decedent's behavior, including the exercise of rights under the policies. The court distinguished between so-called "intent facts," those relating to the conduct and understanding of the insured and his father, and "policy facts," those revealed by the insurance contract itself. The court relied on the latter, in applying the provisions of § 2042.

In contrast, in Estate of Fruehauf v. Commissioner, 427 F.2d 80 (6th Cir. 1970), the court rejected the notion that the mere possession by a decedent in a *fiduciary capacity* of incidents of ownership in a policy of insurance on his own life invariably requires inclusion of the proceeds in his gross estate. (In that case, however, the court went on to find that inclusion was required because the decedent was authorized, as executor and as trustee, to exercise the fiduciary powers for his own individual benefit.)

With respect to incidents of ownership held by the decedent as a fiduciary and only for the benefit of persons other than himself, the court in Estate of Skifter v. Commissioner, 468 F.2d 699 (2d Cir. 1972), relying on case law under § 2038, held that the decedent's fiduciary powers did not require inclusion of the insurance proceeds in his gross estate under

§ 2042 because those powers were not created by the decedent himself but were conferred on him by another person long after he had divested himself of all interest in the insurance policies on his life. The court in Rose v. United States, 511 F.2d 259 (5th Cir. 1975), reached a contrary result, based on the language of § 2042 referring to incidents of ownership *possessed* by the decedent. Nevertheless, the Service has repudiated its victory in *Rose* and has accepted the reasoning and result of *Skifter,* at least in cases where the decedent's powers are held in a fiduciary capacity and are not exercisable for his personal benefit, provided that the decedent did not transfer the policy to the trust and did not acquire his powers as part of a prearranged plan. Rev. Rul. 84–179, 1984–2 C.B. 195.

A particular problem has arisen in determining whether a decedent has incidents of ownership in group term life insurance of the kind commonly provided by an employer for its employees. One incident of ownership is the right to designate the beneficiary who will receive the proceeds at the death of the insured person; another is the right to convert the group term policy to an individual policy upon termination of employment. The question is whether the employee can effectively dispose of all incidents of ownership in the group term policy so as to prevent the proceeds from being included in his gross estate.

Initially, the Service took the position that the proceeds of the group term policy would be includable in the gross estate of the insured employee if he had the power to cancel the insurance by terminating his employment or to control the disposition of the insurance through exercise of a conversion privilege upon termination of his employment. Rev. Rul. 69–54, 1969–1 C.B. 221. Subsequently, however, the Service abandoned that position and ruled that a power to cancel coverage or to convert to an individual policy upon termination of employment is merely a "collateral consequence" of leaving one's job and not an "incident of ownership," because of its potentially costly related consequences. Rev. Rul. 72–307, 1972–1 C.B. 307; Rev. Rul. 84–130, 1984–2 C.B. 194. This result may seem to be in tension with the rationale of the *Noel* case, *supra,* under which the relevant factor is the legal existence of a power to exercise ownership rights, and not the actual ability to exercise the power, much less the potential related cost of doing so.

There is a split of authority on the question of whether the right of an insured person to elect a settlement option relating solely to the time and manner of payments (but not a right to designate beneficiaries) is an incident of ownership that will cause life insurance proceeds to be included in the insured person's gross estate. The court in Estate of Lumpkin v. Commissioner, 474 F.2d 1092 (5th Cir. 1973), held that since such a power would cause inclusion under §§ 2036 and 2038, it was also sufficient for inclusion under § 2042. Initially, the Service announced that it would follow *Lumpkin* and not the "economic benefit" theory of the *Skifter* case, *supra.* Rev. Rul. 76–261, 1976–2 C.B. 276. However, the same group term policy included in *Lumpkin* was excluded from the decedent's estate in Connelly's

Estate v. United States, 551 F.2d 545 (3d Cir. 1977), on the rationale that the "economic benefit" theory of *Skifter* made § 2042 inapplicable. The Service subsequently revoked Rev. Rul. 76–261 in reliance on the reasoning of *Skifter*. Rev. Rul. 84–179, 1984–2 C.B. 195.

This is, in sum, a difficult area of the law, made all the more complicated by the uncertainties inherent in applying §§ 2036 and 2038 in their own context and then applying similar rules by analogy in the § 2042 context.

Insurance; Amount Included. The term "insurance" refers to life insurance of every kind and even includes, for example, death benefits paid by fraternal beneficial societies operating under the lodge system. Reg. § 20.2042–1(a)(1). It includes such things as a New York Stock Exchange Gratuity Fund which provided death benefits comparable to life insurance. Commissioner v. Treganowan, 183 F.2d 288 (2d Cir. 1950), cert. den., 340 U.S. 853 (1950). The term also includes proceeds payable under an accidental death insurance policy, including flight insurance. Commissioner v. Estate of Noel, 380 U.S. 678 (1965).

The amount included in the gross estate under either of the two inclusionary rules of § 2042 is the full amount receivable under the policy. If the proceeds are to be paid over a period of years, the amount included in the gross estate is the lump sum which the insured or the beneficiary could have elected to receive at death or, if no such option was available, the sum used by the insurance company in determining the amount of the annuity. Reg. § 20.2042–1(a)(3).

Insurance in Community Property Situations. If a life insurance policy is classified as community property under applicable state law and the insured spouse dies first, half of the proceeds belong to the surviving spouse and will be excluded from the decedent's gross estate; as a result, only half of the proceeds will be included in the gross estate under § 2042. For example, if a community property policy on the husband's life is made payable to his estate, and the husband dies first, half of the proceeds will be considered to be receivable by or for the benefit of his estate under § 2042(1). Reg. § 20.2042–1(b)(2). Similarly, if the policy is made payable to the couple's child, the insured husband will be deemed to possess an incident of ownership in only half of the policy and therefore half of the proceeds will be included in his gross estate under § 2042(2). If the beneficiary designation remains revocable until the husband's death, and the wife allows her one-half share of the proceeds to be paid to the child as designated beneficiary, she will be deemed to have made a completed gift of half of the proceeds at the husband's death. Reg. § 20.2042–1(c)(5).

The analysis is slightly different if the non-insured spouse dies first. Section 2042 applies only to proceeds of insurance on the life of the decedent; a policy on the life of another person is included, along with other property owned at death, under § 2033. Thus, in the above example, if the wife predeceases the husband, her one-half community interest in the policy, measured by its replacement cost or interpolated terminal reserve value, will be included in her gross estate under § 2033. Reg. § 20.2042–1(c)(5). Later, at the husband's death, if ownership of the policy is still shared equally between the husband and the wife's successors, half of the proceeds will be includable in the husband's gross estate under § 2042. Rev. Rul. 75–100, 1975–1 C.B. 303; see also Estate of Cavenaugh v. Commissioner, 51 F.3d 597 (5th Cir. 1995); Estate of Cervin v. Commissioner, 111 F.3d 1252 (5th Cir. 1997).

The situation becomes a bit more complicated if the insured spouse pays additional premiums on a community property insurance policy after the death of the non-insured spouse. In that case, the additional premium payments may alter the proportional ownership interests of the insured spouse and the successors of the deceased, non-insured spouse in the policy. Scott v. Commissioner, 374 F.2d 154 (9th Cir. 1967), involved a community property policy on the husband's life. The wife died, leaving her one-half interest in the policies by will to their two sons, and after her death the husband continued to pay the premiums on the policies from his own separate funds. At the husband's death, the proceeds were paid to the sons as designated beneficiaries. The court held that the proceeds attributable to the premiums paid by the husband *after* his wife's death were includable in his gross estate. Only half of the proceeds attributable to premiums paid from community funds *prior* to the wife's death were includable in his gross estate, since the other half of the policy was owned by the wife and passed to the sons at her death.

If a husband and wife purchase insurance policies on the life of each of them, naming the non-insured spouse as owner and designated beneficiary of the policy on the other spouse's life, and the policies are classified as community property, half of the proceeds paid on the husband's death are includable in his gross estate under § 2042(2) and half of the value of the policy on the wife's life is includable under § 2033. Rev. Rul. 67–228, 1967–2 C.B. 331. This result follows from the general rule that the value of an insurance policy owned by the decedent on the life of another person is includable in the decedent's gross estate under § 2033. The valuation of an unmatured policy can be tricky. Some guidance on this matter is provided by Reg. § 20.2031–8(a).

Simultaneous Death. A special problem is presented if a husband and wife each own an insurance policy on the other spouse's life with the owner designated as primary beneficiary, and the spouses die under circumstances such that the order of their deaths cannot be determined. Under the "simultaneous death" provision of applicable state law, the proceeds of each policy will be paid to the contingent beneficiary, as if the owner-beneficiary spouse had failed to survive the insured spouse. In such cases, the courts have held that the policy owned by each spouse on the other's life is includable in the owner's gross estate, at its replacement cost or interpolated terminal reserve value, under § 2033.

Estate of Wien v. Commissioner, 441 F.2d 32 (5th Cir. 1971).

§ 2042 and Other Inclusionary Rules. If, at the time of his death, the decedent did not possess any of the incidents of ownership in an insurance policy on his own life, and the policy is not payable to or for the benefit of his estate, none of the proceeds are includable in the decedent's gross estate under § 2042. See Reg. § 20.2042–1(c)(1). Section 2042 does not apply to the value of rights in an insurance policy on the life of a person other than the decedent (though some other inclusionary rule might apply to such property).

In determining whether proceeds of an insurance policy on the decedent's own life are includable in his or her gross estate under § 2042, it makes no difference whether the premiums on the policy were paid by the insured decedent or by another person. This represents an important change from prior law. Under early Treasury regulations and later under the statute itself, proceeds of insurance on the life of the decedent were includable in his gross estate if the decedent had paid the premiums directly or indirectly, whether or not he held any of the incidents of ownership and regardless of the person to whom the proceeds were payable.

This "premium payment test" was eliminated with the enactment of § 2042 as part of a comprehensive revision of the Code in 1954. As a result, a taxpayer now may plan his affairs so as (a) never to hold the incidents of ownership or (b) to dispose of them at least three years before death; thus he can avoid an estate tax on life insurance proceeds which become payable at his death by reason of his payment of premiums during his life. To achieve this result, many planners recommend that life insurance policies be held in an irrevocable trust, with all incidents of ownership in the hands of a third-party trustee. Such a trust arrangement should be structured with care to ensure that the insured person neither holds any incidents of ownership under § 2042 nor retains any other interests or powers that could give rise to inclusion in his gross estate under §§ 2035–2038. Along with other tax and non-tax features of life insurance, the estate tax rules of § 2042 make life insurance an attractive and widely used form of individual estate planning.

From time to time it is suggested that the premium payment test of pre-1954 law should be reinstated so as to require inclusion in the gross estate of the proceeds of life insurance when the premiums have been paid by the decedent, regardless of who holds the incidents of ownership or who is designated as the beneficiary of the proceeds. Some critics view the present state of the law as permitting a transfer that bears a marked similarity to a testamentary disposition of property to be made without estate tax, if the insured decedent divests himself of the incidents of ownership in policies on his life but goes on paying the premiums until his death. Against this view of life insurance as inherently testamentary weighs a contrary policy consisting of a Congressional desire to encourage the purchase of life insurance as a means of providing for surviving dependents of the decedent.

Proceeds of life insurance that are not includable in the decedent's gross estate under § 2042 may turn out to be includable under some other estate tax provision. In this regard, special attention should be paid to the three-year rule of § 2035(a). If the decedent takes out an insurance policy on his own life, then makes a gift of the policy to another person and dies within three years after the gift, the proceeds will be includable in his gross estate under § 2035, even though he held none of the incidents of ownership at death and none of the proceeds were payable to his estate. In other words, the proceeds will be includable if the decedent held any of the incidents of ownership at any time within three years of death, due to the interaction of §§ 2035 and 2042, unless they were all disposed of before death for an adequate and full consideration. (Nevertheless, in determining the amount includable under § 2035, a pro-rata exclusion may be allowed for any premiums paid by the donee after the transfer, by analogy to improvements or additions to property made by the donee.)

Suppose the decedent caused an insurance policy to be taken out on his own life, with another person listed as the sole owner of the policy; the decedent paid all the premiums on the policy, and died within three years after the policy was taken out. At one time the Service enjoyed considerable success in arguing that the decedent had made a constructive transfer of the policy and that the full amount of the proceeds should be drawn back into his gross estate under § 2035. See Bel v. United States, 452 F.2d 683 (5th Cir. 1971), cert. den., 406 U.S. 919 (1972).

Similarly, even if the decedent transferred the policy more than three years before death, retaining no incidents of ownership but kept the policy in force by making premium payments until death, the Service insisted that at least the proportion of the proceeds attributable to the premiums paid by the decedent within three years of death should be included in the decedent's gross estate. Rev. Rul. 67–463, 1967–2 C.B. 327. After losing several court cases, notably First National Bank of Midland v. United States, 423 F.2d 1286 (5th Cir. 1970), the Service modified its position and ruled that only the amount of the premiums paid by the decedent within three years of death would be included. Rev. Rul. 71–497, 1971–2 C.B. 329.

As a result of the 1981 amendments to § 2035, however, courts have held that the three-year rule of § 2035(a) no longer has any application to an insurance policy on the decedent's life unless the decedent actually held incidents of ownership of the policy within three years of death. Thus, if the decedent neither owned nor transferred any incidents of ownership, the proceeds will not be drawn back into his gross estate under § 2035, even if the decedent instigated and controlled the purchase of the policy within three years of death and paid all of the premiums. See Estate of Perry v. Commissioner, 927 F.2d 209 (5th Cir. 1991). The payment of premiums on a policy owned by another person was not a transfer of an interest in the policy, nor did the decedent make a transfer of any incidents of ownership that would, if retained until death, have called § 2042 into play. See § 28, *supra*.

Also, although § 2042 does not apply to insurance on the life of a person other than the decedent, some value may be includable in the decedent's gross estate by reason of holding such a policy, under § 2033 or some other provision. A transfer of such a policy within three years of death will not cause § 2035 to apply, however, since § 2033 is not one of the sections enumerated in § 2035(a).

An insurance policy on the life of the decedent or, for that matter, on the life of someone else, can be the subject of an inter vivos disposition that is incomplete until the death of the decedent and hence will produce inclusion in his gross estate under §§ 2036–2038. For example, if the owner of a life insurance policy makes a revocable transfer of the policy or the right to proceeds at maturity, the transferred interest will be drawn back into the owner's gross estate at death by § 2038. Similarly, if a wife takes out an insurance policy on the life of her husband, naming herself as beneficiary, and elects at the husband's death to receive interest only on the proceeds for life with the principal amount to be paid at her death to designated beneficiaries, the proceeds will be includable in the wife's gross estate under § 2036. See Pyle v. Commissioner, 313 F.2d 328 (3d Cir. 1963).

A § 2036 question arose in Fidelity-Philadelphia Trust Co. v. Smith, 356 U.S. 274 (1958), with respect to a life insurance-annuity package. In that case, the decedent purchased three single-premium insurance policies on her own life, without the requirement of a medical examination. As a condition for issuing each policy, the insurance company required that the decedent also purchase a separate, single-premium, non-refundable life annuity policy. The size of each annuity was calculated so that, in the event the annuitant-insured died prematurely, the proceeds to be paid out under the life insurance policy would be covered by the combined premium payments, less the annuity payments already made, plus interest. The decedent then irrevocably assigned all incidents of ownership in the life insurance policies but retained the annuity policies and continued to receive annuity payments until her death. The Service characterized the entire transaction as a transfer of property by the decedent with a retained income interest (in the form of the annuity payments). Therefore, the Service argued, the life insurance proceeds which were payable to the decedent's children at her death should be included in the decedent's gross estate under § 2036. The Court, however, determined that the life insurance policies and the annuity policies were separate items of property which could be assigned or retained independently of one another, and rejected the Service's attempt to aggregate the two types of policies into one investment. Accordingly, since the decedent retained no interest in the transferred life insurance policies, the proceeds of those policies were not includable in her gross estate. Had the facts shown that the transactions were indivisible, the result might well have been different.

Death benefits not classified as life insurance under § 2042 may nevertheless be taxed as annuities, under I.R.C. § 2039 (discussed in § 43, *infra*). For example, in Estate of Montgomery v. Commissioner, 56 T.C. 489 (1971), aff'd, 458 F.2d 616 (5th Cir.), cert. den., 409 U.S. 849 (1972), the decedent had purchased an insurance-annuity package which involved no economic risk of loss because the total proceeds payable under the policies were offset by the combined annual premiums. The court viewed the arrangement as a single contract for the investment of funds in return for fixed monthly payments to the decedent for life (an annuity) coupled with a fixed payment at his death to designated beneficiaries. As a result, the amount of the death benefit was includable in the decedent's gross estate under § 2039.

Since the provisions of § 2042 are not exclusive, one or more other provisions may apply to produce a different or larger inclusion in the gross estate than would occur under § 2042. Sections 2036–2038 are likely candidates, but a transaction that meets the requirements of those sections will, if it involves life insurance, probably satisfy the requirements of § 2042 as well. Section 2039 is expressly made inapplicable to life insurance as such, and § 2040 applies only if the decedent had a joint-and-survivor interest with others in the property at his or her death. Under § 2041, a power of appointment that would produce inclusion would also constitute an incident of ownership under § 2042. Therefore, it seems that § 2035 is the principal provision that is likely to reach life insurance proceeds that are not otherwise includable under § 2042. (As an exercise in statutory interpretation, it may be interesting to speculate about the taxability of life insurance proceeds on the life of the decedent if § 2042 were removed from the Code.)

Life insurance is often used in a business context, for example in order to provide funds for the redemption or purchase of a decedent's interest in a closely held corporation or partnership. Great care must be used in planning such life insurance arrangements in order to minimize taxes and also to maximize the non-tax utility of insurance. One pitfall to watch for is the danger that the gross estate might include not only the business interest owned by the decedent, but also the insurance carried on his life in order to enable the surviving shareholders or partners to purchase the decedent's business interest. For example, in Connelly v. United States, 70 F.4th 412 (8th Cir. 2023), aff'd, 602 U.S. 257 (2024), the decedent was the controlling shareholder of a corporation which took out an insurance policy on the decedent's life and used the proceeds to redeem the decedent's stock from his estate after his death. Although the insurance proceeds were not includable in the decedent's gross estate under § 2042, they were taken into account as a corporate asset in valuing the decedent's stock for estate tax purposes.

§ 42 LIFE INSURANCE: GIFT TAX CONSEQUENCES

The abolition of the premium payment test in the estate tax has created a strong incentive for inter vivos transfers of life insurance policies which, if retained until death, would cause the proceeds to be included in the insured person's gross estate under the "incidents of ownership" test of I.R.C. § 2042. A taxpayer can remove the proceeds of the insurance from his gross estate by transferring all incidents of ownership during life, assuming the transfer will not produce inclusion under some provision other than § 2042. To avoid such other inclusionary rules, the transferor must be careful not to make the transfer within three years of death (see § 2035) and must not retain any right to income from the transferred property or any power to revoke the transfer or change beneficial enjoyment or any reversionary interest (see §§ 2036–2038).

The price of making an inter vivos gift of life insurance, to minimize estate taxes or for any other purpose, is exposure to gift taxation. Just like any other item of property, a life insurance policy can be the subject of a transfer by gift, potentially taxable as such under the gift tax, whether the policy given away is one on the life of the donor or on the life of some other person. Also, a gift may take place if one person (the donor) pays premiums on a life insurance policy owned by another person (the donee), whether or not the policy itself was ever the subject of a transfer. The payment of premiums itself amounts to a gift when the policy is owned by someone other than the person paying the premiums.

As the regulations elaborately state, if the insured purchases a life insurance policy or pays a premium on a previously issued policy, the proceeds of which are payable to a beneficiary or beneficiaries other than his estate, and with respect to which the insured retains no reversionary interest in himself or his estate and no power to revest the economic benefits in himself or his estate or to change the beneficiaries or their proportionate benefits (or if the insured relinquishes by assignment, by designation of a new beneficiary or otherwise, every such power that was retained in a previously issued policy), the insured has made a gift of the value of the policy, or to the extent of the premium paid, even though the right of the assignee or beneficiary to receive the benefits is conditioned upon surviving the insured. Reg. § 25.2511–1(h)(8). Although this portion of the regulations refers to a gift by the insured person under the policy in question, it is equally clear that a donor may make a gift for gift tax purposes by transferring ownership rights in a policy or by making premium payments on a policy insuring the life of some other person.

As indicated by the regulations, the time when a transfer of a life insurance policy is complete for gift tax purposes is when the donor has divested himself or herself of all dominion and control (i.e., all incidents of ownership) over the policy. Reg. §§ 25.2511–2 and 25.2511–1(h)(8). If the donor retains the power to name the beneficiary of the proceeds at the death of the insured person, no gift tax will be imposed at the time of transfer. If the donee surrenders the policy for its cash value, however, a completed gift will be deemed to take place at that time. (If the donee does not surrender the policy and the donor-insured retains the power to designate a beneficiary until his death, the proceeds will be included in the donor's gross estate at that time under § 2042. In this way, the regulations seek to coordinate the gift and estate tax treatment of transfers of life insurance policies.)

When a donor makes a gift of a life insurance policy, valuation of the policy for gift tax purposes is determined under the principles set forth in the regulations. In general, the valuation of a policy is determined by its cost or by the price of comparable contracts issued by the same company. If the policy has been in force for some time and is not fully paid-up, so that valuation through the cost method is not readily ascertainable, the value may be approximated by adding to the interpolated terminal reserve value of the policy at the date of the gift the proportionate part of the gross premium last paid before the date of the gift which covers the period extending beyond that date. If, however, because of the unusual nature of the contract such an approximation is not reasonably close to the full value, this method may be unavailable. See Reg. § 25.2512–6(a). (The formula for determining the value of an insurance policy transferred inter vivos for gift tax purposes is essentially the same as the formula for determining the value of a policy owned by a decedent on the life of another person for estate tax purposes. See Reg. § 20.2031–8(a).)

When life insurance is the subject of, or vehicle for, a gift transfer, the question arises whether one or more annual per-donee exclusions will be available to the donor under I.R.C. § 2503(b). If the gift qualifies for an annual exclusion, the first $10,000 (indexed for inflation, $19,000 in 2026) will not be taxed. Since

§ 2503(b) allows an exclusion in the case of a gift *other than a gift of a future interest* made to any person by the donor, it is necessary to determine whether a gift of life insurance is a gift of a present interest or a future interest. This question arises both when the gift consists of an assignment of ownership rights in a policy and when the donor pays premiums on a policy owned by another person.

In general, a gift of a life insurance policy, even one having no immediate cash value, will be treated as a gift of a present interest for purposes of determining the gift tax exclusion under § 2503(b). See Reg. § 25.2503–3(a); Rev. Rul. 55–408, 1955–1 C.B. 113. Of course, to be a gift of a present interest, the transfer must give to the donee all present rights and interests in the policy, including the right to surrender it for its cash value (if any), the right to borrow against it, the right to designate a beneficiary, and so on. If the rights or interests of the donee are restricted, for example, by the terms of a trust or some other instrument of transfer, the gift may be deemed to be a transfer of a future interest which will not qualify for the annual exclusion. See Reg. § 25.2503–3(a) and (b).

Community property law, if applicable, complicates the gift tax treatment of a transfer of a life insurance policy or the payment of premiums on a policy owned by another person. The regulations provide some guidance. For example, if a husband and wife use community funds to purchase insurance on the husband's life with a third person revocably designated as beneficiary, and if under state law the transfer by the wife of her interest becomes absolute at the death of the insured husband, the wife will make a completed gift at the husband's death of half of the insurance proceeds. Reg. § 25.2511–1(h)(9).

More generally, under the community property systems in effect in several states, the husband and the wife are each deemed to have equal, present, vested interests in community property, including an insurance policy on the life of one spouse. This principle applies broadly to a transfer of the policy to a third person by the spouses during their lives. If such a transfer is complete when it is made, the gift will be subject to gift tax at that time. However, if the transfer is made in such a form as to be revocable by both spouses or by one spouse alone (e.g., where the transfer is made by one spouse without the consent of the other, in violation of the latter's community property rights), then no gift tax will be imposed until the transfer is complete and no longer revocable. Thus, if the husband makes a gift of community property life insurance in fraud of the wife's rights and without her knowledge, and if under state law she is entitled to recall the transfer within a reasonable period after discovering it, the gift will not be complete until she has consented to the gift or until the reasonable period of recall has elapsed. If the wife has not given her consent and if as a result she can call back the entire transfer during the husband's life, but can recall only half the transfer after his death, there is no assurance that the beneficiary will receive anything until the time of the husband's death or the wife's consent, and therefore no gift will occur at the time of the initial transfer. In other words, to analyze the tax consequences of a gift of community property life insurance by one spouse, the courts look to the spouses' respective rights and interests under applicable state law.

CHAPTER 8

ANNUITIES AND EMPLOYEE DEATH BENEFITS: ESTATE TAX AND GIFT TAX

§ 43 ESTATE TAXATION OF ANNUITIES: § 2039

I.R.C. § 2039 sets forth the basic estate tax rules for the taxation of annuities. Section 2039 is not exclusive, however, and the possibility remains that some other estate tax section will apply. (That possibility will be discussed briefly after an examination of § 2039.)

In order to understand § 2039 and the problem to which it is addressed, one must understand something about the nature of an annuity and how it can present matters of interest to an estate tax system. An annuity is defined as one or more payments or the right to receive such payments, for a period of time, such as for life or for a term of years or for some other period. Sometimes an annuity is purchased by the person entitled to receive payments under it, sometimes the annuity is received as a gift, and sometimes it is provided by an employer to an employee as a form of compensation. For estate tax purposes, the purchased annuity provides the best illustration. Thus, if a taxpayer transfers property to an annuity company (or any other person) in return for a promise by the transferee (called the issuer) to pay $8,000 a year to the taxpayer (called the annuitant), the taxpayer has purchased an annuity and each annual payment is a payment of the annuity. If the stream of $8,000 annuity payments is to last as long as the taxpayer remains alive, without any additional promises, the arrangement would be called a single-life, non-refund annuity.

A single-life, non-refund annuity does not present an estate tax problem and is not taxable upon the death of the annuitant. It resembles a life estate which expires upon the death of the person who purchased it. Nothing passes to any other person at that time and no taxable transfer has been made. So to speak, the decedent "used up" the property during life.

Other annuity arrangements, however, do amount to transactions to which the estate tax should, and will, apply. For example, some annuity contracts provide that if the annuity period comes to an end before a specified minimum amount has been paid out, the issuer will pay a refund to the estate of the annuitant. Such a refund feature often accompanies a single-life annuity contract. At the death of the annuitant, a refund will (or may) be payable to the annuitant's estate or to designated beneficiaries.

Other contracts provide that upon the death of the primary annuitant the annual payment he or she has been receiving will be paid to another person for the life of the other person. This is a so-called self-and-survivor annuity. Another kind of annuity contract, called a joint-and-survivor annuity, provides that a specified sum is to be paid each year to two annuitants jointly while both are living, and after one of them dies the same amount, or a smaller amount, is to be paid to the survivor for his or her life.

Unlike the single-life, non-refund contract, an annuity that provides for payments to another beneficiary after the death of the primary annuitant will produce estate tax consequences, either under § 2039 or § 2033 or possibly under some other provision. This follows because such an annuity consists, at least in part, of an arrangement to dispose of wealth at death. It provides for a transfer of property at death and thus substitutes for an ordinary testamentary disposition. Section 2039, enacted in 1954, is designed to reach such annuity transfers.

The basic rule of § 2039 is as follows. The gross estate shall include the value of an annuity or other payment receivable by any beneficiary by reason of surviving the decedent, under any form of contract or agreement entered into after March 3, 1931 (other than as insurance under policies on the life of the decedent) if, under that contract or agreement, an annuity or other payment was payable to the decedent, or the decedent possessed the right to receive such annuity or payment, either alone or in conjunction with some other person for his life or for any period not ascertainable without reference to his death or for any period which does not in fact end before his death.

The term "annuity or other payment," as used with respect both to the decedent and the beneficiary, refers to one or more payments extending over any period of time, whether they are equal or unequal in amount, conditional or unconditional, periodic or sporadic. The term "contract or agreement" includes any arrangement, understanding, or plan. An annuity or other payment was "payable to" the decedent if at the time of his death he was in fact receiving an annuity or other payment, whether or not he had an enforceable right to have the payments continued. Also, the decedent "possessed the right to receive" an annuity or other payment if, immediately before his death, he had an enforceable right to receive payments at some time in the future, whether or not at the time of his death he had a present right to receive payments. Reg. § 20.2039–1(b). (That section of the regulations also contains some helpful examples.)

The general rule, stated in § 2039(a), clearly means that nothing will be included in the gross estate of a decedent who, before his or her death, was receiving annual payments under a single-life, non-refund annuity. Thus, if Mary, having reached retirement age and wishing to provide for her support during her remaining years, transfers $100,000 in cash to an annuity company in return for the company's agreement to pay her $8,000 a year for the rest of her life, there will be no inclusion in Mary's gross estate under § 2039 at her death. Since no beneficiary will receive any payment by reason of surviving Mary, § 2039 does not apply. This result accords with that obtained under § 2033 when an interest in property that was not transferred by the decedent expires at his or her death. For example, if Mary's parent had transferred property in trust to pay income to Mary for life, with remainder at her death to another beneficiary, there would be no inclusion in Mary's gross estate at the time of her death by reason of the life estate granted by her parent. (Also, § 2036 would not apply because Mary was not the grantor of the trust.) Thus, the tax result is just as if Mary had spent her entire $100,000 during her life (as in fact she did) and then died owning nothing that would pass to any other person.

Similarly, if during her life Mary had purchased an annuity contract that was to go into effect only upon Mary's death and at that time to start paying annual amounts to her surviving spouse or child, there would be no inclusion in her gross estate under § 2039 since Mary had no right to receive any payments during her life. See Kramer v. United States, 406 F.2d 1363 (Ct. Cl. 1969). (The gift tax would apply, however, at the time of purchase.)

In other words, § 2039 confines its rule of estate tax inclusion to survivor annuities, whereby a beneficiary receives one or more payments by surviving the decedent, and it applies to such arrangements only if the decedent, at the time of his death, was in fact receiving annuity payments or had a right to receive future payments. Thus, § 2039 is aimed at refund or survivorship annuities, and it taxes only the value of payments to be made to the estate or the survivor. In fact, the simple refund-to-the-estate annuity is covered by § 2033.

Before the enactment of § 2039 in 1954, annuities were subject to estate taxation, if at all, under other provisions such as §§ 2033, 2036, or 2038. The enactment of § 2039 provided a single, targeted rule for annuities which removed some uncertainties and also dealt specifically, in § 2039(b), with the problem of annuities purchased in part by contributions of the decedent and in part by contributions of others.

Section 2039(b) provides that the inclusionary rule of § 2039(a) shall apply only to such part of the value of the annuity or other payment receivable under the contract or agreement as is proportionate to that part of the purchase price contributed by the decedent. Therefore, if the requirements of § 2039(a) were met in the above example, but Mary's husband had contributed part of the purchase price of the annuity, not all of the value passing to the surviving beneficiary at Mary's death would be includable in her gross estate.

Section 2039 also deals with the important problem of how to tax a refund or survivor annuity that has been purchased by an employer for an employee. Prior to 1954, employee annuities established by the employer, with contributions made only by the employer, often were not included in the employee's gross estate at death even if the annuity payments shifted at that time from the employee to the surviving beneficiary. In 1954 Congress became convinced that such employee annuities should be taxed just as if the employee annuitant had made all the contributions himself, since they were rooted in the employee's work and constituted compensation for it. As a consequence, § 2039(b) specifically provides that any contribution by the decedent's employer or former employer to the purchase price of an annuity contract or agreement is to be considered as contributed by the decedent if made by reason of his or her employment. Accordingly, if the other tests of § 2039 are met, inclusion in the employee's gross estate will follow even if the employee has not directly or personally contributed a penny to the purchase of the annuity. Of course, if an employer pays a death benefit to surviving beneficiaries selected solely by the employer and if the employee did not receive or have any right to receive payments before death, none of the death benefits will be includable in the employee's gross estate under § 2039. See Kramer v. United States, 406 F.2d 1363 (Ct. Cl. 1969). (However, if the employee had the power to designate the beneficiaries, the employee's power might cause the death benefit to be includable in the gross estate under § 2038 or § 2041 (discussed in § 32, *supra,* and § 45, *infra,* respectively), even if § 2039 did not apply because nothing was payable to the employee during his lifetime.)

Section 2039 requires a "contract or agreement." Therefore benefits paid to an employee or his survivors under a statutory program such as Social Security, which is funded with "contributions" in the form of payroll taxes, will not be treated as a § 2039 annuity. Rev. Rul. 81–182, 1981–2 C.B. 179. Similarly, an informal or gratuitous plan or an occasional transfer to employees or their surviving dependents will not amount to a "contract or agreement" so as to produce inclusion under § 2039. See Estate of Barr v. Commissioner, 40 T.C. 227 (1963), where the court held that voluntary and gratuitous death benefits were not includable in an employee's gross estate under either § 2033 or § 2039.

In applying § 2039, courts often read various employee benefit plans together as an integrated package constituting a contract or agreement within the meaning of the statute. For example, in Gray v. United States, 410 F.2d 1094 (3d Cir. 1969), an employee had vested rights in a retirement annuity under a retirement plan, although he died before reaching retirement age. The court viewed the retirement plan, together with a survivor plan which provided for payments to the employee's designated beneficiary, as components of a single contract or agreement, and held that the payments to the surviving beneficiary were includable in the employee's gross estate under § 2039.

Section 2039 requires that an annuity or other payment was *payable to* the decedent or that the decedent possessed the *right to receive* such annuity or payment for life or a related period, as a condition for including survivor benefits in the decedent's gross estate. This requirement is met if the decedent was in fact receiving payments at the time of his death, whether or not he had an enforceable right to have such payments continued, or, alternatively, if immediately before his death the decedent had an enforceable right to receive payments at some time in the future, whether or not he had a present right to receive payments. Reg. § 20.2039–1(b)(1). Thus, for example, the statutory requirement is satisfied if the employee at the time of his death had vested rights in a plan providing retirement benefits, even if the employee died before receiving any of those benefits. Reg. § 20.2039–1(b)(2) (Example 3); *Gray, supra.* If the payments had not yet commenced at the employee's death and were subject to forfeiture at the option of the employer, there would be no inclusion under § 2039, since the employee would not have an enforceable right to future payments. However, if the decedent's right to payments was not forfeitable, or the conditions for forfeiture were within the employee's control, he would be deemed to have an enforceable right to the payments, even if they were to be made only in the future. See Estate of Wadewitz v. Commissioner, 339 F.2d 980 (7th Cir. 1964). (It is possible, of course, that the death of the employee itself ends any possibility of forfeiture or other conditions, including unilateral revocation by the employer, in which event the vesting of the benefits in the spouse or other beneficiary will become taxable under § 2039, assuming the requirement of lifetime payments is met.)

Courts have held, and the Service agrees, that the requirement of lifetime payments is not satisfied by payments in the nature of regular wages or by benefits that replace such wages during an employee's temporary absence from work due to sickness or accident. Estate of Fusz v. Commissioner, 46 T.C. 214 (1966); Rev. Rul. 77–183, 1977–1 C.B. 274. Furthermore, it has been held that benefits payable only in the event of total and permanent disability, which did not in fact occur during the decedent's lifetime, are not sufficient to meet the requirement of lifetime payments under § 2039. See Estate of Schelberg v. Commissioner, 612 F.2d 25 (2d

Cir. 1979); but cf. Estate of Bahen v. United States, 305 F.2d 827 (Ct. Cl. 1962), reaching a contrary result.

The amount included in the decedent's gross estate under § 2039 is the value, determined at the date of death (and pro-rated for the decedent's contribution), of the payments to be made to the surviving beneficiary. So, if Mary transferred $100,000 to an annuity company to pay her $8,000 a year for her life and at her death to pay $8,000 per year to her husband for his life, and if Mary is survived by her husband, the value (at the date of her death) of her husband's right to receive $8,000 a year, given his life expectancy, is the amount to be included in Mary's gross estate. The amount subject to estate tax is measured not by the payments received by Mary before her death, but rather by the value of the interest transferred by her or passing from her at death to the surviving beneficiary. If Mary, her employer, and her husband each contributed one-third of the cost of the contract, only two-thirds of the value of the survivor benefit (i.e., the portion attributable to Mary's own contributions and those of her employer) would be included in her gross estate; the one-third share attributable to her husband's contributions would be excluded. Reg. § 20.2039–1(c).

Section 2039 has no application to an amount which constitutes the proceeds of insurance under a policy on the decedent's life. Reg. § 20.2039–1(a). This exemption leaves, in some cases, the difficult problem of drawing a line between insurance and other types of survivor benefits. See All v. McCobb,

321 F.2d 633 (2d Cir. 1963), holding that payments to a surviving beneficiary were not life insurance, in the absence of shifting or distribution of mortality risk or other indicia of life insurance under the standards of Helvering v. Le Gierse, 312 U.S. 531 (1941), and hence were includable under § 2039. Payments exempted from § 2039 by the "life insurance" clause will then be tested under § 2042, which deals specifically with proceeds of insurance on the decedent's life. However, § 2039 can apply to the annuity portion of an annuity-life insurance package, or to a life insurance policy that has been recharacterized as an annuity. See Estate of Montgomery v. Commissioner, 56 T.C. 489 (1971), aff'd, 458 F.2d 616 (5th Cir.), cert. den., 409 U.S. 849 (1972).

The fact that an annuity or other payment is not includable in the decedent's gross estate under § 2039 does not prevent it from being included under some other provision of the estate tax. For example, if the annuity contract provides for a refund payable to the estate of the primary annuitant at his death, the refund will be includable in the gross estate under § 2033 regardless of any other inclusion under § 2039.

A private annuity, that is to say a transfer of property by the decedent to someone other than a commercial annuity company, often a family member or associate, in return for a promise of payments, may give rise to inclusion in the gross estate under § 2039 if there are payments to a survivor after the transferor's death. Even if § 2039 does not apply, such a transfer must also be tested under §§ 2036 and 2038 to see whether the transferor retained a "taxable string" described in those provisions. If the transaction amounts to a transfer of property with a retained life estate, either because the transferred property is security for the promised annuity payments to the transferor or because those payments are directly geared to the income from the transferred property, § 2036 may require inclusion of the entire value of the transferred property (not just the value of the survivor's annuity, the amount that would be includable under § 2039).

For many years, annuities or other payments under certain "qualified plans" were exempted from inclusion in the gross estate by former § 2039(c), a provision whose intricacies lie beyond the scope of this discussion. The exclusion for qualified plan benefits was cut back in 1982, and then repealed in 1984 for decedents dying after 1984 (with a limited "grandfather" exception). It was thought that qualified plan benefits payable to a surviving spouse were sheltered from tax by the unlimited marital deduction and that benefits payable to other beneficiaries should be subject to tax to the extent they exceeded the amount sheltered by the unified credit.

§ 44 ANNUITIES: GIFT TAX

In the absence of a specific statutory provision, the application of the gift tax to inter vivos transfers of annuities is governed by general gift tax principles. For example, a taxable gift may occur if one person purchases an annuity solely for the benefit of another. (Of course, it is possible that such a transaction involves compensation for services or the purchase of property, with potential income tax, but not gift tax, consequences to follow.) Also, if one person purchases an annuity that will benefit both himself and someone else, at once or later, a gift may be involved, since the purchaser is making a transfer in part to or for the benefit of the other person. Further information must be obtained to ascertain when the transfer is complete, what offsetting consideration, if any, has been received, whether the transfer is at arm's length and in the ordinary course of business and, altogether, what amount must be included in the gift tax base. Also, a problem may arise with respect to a gift of a future interest in an annuity setting.

At the death of a married employee who was covered by a qualified plan, the surviving spouse is entitled to receive specified survivor benefits, unless the spouse waived those benefits during the covered employee's lifetime. If the spouse waives the right to such benefits, before the employee's death, the waiver will not be treated as a transfer by gift for gift tax purposes. I.R.C. § 2503(f). (I.R.C. § 2517, which formerly contained special rules for certain annuities under qualified plans, was repealed in 1986.)

CHAPTER 9

POWERS OF APPOINTMENT: ESTATE AND GIFT TAX CONSEQUENCES

§ 45 POWERS OF APPOINTMENT—ESTATE TAX CONSEQUENCES: § 2041

Under I.R.C. § 2041, a decedent's gross estate includes the value of property with respect to which the decedent possessed, exercised or released certain powers of appointment. The rules for inclusion vary with the nature of the power, the time it was created and whether or how it was held, exercised or released.

A power of appointment is a power over property held in trust or otherwise, exercisable either during life or at death (or both), to determine who shall become the owner of property or the recipient of income. For estate tax purposes, moreover, the term "power of appointment" includes all powers which are in substance and effect powers of appointment, regardless of the nomenclature used in creating the power and regardless of local property law connotations. For example, a power to appropriate or consume the principal of a trust is a power of appointment, as is a power to affect the beneficial enjoyment of trust property or its income by altering, amending or revoking the trust instrument or terminating the trust. Reg. § 20.2041–1(b)(1). Thus, a decedent's power, as one of four co-trustees under a trust set up by his father, to terminate the trust, and thereby accelerate his own remainder interest, if all four agreed that such termination was "in the interest of the beneficiary," constitutes a general power of appointment sufficient to include the trust corpus in his gross estate under § 2041. Maytag v. United States, 493 F.2d 995 (10th Cir. 1974).

Powers of appointment are classified in two categories according to the appointees who may be designated as the takers of the property. Traditionally, a so-called *general power* of appointment is one exercisable in favor of an unrestricted group of beneficiaries. A so-called *special* or *limited power* is one that, by its terms, can be exercised in favor only of a restricted or specified group of beneficiaries. The term "general power of appointment" takes on a more specialized meaning in the estate tax, as will be discussed below. See I.R.C. § 2041(b)(1); Reg. § 20.2041–1(c).

Unlike §§ 2036–2038, § 2041 is not a "grantor section." Indeed, the regulations provide that § 2041 has no application to powers reserved by the decedent to himself within the scope of §§ 2036–2038, nor does it apply to the decedent's power to dispose of his own property. Therefore, the "grantor sections" will apply exclusively in the case of a reserved or retained power. Similarly, § 2033 will apply to a transfer of the decedent's own property. Reg. § 20.2041–1(b)(2). In contrast, § 2041 is aimed at a power, conferred on the decedent by another person, to designate the recipients of property or interests not already owned by the decedent. Thus, the holder of a general power of appointment need not have any beneficial interest in the property, such as a life estate or a remainder interest (though he may have such an interest), for the power to be taxable under § 2041. It is enough that the power meets the definition of a general power of appointment and was held or exercised or released by the decedent in the manner described in the statute.

From the nature of a power of appointment, one can easily infer that estate tax consequences may and should be involved. For example, if the decedent held a power of appointment which could have been exercised to make him the owner of property held in trust, and the decedent exercised the power by will in favor of another person, the exercise of the power is functionally equivalent to a testamentary gift of property and will be taxed accordingly. Indeed, the mere possession of such a power, even if it is not actually exercised, may be viewed as approaching beneficial ownership of the property subject to the power.

Originally, the estate tax statute did not contain a provision specifically aimed at taxing property subject to a power of appointment. Under property law concepts, the holder of a power of appointment (without any beneficial interest) was viewed merely as exercising a kind of fiduciary authority over the property so that the property was actually being transferred from the original owner to the ultimate beneficiary. Accordingly, the holder of a power of appointment who had no other beneficial interest in the property or income was not viewed as himself making a transfer of property when he exercised the power at death or during life, much less if he merely held the power without exercising it, in which event the property would pass by default. Consequently, in an early case, the Supreme Court held that property subject to a general power of appointment held by the decedent at death was not includable in her gross estate. United States v. Field, 255 U.S. 257 (1921). In the *Field* case, the decedent actually exercised the power of appointment by will and thus the situation looked very much like a transfer of property at and by reason of the decedent's death; nevertheless, the Court held against inclusion. Later, the Service attempted to use the predecessor of § 2033 to include property subject to a power of appointment and in which the holder also held a life estate, on the ground that the holder of the power was the constructive or substantial owner of the property. However, the Supreme Court refused to apply the constructive ownership doctrine in the estate tax context. See Helvering v. Safe Deposit & Trust Co., 316 U.S. 56 (1942).

When the courts failed to include in the gross estate property subject to a power of appointment, exercised or not, Congress took action. From 1918 until 1942, the statute required inclusion in the gross estate of property *passing* under a *general* power of appointment that was *exercised* by the decedent by will (or during life under circumstances that would have caused inclusion if the exercise had actually been a transfer of property). Under these statutory requirements, the Supreme Court held, in Helvering v. Grinnell, 294 U.S. 153 (1935), that the mere exercise of a general power of appointment was not sufficient to require inclusion, if the property did not actually pass under the exercise of the power. (In that case, the appointees had renounced the shares appointed to them under the power.)

In 1942, Congress expanded the coverage of the statute dealing with powers of appointment to include property subject to a power that was *held but not actually exercised,* on the ground that the possession of the power resembled ownership and that non-exercise of the power also constituted dominion and control over the property and its disposition. The 1942 legislation was applicable to preexisting powers actually exercised by decedents who died after the new law was enacted in 1942. Some aspects of the 1942 legislation generated much controversy and dissatisfaction. As a consequence, the law was changed in 1951 with the enactment of a new provision which eventually was codified in 1954 as § 2041. Section 2041 still distinguishes between pre- and post-1942 powers and restores much of the pre-1942 law with regard to earlier powers. Therefore, the non-exercise of a pre-1942 power results in no estate tax and the release of such a power is permitted without imposition of tax. Under the regulations, the date of the creation of a power is controlled by the effective date of the instrument that created the power. Reg. § 20.2041–1(e).

I.R.C. § 2041 provides, in general, that the value of the gross estate shall include the value of all property with respect to which the decedent *has* at the time of his death a *general* power of appointment (created after October 21, 1942). It also includes all property with respect to which the decedent has at any time *exercised* or *released* a general power of appointment by a disposition which is of such a nature that if it were a transfer of property owned by the decedent, such property would be includable in the decedent's gross estate under §§ 2035–2038. I.R.C. § 2041(a)(2). As to general powers of appointment created on or before October 21, 1942, the gross estate includes the value of all property with respect to which the decedent actually *exercised* a general power of appointment, either by will or by a disposition of such a nature that if it were a transfer of property owned by the decedent, such property would be includable under §§ 2035–2038. I.R.C. § 2041(a)(1). The different rules for powers created before and after the crucial date reflect the change in the law made on that date, a change which has not been applied retroactively. The difference between the pre- and post-1942 rules is significant—the difference between actually exercising a power of appointment and merely holding it. The following discussion will concentrate on the post-1942 rule, as it now has become preeminent in importance.

Putting aside for the moment some technicalities and the different rules applicable to pre-1942 powers of appointment, one may observe generally that § 2041 will require inclusion in the decedent's gross estate of property which he may never have owned during his life and which he may never have personally possessed or enjoyed and whose ownership or receipt he has never actually determined by the exercise of a power of appointment. In other words, the mere possession of a general power of appointment, as defined in the statute, is treated as the possession of such an important component of ownership that the holder of the power should be subject to an estate tax. The holder of such a power is treated just as if he had owned the property and transferred it at his death or otherwise had determined who would take "his" property at his death. Unlike §§ 2035–2038, § 2041 is not a "grantor section" and, therefore, an inter vivos transfer of an interest in the property is not a prerequisite to the application of § 2041. A general power held by Tom over property placed in trust by Alice can cause inclusion in Tom's gross estate at his death.

The mere possession or even the exercise of a power of appointment that is *not* a "general power of appointment" (as defined in the statute) will not produce inclusion in the holder's gross estate of the property that is subject to the power or that passes by the exercise of the power. Hence, it becomes crucial to differentiate between a "general power of appointment" and a so-called "special power of appointment."

Section 2041(b)(1) defines a *general power* of appointment, for purposes of the inclusion rules in § 2041(a), as a power which is exercisable in favor of the decedent, his estate, his creditors or the creditors of his estate, with certain exceptions specified in the statute. The language of the statute is cast in the alternative and it is clear that the power to appoint property to any of the specified appointees is sufficient to make the power a general power. A power is *not* a general power if it is (a) exercisable only in favor of one or more designated persons or classes of persons other than the decedent, his estate, his creditors or the creditors of his estate, or (b) expressly not exercisable in favor of the decedent, his estate, his creditors, or the creditors of his estate. Reg. § 20.2041–1(c)(1). In general, then, a "general power of appointment" for statutory purposes is a power of appointment (broadly construed) that is exercisable in favor of the decedent directly, or indirectly by appointment to his creditors or to his estate. An important statutory exception is made for a power to consume, invade or appropriate property for the benefit of the decedent when that power is limited by an ascertainable standard relating to the health, education, support, or maintenance of the decedent, and another exception is provided for powers held jointly by the decedent and another person, such as the creator of the power or someone having a substantial adverse interest. See I.R.C. § 2041(b)(1); Reg. §§ 20.2041–1(c)(2) and 20.2041–3(c).

Thus, § 2041 uses the term "general power" to describe something that might be labeled a "beneficial power," that is to say a power which can be exercised to confer a financial benefit on the holder of the power. By so doing, the statute includes in the gross estate property which the decedent might have obtained for his own personal benefit by exercising an inter vivos power of appointment in his own favor, or which he might have "sold" by exercising an inter vivos power of appointment in favor of someone else in return for a payment or other favors to him.

Section 2041 also requires inclusion of property which the decedent could not have personally enjoyed during life because his power was exercisable only by will but which he could appoint through his estate to beneficiaries he himself selected, by exercise of the testamentary power. By also requiring the inclusion of property subject to a general power exercisable by will even though that power was not in fact exercised, the statute requires inclusion of property whose disposition or ownership at and after the decedent's death evidently was satisfactory to him (because he could have changed the result by exercising the power but in fact chose not to do so).

As to post-1942 powers, the first question is whether the decedent had a *general* power of appointment at the time of his death. If he held a general power, it is taxable to him whether or not actually exercised. The decedent will be deemed to have such a general power at the time of his death even if the exercise of the power will not be effective until a stated time after the exercise or even if the holder must give advance notice before exercising the power and the required notice has not been given before his death. I.R.C. § 2041(a)(2). However, if a power of appointment is exercisable only upon the occurrence of an event or contingency which did not in fact take place or occur before death and is not within the control of the decedent, the decedent will not be deemed to hold the power at his death. Reg. § 20.2041–3(b).

If the decedent's power is one that is *not* a general power as defined in the statute, no inclusion will follow even if he exercises the power—with one exception. Section 2041(a)(3) provides that property will be included in the gross estate if the decedent by will (or by a disposition of such a nature that if it were a transfer of property owned by the decedent such property would be includable under §§ 2035–2037) exercises a post-1942 power of appointment (whether general or special) by creating another power which can be validly exercised under applicable state law so as to postpone the vesting of any estate or interest in the property, or to suspend the absolute ownership or power of alienation of such property, for a period ascertainable without regard to the date the first power was created. For example, if the decedent was the life beneficiary of a trust with a $100,000 corpus, and had the power to appoint the property only to his descendants, the entire $100,000 would be included in his gross estate if by will he appointed one of his children as life beneficiary and gave that child a power to appoint the remainder and this second power could be validly exercised so as to postpone the vesting of any interest beyond some period running from the date the first power was created. See Reg. § 20.2041–3(e).

The purpose of this somewhat arcane rule is to prevent a succession of untaxed special powers from producing an indefinite suspension of the absolute ownership of property, even if such an arrangement is permissible under applicable state law. But for this rule, a special power (i.e., a non-general power) could be created and then exercised to create another special power, and so on and on without tax. Property could thus be transferred from one generation to another indefinitely without imposition of an estate tax. Section 2041(a)(3) blocks this possibility.

The second question under § 2041 is whether a general power of appointment, though not *held* at death, may nevertheless result in inclusion by reason of its *prior exercise*. Section 2041 requires inclusion not only if a post-1942 general power is held or exercised at death, but also if such a power was exercised or released by the holder during life under certain circumstances, by analogy to the inclusionary rules of §§ 2035–2038, which are incorporated by reference in § 2041(a)(2). This provision requires inclusion in the decedent's gross estate of property with respect to which the decedent at any time (i.e., during life) exercised or released a general power of appointment by a disposition equivalent to a §§ 2035–2038 transfer of property actually owned by him. For example, inclusion would be required if the decedent exercised a general power to appoint a remainder to another person while retaining a life estate, by analogy to § 2036(a)(1); the same result would hold for an inter vivos exercise subject to a retained power of revocation, by analogy to § 2038. See also Reg. § 20.2041–3(d). For a similar rule applicable to pre-1942 general powers, see I.R.C. § 2041(a)(1); Reg. § 20.2041–2(c).

A *release* of a post-1942 general power of appointment is treated as the equivalent of an exercise of the power. Thus, property subject to such a power will be included in the gross estate of the holder if he releases the power by a disposition equivalent to a §§ 2035–2038 transfer of property actually owned by him. Moreover, the *lapse* of such a power during the holder's life is treated the same as a release and hence equivalent to an exercise of the power, to the extent that the property subject to the power at the time of the lapse exceeded the greater of $5,000 or 5% of the value of the property from which an exercise of the lapsed power could have been satisfied. I.R.C. § 2041(b)(2).

The typical lapse situation occurs when the life income beneficiary of a trust has the power to invade the corpus up to a certain amount of money in each calendar year. If the beneficiary does not exercise that power during the year, then the power will automatically lapse and the amount, if any, that exceeds the greater of $5,000 or 5% will be considered a taxable release under § 2041(a)(2), since the holder of the lapsed power has allowed property which he could have obtained for himself (by exercising the power) to pass instead to the remainder beneficiary while retaining a life estate. See Reg. § 20.2041–3(d)(3) through (d)(5).

Section 2041(a)(2) does *not* require inclusion in the gross estate if a post-1942 general power of appointment is irrevocably exercised, released or allowed to lapse *during life,* if the exercise or release is not equivalent to a §§ 2035–2038 transfer of property actually owned by him. See Reg. § 20.2041–3(d)(2). Moreover, a disclaimer of a power will not be treated as a transfer by the holder of the power for gift or estate tax purposes, if the disclaimer meets the requirements of § 2518, discussed in § 20, *supra.* Reg. § 20.2041–3(d)(6).

The amount of property to be included in the gross estate when § 2041 applies to a power of appointment depends on which portion of § 2041 is called into effect. If a pre-1942 power is involved, § 2041 will include only the property with respect to which the power was exercised. In the case of a post-1942 power, the gross estate will include all the property subject to the power that the decedent held at death or that he exercised or released during life in a disposition equivalent to a §§ 2035–2038 transfer. (A special rule applies to lapsed powers, as noted above.) If a power of appointment exists only as to part of an entire group of assets or only over a limited interest in property, § 2041 applies only to such part or interest. Reg. § 20.2041–1(b)(3).

By virtue of the broad definition of "general power of appointment" in the statute and the regulations, an overlap between § 2041 and §§ 2035–2038 becomes possible. In the event of such an overlap, § 2041 will *not* have the effect of reducing the amount includable in the gross estate under other provisions of the Code. Powers reserved by the decedent to himself in connection with a transfer of his own property are governed exclusively by the "grantor sections," not by § 2041. See Reg. § 20.2041–1(b)(2).

By way of a last word, it should be mentioned that a tax advisor has at his or her disposal a very useful estate planning tool in the form of the non-taxable power of appointment. By steering clear of the inclusionary rules of § 2041, an individual can pass important powers over the disposition of property to a succeeding beneficiary or generation while keeping the property in trust or otherwise within restrictions that would be lost if outright ownership were conferred and without the tax liability attendant on outright ownership, subject only to the tax on generation-skipping transfers.

§ 46 POWERS OF APPOINTMENT—GIFT TAX: § 2514

In many respects, the rules of the gift tax with respect to powers of appointment complement the rules of the estate tax. The general rule of the gift tax, embodied in § 2514(b), is that the *exercise* or *release* of a post-1942 general power of appointment shall be deemed a transfer of property by the individual possessing the power. A *lapse* of the power is treated as a release of the power by § 2514(e), but only to the extent that the property subject to the lapsed power at the time of the lapse exceeds the greater of $5,000 or 5% of the value of the property from which an exercise of the lapsed power could have been satisfied. A *disclaimer* of such a power shall not be deemed a transfer by the holder for gift tax purposes, if the disclaimer meets the requirements of § 2518 (discussed in § 20, *supra*). A statutory definition of what is a "general power of appointment" for gift tax purposes can be found in § 2514(c); it is almost identical to the estate tax definition in § 2041(b). See Reg. § 25.2514–1.

Since the mere possession of a post-1942 general power of appointment causes estate tax consequences, some incentive is created to exercise or release such a power during life. By treating a lifetime exercise or release as a taxable event, the gift tax rule of § 2514 backstops the estate tax and prevents easy, tax-free avoidance of § 2041.

Slightly different rules are applicable with respect to pre-1942 powers. Under § 2514(a), the exercise of a pre-1942 general power is taxable as a transfer of property by the person possessing the power. However, failure to exercise a pre-1942 general power or the complete release of such a power is not deemed to be an exercise of the power and hence is not a taxable transfer. Furthermore, a pre-1951 partial release of a pre-1942 general power, the effect of which is to cut down the general power to a special power, is not treated as a taxable gift at the time of the release and the exercise of the reduced power at a later time will not give rise to gift or estate tax. I.R.C. § 2514(a). In other instances, a partial release and subsequent exercise or release will be telescoped and treated as an exercise or release of a general power.

Finally, paralleling the special rule in the estate tax, § 2514(d) declares that the inter vivos exercise of a post-1942 power by creating another power which can be validly exercised under applicable state law so as to postpone the vesting of any estate or interest in the property, or to suspend the absolute ownership or power of alienation of such property, for a period ascertainable without regard to the date the first power was created will be treated as a transfer of property by the holder of the power, to the extent of the property subject to the second power.

The regulations under § 2514 provide substantial explanatory material. See Reg. §§ 25.2514–1 through 25.2514–3. Many of the definitions and other rules in the gift tax provisions coincide with or parallel the estate tax regulations on the same points. For example, the gift tax regulations, echoing the estate tax regulations, state that the term "power of appointment" does not include powers reserved by a donor to himself. Reg. § 25.2514–1(b)(2). Nor is any provision of § 2514 or of the regulations thereunder to be construed to limit the application of any other section of the Code or the regulations. Specifically, the power of the owner of property to dispose of his own beneficial interest is not a power of appointment, and the interest is includable in the amount of his gifts to the extent that it would be includable under § 2511, without regard to § 2514. So, if Tom (after October 21, 1942) creates a trust to pay income to his wife Alice for life, with power in Alice to appoint the entire trust property during her lifetime to a class consisting of her children, and a further power to dispose of the entire corpus by will to anyone (including her estate), and if Alice exercises the inter vivos power in favor of her children, she has made a completed gift of her life estate under § 2511, without regard to § 2514. (Alice has also relinquished her testamentary general power, resulting in a completed gift of the remainder under § 2514.) See Reg. § 25.2514–1(b)(2).

If the power of appointment exists only as to part of an entire group of assets or only over a limited interest in property, § 2514 applies only to such part or interest. Reg. § 25.2514–1(b)(3).

To sum it up, the gift tax treats a person who exercises or releases a post-1942 general power of appointment in favor of someone else, even in favor of the taker in default, much as it treats an owner of property who transfers the property to another. (The same approach is taken to the exercise of a pre-1942 power, but a complete release or a failure to exercise a pre-1942 power is treated differently.) The exercise or release of such a power will be taxable as a gift even though the property never actually belonged to the holder of the power; by exercising or releasing a general power in favor of someone else, he is deemed to be giving up the power to take property for himself and transferring it (or allowing it to pass) to the appointee instead. In contrast, the exercise or release of a non-general power of appointment is not treated as a transfer of property for gift tax purposes (except in particular circumstances when it might be used to postpone vesting or suspend the power of alienation, as set forth in § 2514(d)). In the case of a non-general power, there is no constructive transfer by gift from the holder of the power to the appointee. The exercise of the power merely gives effect to the transfer from the original owner (who created the power) to the appointee.

Although § 2514 attempts to spell out when dealings with a power of appointment constitute a transfer, the gift tax consequences of such a transfer must be determined in the light of other gift tax principles as to completion, consideration, disclaimer, and the amount and value of the gift, if any.

CHAPTER 10

INCLUSION AND VALUATION

§ 47 INCLUSION AND VALUATION: INTRODUCTION

The question of what property or interest must be *included* in the gross estate of a decedent is a question separate from the *valuation* to be placed on the included property or interest. When applying an estate tax inclusion rule, the first question is whether any interest will have to be included in the decedent's gross estate as a result of the rule in question. Once it has been determined that an interest is to be included, the valuation of that interest must then be ascertained by determining the value of the property in which the interest is held and then by determining the value of the interest that is to be included in the gross estate, if that interest is less than all of the property.

Preceding chapters of this book have dealt with the extent of inclusion or with the determination of which interest is to be included under the various rules of the estate tax. Similarly in the gift tax area, the question has been what property or interest is the subject matter of the gift and thus includable in the base for the gift tax. This chapter turns first to the question of how property or an interest in property that is admittedly includable in the gross estate shall be valued for *estate tax* purposes and, later, how property or an interest that is admittedly the subject of a taxable gift shall be valued for *gift tax* purposes. From time to time, dimensions of the inclusion question will crop up again, but the primary focus will be upon the separate issue of valuation.

§ 48 VALUATION—ESTATE TAX: § 2031

When property owned by the decedent is included in the gross estate under I.R.C. § 2033, the value of the property is determined as of the date of death, unless the executor elects the alternate valuation date (see § 51, *infra*). The date of death rule is established by § 2031(a), which states that the value of the gross estate shall include, to the extent provided for in the estate tax inclusion provisions, the value of all property, wherever situated, at the time of death.

The regulations under § 2031 provide elaborate guidance concerning the method of valuation to be used for property included in the gross estate and valued at the time of death. (Regulations under § 2032 supplement the rules under § 2031 in order to cope with special problems that may arise as a result of the election of the alternate valuation date.)

In general, property included in the gross estate is valued at its *fair market value* at the time of the decedent's death (or on the alternate valuation date under § 2032). In general, fair market value is defined as the price at which the property would change hands between a willing buyer and a willing seller, neither being under any compulsion to buy or sell and both having reasonable knowledge of relevant facts. Reg. § 20.2031–1(b). Fair market value is not to be determined by a forced sale price, nor by the sale price of an item in a market other than that in which the item is most commonly sold to the public. Therefore, if an item of property includable in the decedent's gross estate is generally obtained by the public in the retail market, the fair market value is the price at which the item or a comparable item would be sold at retail. In the case of an automobile, for example, it is the price for which an automobile of the same or similar description could be purchased by a member of the general public and not the price for which the particular automobile would be purchased by a dealer in used automobiles. The regulations go on to say that all relevant facts and elements of value as of the applicable valuation date shall be considered in every case. Reg. § 20.2031–1(b).

The regulations provide specific rules for the valuation of property, such as stocks and bonds, based on the value of each unit of property. See Reg. §§ 20.2031–1(b) and 20.2031–2. Specifically, stocks and bonds are valued at their fair market value per share or bond on the applicable valuation date. Fair market value is based upon selling prices where possible and otherwise on bid and asked prices, as described in Reg. § 20.2031–2(a) through (d). If such prices do not reflect fair market value, other factors may be considered. Reg. § 20.2031–2(e). If selling prices or bid and asked prices are completely unavailable, then the fair market value of the stocks or bonds is to be determined by taking into account the soundness of the security, the interest yield, the date of maturity and other relevant factors in the case of bonds, and in the case of stock, the company's net worth, prospective earning power and dividend-paying capacity, and other relevant factors. Reg. § 20.2031–2(f). The statute itself provides that unlisted stock or securities whose value cannot be determined by reference to bid and asked prices or by reference to sale prices shall be valued by taking into consideration, in addition to all other factors, the value of stock or securities of corporations engaged in the same or a similar line of business which are listed on an exchange. I.R.C. § 2031(b). The regulations go on to provide additional rules to govern securities that have been pledged, or that are subject to an option or contract to purchase, or stock that is selling "ex-dividend" on the date of the decedent's death. See Reg. § 20.2031–2(g) through (i). (For special valuation rules applicable to certain rights and restrictions, see I.R.C. § 2703, discussed in § 49, *infra.*)

An interest in a business, whether a partnership or proprietorship, is also valued at the net amount that a willing purchaser would pay to a willing seller. The net value is determined on the basis of all relevant factors, including a fair appraisal of the assets and earning capacity of the business and other factors. Reg. § 20.2031–3. (For special gift tax valuation rules applicable to gifts of certain interests in a family corporation or partnership, see I.R.C. § 2701, discussed in § 49, *infra.*)

Promissory notes are valued at the amount of unpaid principal and interest accrued to the date of death, unless the executor can establish that the value is lower or that the notes are worthless. Reg. § 20.2031–4. Cash on hand or on deposit is, of course, to be valued at the amount thereof. Reg. § 20.2031–5.

Household and personal effects similarly are to be valued at the price that a willing buyer would pay to a willing seller. Special rules are provided for small and miscellaneous items, items of substantial value, and items disposed of prior to investigation. Reg. § 20.2031–6.

Somewhat more complex rules are necessary to determine the valuation of annuities, life estates, terms of years, remainders, and reversions. In general, the fair market value of such an interest is its present value, determined under the regulations in accordance with actuarial principles. Reg. § 20.2031–7. The interest rate to be used in calculating present value for this purpose is prescribed by statute and adjusted each month. See I.R.C. § 7520(a). In addition, in valuing an annuity or a life estate, remainder, or reversionary interest, it is often necessary to estimate the longevity of a particular living individual. Usually such interests will be valued on the assumption that the particular measuring life will turn out to be equal to the average life expectancy for a person of the same age, based on current national mortality experience. See I.R.C. § 7520(c). The regulations contain valuation tables with examples and explanations of standard present value calculations. See Reg. §§ 20.2031–7 and 20.7520–1 through 20.7520–3. In unusual cases involving more complex conditions or restrictions, the value of an interest may be determined by the use of special actuarial factors or with the assistance of the Internal Revenue Service.

The regulations provide rules for the valuation of certain life insurance and annuity contracts and for the valuation of shares in an open-end investment company (i.e., a mutual fund). See Reg. § 20.2031–8. The former provision in the regulations requiring that shares in a mutual fund be valued at the public offering price (i.e., replacement cost), rather than at the redemption price for which those shares could be sold back to the mutual fund itself, was held to be invalid by the Supreme Court in United States v. Cartwright, 411 U.S. 546 (1973). As a result, the regulations have been amended to provide that mutual fund shares will be valued at the (lower) redemption price, rather than at the fund's asking price. Reg. § 20.2031–8(b).

The general rule requiring that property owned at death be included in the gross estate at fair market value, whether determined on the date of death or at the alternate valuation date, is simpler to state than to apply. Even expert appraisers will often differ on the value of a particular piece of tangible property, and the variation among appraisals of an intangible ownership right or an interest in a going business can be very substantial. Special rules attempt to take into account some particular market problems. For example, the "blockage rule" allows a discount in valuing an unusually large block of stock held by the decedent to reflect the effect on the market price that could be expected if all of the shares were released for sale at one time. See Reg. § 20.2031–2(e).

In valuing a closely held business, courts frequently allow substantial discounts from a proportionate share of the total value of the business (whether based on the value of the underlying assets or on capitalized income or on some combination thereof) to reflect lack of marketability and, in appropriate cases, lack of control. On the other hand, a controlling interest may well be valued at a premium over the market price per share for a noncontrolling interest. Reg. § 20.2031–2(e). In Estate of Bright v. United States, 658 F.2d 999 (5th Cir. 1981), the decedent and her husband had owned 55% of the common stock of several closely held corporations as community property. In valuing the decedent's interest, which passed to her husband as executor and trustee under her will, the Service sought to treat the decedent as owning half of a 55% block, with its attendant control premium, on the ground that the 55% block remained intact in the hands of the husband. The court, however, rejected the notion of "family attribution" and held that the decedent's interest was equivalent to a separate (noncontrolling) 27½% interest and should be valued accordingly. The Service now agrees that a minority discount will not be denied merely because a transferred interest, if aggregated with interests held by other family members, would be part of a controlling interest. Rev. Rul. 93–12, 1993–1 C.B. 202.

Another problem involves restrictive agreements and agreements for the purchase or sale of business interests and their impact on valuation for estate tax purposes. For many years the Service took the position that a restrictive agreement generally constituted a factor to be considered in determining fair market value, and might even be sufficient to establish the value for estate tax purposes of property owned by a decedent. Rev. Rul. 59–60, 1959–1 C.B. 237; Reg. § 20.2031–2(h). In numerous cases, courts were called on to determine the weight to be afforded to such restrictions. The standards developed by the courts are now reflected in the special valuation rules of I.R.C. § 2703 (discussed in § 49, *infra*), which apply to rights and restrictions created or substantially modified after October 8, 1990.

§ 49 SPECIAL VALUATION RULES: §§ 2701–2704

During the 1970s and 1980s, planners developed and refined various "estate freezing" techniques which often allowed taxpayers to pass property to younger generations at artificially low values for estate and gift tax purposes. Congress initially responded in 1987 with former I.R.C. § 2036(c), which addressed a broad range of transactions by requiring that interests transferred during life be drawn back into the transferor's gross estate at death. This provision, as amended in 1988, was widely perceived as unduly complex, vague, and intrusive. See § 31, *supra*.

In 1990, Congress opted for a different approach, focusing not on the *inclusion* in the gross estate of interests previously transferred by the decedent during life but rather on the *valuation* of those interests at the time of the inter vivos transfer. The

1990 legislation retroactively repealed former § 2036(c) and added a new Chapter 14 (I.R.C. §§ 2701–2704) to the Code. Chapter 14 provides elaborate special valuation rules for certain transfers between family members of interests in corporations, partnerships, and trusts. Section 2701 applies to estate freezing transactions involving inter vivos transfers of interests in family-controlled corporations and partnerships. Section 2702 applies to similar transactions involving inter vivos transfers in trust. Section 2703 governs the effect of rights and restrictions on the use or transfer of property for transfer tax purposes, and § 2704 deals with transfers of interests in family-controlled corporations and partnerships subject to lapsing rights and restrictions. The valuation rules of §§ 2701–2704 generally apply to transfers taking place after October 8, 1990.

I.R.C. § 2701. Section 2701 is aimed at a "preferred equity freeze" in which the owner of a family corporation or partnership makes an inter vivos transfer, to a younger family member, of a junior equity interest with a disproportionate share of potential future appreciation, while retaining a senior equity interest with limited distribution rights. To illustrate: Suppose Mother owns all the outstanding stock of a corporation, consisting of one share of voting common stock and 99 shares of voting preferred stock. Mother gives the common stock to Son, but retains all of the preferred stock, which carries a fixed *noncumulative* dividend and a fixed liquidation preference. Under general valuation principles, assuming the corporation as a whole is worth $1 million, Mother might value her retained stock at $990,000 (attributable to her voting control and substantial distribution rights), leaving a residual value of only $10,000 for the common stock given to Son. Although Mother will eventually be subject to gift or estate tax when she disposes of her retained stock, the value of that stock will presumably remain "frozen" in her hands, while all of the subsequent appreciation in the corporation will pass tax-free to Son. In fact, Mother might be able to shift additional value to Son simply by failing to exercise her discretionary distribution rights.

Section 2701 deals with this type of transaction by treating the donor's retained interest as having little or no value for gift tax purposes, with the result that the value of the transferred interest is artificially inflated at the time of the inter vivos transfer. Thus, in the above example, Mother's retained preferred stock would be valued at zero, and the entire value of the corporation would be allocated to the common stock transferred to Son, producing a taxable gift of $1 million. The reason for this seemingly harsh approach is that the nature of the retained and transferred interests makes it extremely difficult to value them accurately under general valuation principles. If Mother and Son were dealing at arm's length, Mother would have the opportunity and the incentive to maximize the return on her retained preferred stock through her voting control. Given the family relationship, however, she may be inclined to forego benefits to herself and thereby allow income and appreciation to be shifted to the common stock that she gave to Son. The special valuation rules of

§ 2701 are intended to remove the opportunity for taxpayers to manipulate the respective values of the retained and transferred interests for gift tax purposes by means of discretionary rights and powers which may in fact never be exercised.

In general, § 2701 may apply when a person makes an inter vivos transfer of an equity interest in a corporation or partnership to a member of his or her family, if the transferor or another family member retains a preferred equity interest in the same corporation or partnership. Under the special valuation rules, a distribution right (in the case of a family-controlled corporation or partnership) or a liquidation, put, call, or conversion right attributable to the retained interest will be valued at zero, producing a corresponding increase in the value of the transferred interest for gift tax purposes. An exception to the zero valuation rule exists for qualified payment rights under the retained interest (e.g., a *cumulative* dividend payable at least annually at a fixed rate on preferred stock); such rights will be valued under general valuation principles. The statute provides a complex network of specially defined terms and detailed technical requirements which are further explained and illustrated in the regulations. See Reg. §§ 25.2701–1 through 25.2701–6.

The statute contains several exceptions for transactions that are not considered to pose substantial problems of tax avoidance. Thus, § 2701 does *not* apply if (1) market quotations are readily available for the retained interest or the transferred interest on an established securities market, (2) the retained interest is of the same class as the transferred interest, or (3) the retained interest is proportionally the same as the transferred interest, without regard to nonlapsing differences in voting power (or, for a partnership, nonlapsing differences with respect to management and limitations on liability). See I.R.C. § 2701(a)(2). Other limitations on the scope of § 2701 are implicit in its operational rules. For example, the statute does not apply if the transferor retains no equity interest in the corporation or partnership, or if the recipient of the transferred interest is not a "member of the transferor's family" as defined in the statute. (The defined term "member of the family" does not include, for example, a brother, sister, nephew, or niece of the transferor.) These exceptions and limitations have great practical importance for taxpayers who wish to avoid the application of the special valuation rules.

I.R.C. § 2702. Section 2702 is aimed primarily at a "grantor retained income trust" in which an individual makes an inter vivos transfer of property in trust for the benefit of a younger family member, while retaining an interest in the trust income for a fixed term of years. For example, suppose Mother transfers property worth $1 million in trust for Son, retaining a 20-year income interest. Under general valuation principles, the value of the remainder interest transferred to Son would be determined under the valuation tables set forth in the regulations. See I.R.C. § 7520. If the applicable factor for a remainder following a 20-year term is 30%, the present value of the remainder, and hence the amount of Mother's taxable gift, would be $300,000. In effect, the valuation tables apportion the total value of the trust property between the income interest and the remainder interest. By implication, then, the present value of Mother's retained income interest would be $700,000. However, Mother may actually receive a much smaller amount, even if she receives all the trust income for the full 20-year term. This could happen, for instance, if the trust property is invested in a manner that produces substantial capital appreciation but little or no current income. Furthermore, if Mother survives the 20-year term, none of the trust property will be drawn back into her gross estate under § 2036. As a result, a good deal of the value of the property at the time of the initial transfer, along with all of the subsequent appreciation, would pass to Son free of transfer tax.

Section 2702 forecloses such tax avoidance opportunities by treating the grantor's retained interest as having no value for gift tax purposes, with the result that the value of the transferred interest will be correspondingly increased. In the above example, Mother's retained income interest would be deemed to have a value of zero, and Son's remainder would accordingly be valued at $1 million. Therefore, Mother would be subject to gift tax on the entire value of the trust property. The rationale for this approach is similar to that offered for the analogous provisions of § 2701. Given the unrealistic apportionment of value between transferred and retained interests under general valuation principles, the statute imposes special valuation rules to remove the opportunity and the incentive for tax avoidance.

In general, § 2702 may apply when a person makes an inter vivos transfer of property in trust to or for the benefit of a member of his or her family, if the transferor or another family member retains another interest in the same trust. Under the special valuation rules, the retained interest will be treated as having a value of zero, producing an increase in the value of the transferred interest for gift tax purposes. The zero-value rule, however, does not apply to a "qualified interest" consisting of a right to receive fixed amounts payable at least annually (an annuity), a right to receive a fixed percentage of the annually-determined value of the trust property, payable at least annually (a unitrust interest), or a noncontingent remainder following an annuity or a unitrust interest. These interests are thought to offer relatively little opportunity for distortion or manipulation, and therefore they are still permitted to be valued under general valuation principles. The statute has no application to a transfer that is entirely incomplete (e.g., a revocable trust). There is also a special statutory exception for personal residence trusts. The regulations provide additional guidance concerning the scope and operation of the statutory rules. See Reg. §§ 25.2702–1 through 25.2702–7.

I.R.C. § 2703. Section 2703 applies to agreements that burden property either by granting to a person other than the owner the right to purchase or use the property at a bargain price or by restricting the owner's right to sell or use the property. A common example is a buy-sell agreement whereby the owners of shares in a family corporation agree that none of them can sell any of their shares to an outsider without first offering the interest to the other owners; the agreement may also provide that when one owner dies, the corporation has an enforceable right to purchase the decedent's shares at a specified price. On one hand, a buy-sell agreement may serve a bona fide business purpose (e.g., maintaining family ownership and control, providing for orderly succession, and avoiding disputes over valuation). On the other hand, the agreement may also serve a tax avoidance purpose. Courts have held that the value of a decedent's shares may be limited for estate tax purposes by a formula price specified in an enforceable agreement, if the estate can be compelled to sell the shares at that price and the decedent could not have sold the shares for a higher price during life. In May v. McGowan, 194 F.2d 396 (2d Cir. 1952), the court held that the formula price specified in a buy-sell agreement established a ceiling on the value of the decedent's shares for estate tax purposes, even though the formula price turned out to be zero. As a result, the decedent's shares passed to his son completely free of estate tax.

The general rule of § 2703(a) provides that the value of property shall be determined for transfer tax purposes without regard to "any option, agreement, or other right to acquire or use the property at a price less than the fair market value of the property (without regard to such option, agreement, or right)," or "any restriction on the right to sell or use such property." This sweeping provision is limited, however, by § 2703(b), which makes the general rule inapplicable if the option, agreement, right, or restriction meets the following requirements: (1) it must be a bona fide business arrangement; (2) it must not be a device to transfer such property to members of the decedent's family for less than full and adequate consideration in money or money's worth; and (3) its terms must be comparable to similar arrangements entered into by persons in an arm's-length transaction. If all three requirements of the § 2703(b) safe harbor are met, the effect of a restrictive agreement on valuation will be governed by applicable judicial and regulatory authority. Further details concerning the application of the statute can be found in Reg. §§ 25.2703–1 and 25.2703–2.

I.R.C. § 2704. Section 2704 provides special rules governing the effect of certain lapsing rights and restrictions on the valuation of interests in family corporations and partnerships for transfer tax purposes. Section 2704(a) provides that a lapse of voting or liquidation rights in a family-controlled corporation or partnership shall be treated as a transfer by the holder of the lapsed rights. The amount of the transfer is equal to the difference between the value of the holder's interests in the corporation or partnership immediately before the lapse (determined as if the rights were nonlapsing) and the value of such interests immediately after the lapse. Section 2704(b) provides that if a person transfers an interest in a family-controlled corporation or partnership to a member of his or her family, any "applicable restriction" shall be disregarded in determining the value of the transferred interest. An applicable restriction is defined as a restriction which effectively limits the ability of the corporation or partnership to liquidate, and which either lapses after the transfer or can be removed by the transferor and his or her family; however, the term does not include any commercially reasonable restriction incident to financing with an unrelated third party or any restriction imposed by federal or state law. A more detailed explanation of the statute and its applications appears in Reg. §§ 25.2704–1 through 25.2704–3.

§ 50 SPECIAL USE VALUATION: § 2032A

There is one exception to the general rule that the value of the gross estate shall be determined by including property at its fair market value. Section 2032A, added to the Code in 1976 and significantly liberalized by subsequent amendments, authorizes the decedent's executor to elect "special use valuation" for estate tax purposes. This election, if available, allows qualifying real property used in a farm or other business to be valued at less than its fair market value. See Reg. §§ 20.2032A–1 through 20.2032A–8.

This special relief was needed because the normal concept of fair market value presupposes that property will be valued at its potential "highest and best use." Therefore the fair market value of a particular piece of property, a farm for example, may well greatly exceed its income potential as a farm, because of the possibilities of developing the land for other, more lucrative uses. In other words, what might be called "speculative value" is reflected in fair market value. If the decedent's heirs wish to keep the property in use as a farm, an estate tax liability based on fair market value may cause severe liquidity problems. Special use valuation serves to ameliorate these liquidity problems and thus to encourage the continued existence of family-owned farms and businesses, by relieving the need to sell the property in order to pay the estate tax.

To qualify for the election, the real property itself must have been owned and used by the decedent or a family member for farming or other business purposes, both prior to and at the time of the decedent's death. The property must pass from the decedent to a "qualified heir," that is, to a member of the decedent's family. In addition, the property must constitute a substantial portion of the gross estate. If all of the statutory conditions are met, the property may be included in the gross estate at its special use valuation rather than at its fair market value; however, the resulting reduction in the includable amount cannot exceed $750,000 (indexed for inflation, $1,460,000 in 2026). One of two separate valuation methods may be elected to determine the special use valuation. There are also recapture provisions, which will impose an "additional estate tax" on the property in the event that the qualified heir transfers the property (other than to a family member) or ceases to use the property for its qualifying use. The additional estate tax is the personal liability of the qualified heir, and the recapture period lasts for ten years after the decedent's death or until the death of the qualified heir, whichever is earlier.

The provisions of § 2032A are labyrinthine. In addition to the internal complexity of the provision, problems can arise relating to its interaction with other aspects of the transfer tax system, for example, the marital deduction. Other trouble spots involve its application in a corporate or partnership context, the continuing requirement of qualifying use, and the transfer tax and income tax consequences of a subsequent transfer within the recapture period. In appropriate circumstances, special use valuation can produce substantial estate tax savings that outweigh the concomitant increase in administrative costs.

§ 51 ALTERNATE VALUATION DATE: § 2032

As an alternative to valuing the property included in the gross estate as of the time of the decedent's death, I.R.C. § 2032 allows the executor to elect to use an alternate valuation date. If the election is made, the property included in the gross estate will be valued as of the alternate valuation date, which is six months after the date of death in the case of property that has not been distributed, sold, exchanged, or otherwise disposed of in the interim; in the case of property that has been distributed, sold, exchanged, or disposed of within six months after death, the alternate valuation date is the date of distribution, sale, exchange, or other disposition. I.R.C. § 2032(a).

The original purpose of an alternate valuation date was to soften the impact of the estate tax when property held by the decedent at death plummeted in value shortly thereafter and before the due date for payment of the estate tax. In particular, the stock market crash in 1929 and the subsequent drop in property values were responsible for the enactment of the relief provision in 1935.

Although it is the purpose of § 2032 to permit a reduction in the amount of tax payable if the gross estate has shrunk in aggregate value during the period after decedent's death, the alternate valuation date is not automatically employed in all such cases but must be elected. If the executor elects the alternate valuation date, the alternate valuation method applies to all of the property included in the gross estate in its entirety; it cannot be applied selectively to specific items of property.

The alternate valuation date can be elected only if the election has the effect of reducing both the value of the gross estate and the total amount of estate and generation-skipping transfer taxes payable (after allowable credits) with respect to property includable in the gross estate. I.R.C. § 2032(c). This restriction was added in 1984 to prevent the election from being used to increase the estate tax value, and hence the income tax basis, of appreciating property without a corresponding increase in the amount of transfer tax payable.

Whenever any provision of the estate tax law refers to the value of property at the date of the decedent's death, such reference shall be deemed to refer to the value of that property used in determining the value of the gross estate, which would mean the alternate valuation date if elected by the executor. I.R.C. § 2032(b). The election of the alternate valuation date is made by the executor on the estate tax return and, once made, is irrevocable. No election is allowed if the estate tax return is filed more than one year after the time prescribed by law (including extensions) for filing. I.R.C. § 2032(d).

Election of the alternate valuation date may create some uncertainty about whether property earned or accrued after death but before the alternate valuation date is to be included in the value of the gross estate. At one time, the regulations took the position that when the alternate valuation date was used, the gross estate would have to include income earned by the estate up to the valuation date. However, the Supreme Court rejected this interpretation of the statute in Maass v. Higgins, 312 U.S. 443 (1941), and the regulations were subsequently amended to exclude such income from the gross estate. Nevertheless, income accrued prior to death but received after death is includable. Reg. § 20.2032–1(d).

In explaining the application of the alternate valuation method when property has been received or disposed of after death but before the valuation date, the regulations use the concepts of "included property" and "excluded property." Property interests existing at the date of the decedent's death which form a part of the gross estate but are valued in accordance with the provisions of § 2032 are referred to as "included property." Furthermore, such property interests remain "included property" for valuation purposes, even though they may undergo a change in form during the alternate valuation period by being actually received or disposed of in whole or in part by the estate. In contrast, property earned or accrued after the date of death and during the alternate valuation period with respect to any property interest existing at the date of the decedent's death which does not represent a form of "included property" itself or the receipt of "included property" is excluded in valuing the gross estate under the alternate valuation method. The regulations refer to such property as "excluded property." Reg. § 20.2032–1(d).

For example, an interest-bearing obligation, such as a bond or a note, may comprise two elements of "included property" at the date of death, namely the principal amount of the obligation itself and interest accrued to the date of death. Interest accrued after the date of death and before the alternate valuation date constitutes "excluded property." However, any payments of principal installments made during the alternate valuation period will be included in the gross estate and valued as of the date of payment. Reg. § 20.2032–1(d)(1). As to leased property, the realty or personalty itself and the rent accrued to the date of death constitute "included property," but any rent accrued after the date of death and before the alternate valuation date is "excluded property." Reg. § 20.2032–1(d)(2). Shares of stock in a corporation and dividends declared to shareholders of record on or before the date of death constitute "included property." Ordinary dividends declared to shareholders of record after the date of death constitute "excluded property." However, if a dividend is declared to shareholders of record after the date of death with the effect that the shares of stock at the subsequent valuation date do not reasonably represent the same "included property" as existed at the date of death, the dividend itself may be treated as "included property" (except to the extent paid out of post-death corporate earnings). Reg. § 20.2032–1(d)(4).

A similar issue may arise if the decedent owned an insurance policy on the life of another person who dies during the six-month period following the decedent's death. In Rev. Rul. 63–52, 1963–1 C.B. 173, the Service ruled that the "appreciation" in the value of the policies by reason of the insured's death was "included property" so that the entire value of the proceeds was includable in the decedent's gross estate.

Under the alternate valuation method, any interest or estate that is affected by mere lapse of time shall be included at its value as of the time of death (rather than as of the alternate valuation date), with adjustment for any difference in its value as of the alternate valuation date that is not due to a mere lapse of time. I.R.C. § 2032(a)(3). Examples of property whose value is affected by mere lapse of time include patents, a life estate for the life of a person other than the decedent, remainders, and reversions. See Reg. § 20.2032–1(f).

§ 52 ESTATE TAX INCLUSION AND VALUATION OF PROPERTY TRANSFERRED DURING LIFE

The preceding sections dealing with valuation problems have focused on the valuation of property includable in the gross estate because it was held by the decedent at death. It is also possible, however, that some interests in property not owned at death will be includable in the gross estate under provisions other than I.R.C. § 2033. More specifically, inclusion may be required of an interest in property transferred by the decedent at some time during life. See, e.g., I.R.C. §§ 2035–2038. When property transferred during life is drawn back into the gross estate, one question is whether the value at which it is to be included should be its value at the date of the lifetime transfer or the value of the same property at the date of death (or the alternate valuation date) if the property has risen or fallen in value in the interim. If income has been earned after the transfer but before the date of death, is the income to be included in valuing the property? Will it be included only if accumulated or reinvested, or even if expended before death? Another question arises if the transferee has made improvements or additions to the property received from the decedent, or if the property has been squandered or disposed of. If the transferee exchanged the gift property or sold it and reinvested the proceeds, is the amount to be included in the decedent's gross estate the value at the date of death of the property received by the transferee in the exchange or the value at death of the proceeds from sale of the gift property? The answers to some of these questions are uncertain, but answers to some others can be given with confidence.

The valuation question throughout §§ 2035–2038 is, in a sense, whether or not the language of the statute is to be taken literally. The terms of § 2031 broadly imply that when property transferred during life is drawn back into the gross estate, the value to be included is the value of the property at the decedent's death (or the alternate valuation date), not the value at the time of the earlier transfer. The language in each of the lifetime transfer provisions, §§ 2035–2038, says that the gross estate shall include the value of all property to the extent of any interest in the property of which the decedent has at any time made a transfer, by trust or otherwise. Literally interpreted and applied, the language of both § 2031 and §§ 2035–2038 would seem to lead to the result that the specific property that was the subject of an includable inter vivos gift (and only that specific property) must be valued at death. If, however, the specific property has been disposed of, must it be traced and valued in the hands of someone else? Might the result turn on whether property was includable because of a transfer within three years of death or, in contrast, because of a retained power over income or corpus? Should the rule be different for sale and reinvestment as distinguished from squandering and as differentiated from accumulated income or capital appreciation?

Transfers Within Three Years of Death. In its present form, § 2035(a) serves essentially as a backstop to the enumerated provisions (§§ 2036,

2037, 2038, and 2042) that would have required inclusion in the gross estate in the absence of a transfer within three years of death. Accordingly, the three-year rule no longer raises special problems of valuation distinct from those other provisions.

The situation was considerably more complicated under the broader version of the three-year rule as it existed prior to the 1981 amendments, when § 2035(a) required that any gratuitous transfer made by the decedent within three years of death be drawn back into the gross estate. Although the regulations promulgated under prior law have been withdrawn and much of the case law interpreting those regulations is no longer directly applicable, the principles developed under prior law remain relevant by analogy in other areas of the estate tax (e.g., in tracing contributions to joint tenancy property under § 2040) and therefore deserve brief mention here. If an outright, "no-strings" lifetime gift was drawn back into the decedent's gross estate, the regulations indicated that the amount to be included was the value of the gift property itself. In the case of a cash gift, it was held that the includable amount was equal to the amount of the cash gift, even if the donee had spent the cash or used it to purchase other property. Humphrey's Estate v. Commissioner, 162 F.2d 1 (5th Cir. 1947), cert. den., 332 U.S. 817 (1947). If the gift consisted of shares of stock, the includable amount would be the value of the very same shares at the decedent's death, whether or not the donee still held them at that time. Rev. Rul. 72–282, 1972–1 C.B. 306. However, neither income received after the time of the gift nor property purchased with such income was included in the gross estate. Furthermore, if the donee made improvements that increased the value of the property after the time of the gift, that increase would not be considered as part of the value of the property to be included in the decedent's gross estate. See generally former Reg. § 20.2035–1(e).

Transfers with Retained Interests or Powers. The statutory language of §§ 2036–2038 has received a somewhat broader interpretation than the similar language of § 2035(a) (as in effect prior to the 1981 amendments), due in large part to differences in the types of transfers involved. Unlike the outright, "no-strings" gifts covered by the old version of § 2035(a), the transfers described in §§ 2036–2038 usually involve retained "strings" in the form of interests in or powers over the transferred property which can be viewed as making the transfer incomplete for estate tax purposes.

Where the taxpayer has retained an interest in or a power over the transferred property, whether it be a power to revoke the transfer or a power to designate the beneficiaries or an interest in the income of the transferred property, it can be argued that the decedent has retained sufficient ownership or control to justify inclusion in the gross estate of something more than merely the value of the particular property transferred during life. To illustrate, if the decedent transferred property but retained a power of revocation, his gross estate should include whatever he could have gotten back until the moment before his death, even if that is larger in value than the property he transferred during life. Similarly, if the decedent retained a power to designate the beneficiaries of property, even though he could not get the property back directly for himself, § 2036(a)(2) arguably should require inclusion of the value of whatever property was subject to his power of designation at the time of his death, even if that is not the same as the value of the property he originally transferred.

To generalize, a power to revoke a transfer or to change the beneficial enjoyment of the property transferred, including any income or appreciation, will cause the full value of what the transferor could have gotten back to be included in the gross estate. In such a case, the transferor retained a power exercisable up to the time of death to recapture the property subject to the power, and will be taxed accordingly. If the power held at death pertained only to some limited interest in the transferred property, then § 2038 would require the inclusion only of the value of that particular interest. See Reg. § 20.2038–1(a); Walter v. United States, 341 F.2d 182 (6th Cir. 1965); Rev. Rul. 70–513, 1970–2 C.B. 194. If the decedent retained a power to designate the beneficiaries of a given amount or percentage of the trust income, only a corresponding portion of the corpus will be included in the gross estate under § 2036(a)(2). See Reg. § 20.2036–1(c); Industrial Trust Co. v. Commissioner, 165 F.2d 142 (1st Cir. 1947).

A related question involves the treatment of the portion of trust property attributable to accumulations of income. The leading case in this area is the Supreme Court's decision in United States v. O'Malley, 383 U.S. 627 (1966). In that case, the decedent had established irrevocable inter vivos trusts to which he transferred income-producing property. He relinquished all rights to the income except a power to distribute that income to the income beneficiaries or to cause it to be accumulated and held for the remainder beneficiaries. In point of fact, he exercised his retained power by choosing to accumulate the income and adding it to the principal of the trusts. The Court held that each addition to trust principal from accumulated income constituted a "transfer" by the decedent within the meaning of § 2036(a)(2) so as to require inclusion in his gross estate of all the trust principal at death, including those portions representing accumulated income.

The *O'Malley* case settles the question of trust income that is actually accumulated under § 2036(a)(2) but leaves other questions unanswered. What if the income was not actually accumulated, although decedent had power to compel accumulation? Or, what if the income was in fact accumulated, though not by virtue of a power exercised by the decedent, and some interest was required to be included because of a power to alter or amend or to designate beneficial enjoyment? Some of the Supreme Court's language in *O'Malley* seems to suggest that a retained § 2036 or § 2038 power makes the transfer incomplete until death for estate tax purposes. Although this language was addressed to the accumulated income question, it suggests a still broader effect—each and every interest that is subject to a retained § 2036 or § 2038 power is to be valued at the date of death and included in the gross estate.

As a general rule, if property was transferred during life and the transferor retained such a power over the property that it must be included in the gross estate under §§ 2036–2038, the value of the property at the applicable valuation date should include accumulated or investment income, since the transfer was not complete until his death. The technical argument that the decedent has not *transferred* the income has been put to rest by *O'Malley*. However, this general principle does not serve to answer all the possible questions that may arise with property that has been traded, sold, improved, consumed, or wasted.

Estate Tax Valuation of Consideration Received for an Incomplete Inter Vivos Transfer. A final question in connection with inclusion in the gross estate under §§ 2035–2038 relates to the valuation of consideration received. Suppose the decedent made an inter vivos transfer subject to a retained interest or power and received in return partial (not adequate and full) consideration in money or money's worth; at the decedent's death, the property is drawn back into the gross estate. To avoid the problem of double inclusion, the statute provides that the gross estate shall include only the excess of the fair market value, at the time of death, of the property otherwise required to be included over the value of the consideration received therefor by the decedent. I.R.C. § 2043(a). Should the consideration received be valued at the time of the inter vivos transfer or at death?

Section 2043(a) is silent on the question, but the regulations take the position that only "the price received by the decedent" is allowable as an offset in calculating the amount includable in the gross estate. Reg. § 20.2043–1(a). The courts agree that § 2043(a) requires a dollar-for-dollar offset based on the value of the consideration received at the time of the inter vivos transfer. An illustrative case is United States v. Righter, 400 F.2d 344 (8th Cir. 1968), in which the decedent transferred shares of stock subject to a retained life estate, resulting in inclusion of the transferred shares in her gross estate under § 2036. (The value of the transferred shares, before any offset for consideration received, was around $379,000.) She received, in exchange, a life interest in other shares transferred by her nephews. At the time of the transfer, the life estate received in the exchange was valued at around $36,000, based on valuation tables in the regulations. As it turned out, however, the decedent outlived her actuarial life expectancy and actually collected around $230,000 in income before her death. The district court held that the includable transfer was to be reduced by the total amount the decedent actually received. Under this rule, the longer the decedent lived, the greater would be the consideration received and the smaller the net addition to the gross estate. On appeal, however, the Eighth Circuit reversed and held that the consideration received was to be taken into account at its value at the date of the inter vivos transfer, not the later date of the decedent's death.

As a conceptual matter, this reading of § 2043(a) is problematic because it seems to compare apples with oranges: The property transferred during life is includable in the gross estate at its value at the date of death (or alternate valuation date) for estate tax purposes, but the amount of the offset allowed for consideration received is measured as of the time of the exchange. Thus, while the value of the transferred property will reflect any appreciation (or accumulated income, in the case of property held in trust) accruing between the time of the exchange and the date of death, the value of the consideration is frozen at its original amount, with no adjustment for "time value." (Compare this dollar-for-dollar approach with the proportional exclusion rule of § 2040(a) in the case of a joint tenancy funded in part with consideration furnished by the surviving joint tenant, discussed in § 40, *supra*.) Accordingly, if at the time of the exchange the consideration received falls short of the value of the property transferred by even a small amount, any appreciation in the value of the transferred property will be fully includable in the gross estate at death. Although the dollar-for-dollar offset may produce harsh results in particular cases, it seems to be firmly entrenched in the regulations and the case law.

§ 53 VALUATION FOR GIFT TAX PURPOSES

Valuation for purposes of the gift tax is governed by principles largely resembling the general principles applicable in the estate tax area. Under I.R.C. § 2512(a), a gift made in property is to be valued at the date of the gift. If property is transferred for less than an adequate and full consideration in money or money's worth, then the amount by which the value of the property exceeded the value of the consideration is deemed a gift. I.R.C. § 2512(b). The value of the consideration offset evidently is to be established as of the date of the gift. The regulations under § 2512 provide detailed guidance to valuation problems under the gift tax (mirroring, in substantial measure, the principles enunciated in the parallel regulations under § 2031). Fair market value is to be determined as of the date of the completed gift, and is defined as the price at which the property would change hands between a willing buyer and a willing seller, neither being under any compulsion to buy or sell and both having reasonable knowledge of the relevant facts. Similar rules about the appropriate markets in which to make comparisons are given, and guidance is set forth for the valuation of stocks and bonds, interests in businesses, promissory notes, annuities, life estates, terms for years, remainders and reversions, life insurance and annuity contracts, and mutual fund shares. See Reg. §§ 25.2512–1 through 25.2512–8.

One important distinction to keep in mind is that each gift of property made during life is ordinarily valued separately from other gifts of similar property, even if all the gifts occur at the same time. For example, if a parent who owns all of the outstanding stock of a family corporation makes simultaneous gifts of 20% of the shares to each of her five children, each gift will be valued as a separate minority interest. Rev. Rul. 93–12, 1993–1 C.B. 202.

In contrast, if the parent held the stock until death and left it by will to her children in equal shares, the stock included in the gross estate would be valued as a single controlling interest for estate tax purposes. By the same token, a single testamentary gift of a large block of stock may qualify for a blockage discount that would not be allowed in the case of separate, smaller gifts made during life. See Reg. § 25.2512–2(e).

The special valuation rules of § 2701 for transfers of interests in corporations and partnerships to family members, and those of § 2702 for transfers of interests in trust to family members, apply exclusively for gift tax purposes. If a person retains an interest that is subject to the special valuation rules of § 2701 or § 2702 and subsequently disposes of the retained interest during life or at death, the valuation of the subsequent transfer will be governed by general valuation principles. The regulations, however, allow adjustments in the amount of the subsequent transfer to prevent double taxation. See the discussion in § 49, *supra*.

There is no alternate valuation date for gift tax purposes. Since the valuation date is the date of the gift, the problems and uncertainties involved in determining when a gift is complete for gift tax purposes affect the valuation question as well as other issues. In actual application, determining the value of a gift when the time of completion is in doubt can turn out to be a difficult matter.

The special valuation rules of § 2032A for certain farms and other businesses are available only for estate tax purposes and have no counterpart in the gift tax area.

CHAPTER 11

EXEMPTIONS AND EXCLUSIONS: GIFT TAX (GIFTS OF FUTURE INTERESTS AND GIFTS TO MINORS)

§ 54 EXEMPTIONS

Prior to the 1976 Act, every individual was allowed a $30,000 lifetime exemption for gift tax purposes and, in addition, a separate $60,000 exemption for estate tax purposes. The 1976 Act consolidated the former exemptions and converted them into a unified credit. The credit is designed to offset the tax that would otherwise be imposed on taxable transfers up to a specified exemption or exclusion amount. Accordingly, it is sometimes referred to as an "exemption equivalent." Unlike the former exemptions, however, the credit offsets the tax at the lowest brackets and hence provides a tax benefit that does not vary with the marginal tax rate applicable to a particular transfer. The credit is not refundable; it can only be used to offset tax otherwise due. See § 72, *infra*.

§ 55 GIFT TAX EXCLUSIONS: § 2503

Section 2503(a) defines "taxable gifts" as the total amount of gifts made during the calendar year, less the deductions provided in §§ 2522 and 2523. In computing taxable gifts, every donor is entitled to an annual, per-donee *exclusion* of $10,000 (indexed for inflation, $19,000 in 2026). The annual per-donee exclusion is authorized in I.R.C. § 2503(b), which states that in computing taxable gifts for the calendar year, in the case of all gifts (other than gifts of future interests in property) made to any person by the donor, the first $10,000 of such gifts to such person shall not be included in the total amount of gifts made during that year. Since a gift of a future interest does not qualify for the annual exclusion, the entire value of a future interest in property must be included in the total amount of gifts for the calendar year in which the gift is made. In other words, the first $10,000 of present-interest gifts made by a donor to a particular donee during a calendar year are automatically excluded in determining the donor's gift tax liability. Thus, a donor who makes gifts of $10,000 to each of six different donees is entitled to six annual exclusions, enabling the donor to make tax-free gifts totaling $60,000 in the current year, and the result will be the same for the following year and every other year in which the donor makes similar gifts. If a gift is made in trust, the beneficiary of the trust (rather than the trust itself) is treated as the donee. Reg. § 25.2503–2(a). (As to the definition of present and future interests, see § 56, *infra.*)

At least one court has applied "substance-over-form" analysis in the gift tax context. In Heyen v. United States, 945 F.2d 359 (10th Cir. 1991), a donor transferred separate blocks of stock, each valued at less than $10,000, to more than 25 intermediate recipients, who promptly endorsed the stock certificates in blank so that the stock could be reissued to members of the donor's family. The court held that the donor "merely used those recipients to create gift tax exclusions to avoid paying gift tax on indirect gifts to the actual family member beneficiaries," and since indirect gifts are subject to gift tax by virtue of § 2511(a), the donor was, in fact, liable for gift tax on the gifts to the ultimate beneficiaries.

The purpose of the annual exclusion is, so to speak, to keep the tax collector from lurking behind the Christmas tree or beside the birthday cake. The exclusion removes the need to keep records of and report small incidental gifts and most ordinary family or holiday transfers. (A more cynical way of stating much the same idea is to say that the per-donee annual exclusion prevents the law from making liars of us all, since many small intrafamily gifts would probably go unreported if they were not exempted from tax.)

The annual exclusion not only exempts many gifts from tax but also relieves taxpayers of a heavy burden of reporting those gifts by filing tax returns. In general, a donor is required to file a gift tax return for any calendar year in which he or she makes any gift that is not fully covered by the annual exclusion, the exclusion for tuition and medical care, the marital deduction or the charitable deduction. I.R.C. § 6019. The return is normally due on April 15 following the close of the calendar year, and the tax is to be paid when the return is filed. I.R.C. §§ 6075(b) and 6151. The annual exclusion under § 2503(b) applies automatically to gifts made to each donee during the calendar year, up to the excludable amount; gifts to any donee in excess of that amount may give rise to gift tax liability. Another annual exclusion becomes available only after the turn of the calendar year; an unused exclusion expires at year end and cannot be carried over or accumulated.

The size of the annual exclusion has been changed from time to time. These changes remain relevant in later years by reason of the way the gift tax is calculated. Although the gift tax is payable on an annual basis, each year's gift tax computation builds on the donor's cumulative taxable gifts made in prior years. To determine the tax payable for a given year, the total taxable gifts made since enactment of the gift tax on June 6, 1932 to the end of the current year must be aggregated and a tentative tax on such gifts must be computed at present rates. From that amount must then be deducted a tentative tax, again determined at present rates, on the total taxable gifts made in prior years. The amount so calculated is the gift tax for the current year. I.R.C. §§ 2501 and 2502. Against the gift tax so computed may be offset any unused portion of the unified credit. I.R.C. § 2505. For purposes of determining the aggregate amount of taxable gifts in past years, exclusions, deductions and exemptions may be taken as they were allowable at the time those gifts were made. I.R.C. § 2504. Consequently, the dimensions of the exclusion allowed in past years remain relevant in determining the current year's tax liability. The excludable amount, originally set at $5,000, was reduced to $4,000 and further reduced to $3,000 where it remained for many years until it was raised to $10,000 for gifts made after 1981. Under § 2503(b)(2), enacted in 1997, the $10,000 amount is subject to periodic increases in round increments of $1,000 to keep pace with inflation; in 2026 the amount of the exclusion was $19,000.

Although there is no statute or regulation directly on point, it has always been assumed that transfers in satisfaction of a support obligation are not gifts subject to transfer taxes. This proposition is supported by inference from numerous cases and rulings. Education and medical care are marginal "gift-support" items which are now expressly excluded from taxable gifts by § 2503(e).

Section 2503(e) excludes amounts paid on behalf of an individual as tuition to an educational organization described in § 170(b)(1)(A)(ii) for the education or training of such individual, or to any person who provides medical care for such individual as payment for such care. Note that the beneficiary need not be a dependent of the donor, nor need the educational institution be tax exempt. However, the payments must be made directly to the educational institution or medical care provider. The exclusion does not apply where the donor gives cash to the beneficiary to defray the cost of current tuition or medical care, or to reimburse the beneficiary for amounts previously paid for such expenses. Reg. § 25.2503–6.

§ 56 GIFTS OF FUTURE INTERESTS: § 2503(b)

The annual exclusion is subject to one very important limitation: the exclusion is available only for gifts of "present interests" in property. No exclusion is allowed for gifts of "future interests" in property. This limitation, contained in I.R.C. § 2503(b), has produced reams of interpretation, litigation, and commentary.

The rule that no annual exclusion will be allowed for gifts of future interests apparently has its roots in the idea that the exclusion should be available only if the donee or donees are known with certainty and only if the value of the interest to be received by each donee can be definitely ascertained. With some gifts of future interests, it is not possible at the time of the gift to know with certainty the identity of the ultimate recipient or the precise value of the interest eventually to be received by each recipient. But these problems are not always present. Nevertheless, the statute denies the exclusion for *all* gifts of future interests, even if it is possible to determine the identity of the ultimate recipient and the value of the particular future interest.

As the regulations put it, no part of the value of the gift of a future interest may be excluded in determining the total amount of gifts made during the taxable year. The regulations go on to say that "future interests" is a term that includes reversions, remainders, and other interests or estates, whether vested or contingent, and whether or not supported by a particular interest or estate, which are limited to commence in use, possession, or enjoyment at some future date or time. Reg. § 25.2503–3(a). Thus the prohibition against an annual exclusion for a gift of a future interest will apply even in the case of an indefeasibly vested remainder where it is possible at the time of the gift to identify the individual who (either personally or through his estate) will eventually receive full beneficial ownership of the property and where there is no possibility of the interest shifting by some contingency or condition to another taker. Furthermore, not even a single exclusion will be allowed if the identity of the donee is unascertained, even if it is quite clear that at least some *one* person will receive full beneficial ownership.

The broad language of the regulations might seem to suggest that any gift whose economic value or enjoyment will be available in part or as a whole at a later time may be treated as a future interest with the result that no annual exclusion would be available. However, the term "future interest" does not refer to the contractual rights that exist in a bond, promissory note (even if it bears no interest until maturity), or in a policy of life insurance the obligations of which are to be discharged by payments in the future. Reg. § 25.2503–3(a). (However, a future interest in such contractual obligations may be created by limitations contained in a trust or other instrument of transfer used in effecting a gift of such obligations.)

In attempting to help describe what *does* constitute a present interest in property, the regulations say that an unrestricted right to the immediate use, possession or enjoyment of property or the income from property (such as a life estate or term certain) is a present interest in property. Therefore, an exclusion is allowable with respect to a gift of such an interest, but not in excess of the value of that interest. Reg. § 25.2503–3(b).

Section 2503(b) states that where there has been a transfer to any person of a present interest in property, the possibility that such interest may be diminished by the exercise of a power shall be disregarded in applying the future interest rule, if no part of such interest will at any time pass to any other person. Thus, for example, if the terms of a trust provide that the income from the trust property is to be paid to A for his life with the remainder payable to B on A's death, and if the trustee has the uncontrolled power to pay the corpus over to A at any time, A's present right to receive the income may be terminated by a distribution of corpus but no portion of the income interest can be diverted to any other person. Therefore, an annual exclusion will be available under § 2503(b) for the value of A's life income interest. Reg. § 25.2503–3(c) (Example 4).

In the case of a transfer in trust, the Supreme Court has held that it is the individual beneficiary, not the trustee, who is the donee for purposes of determining the annual exclusion. Helvering v. Hutchings, 312 U.S. 393 (1941). Therefore, even if the donor of a gift in trust completely divests himself of ownership, dominion and control over the property, he will not be entitled to an annual exclusion unless he can show that an ascertainable beneficiary will receive some present enjoyment from the trust property. As the Supreme Court put it in the leading case of Fondren v. Commissioner, 324 U.S. 18 (1945), the term "present interest" connotes the right to substantial present economic benefit. The question is of the time, not when title vests, but when enjoyment begins. If anything puts the barrier of a substantial period between the wish of the donee or beneficiary to enjoy the gift and actual enjoyment, the gift is one of a future interest.

The determination of what is a future interest for purposes of § 2503(b) can turn out to be very troublesome, particularly in the case of gifts made in trust. Although the underlying rationale of the future interest rule, having to do with the apprehended difficulty in many instances of determining the number of eventual donees and the values of their respective gifts, cannot serve as a perfect guide to the interpretation of the statute, it nevertheless must be kept in mind as providing some guidance to the law. The burden rests with the taxpayer to show that a present interest that is ascertainable in value has been transferred. If an admittedly present interest cannot be valued because it may be reduced or terminated by a power or a succeeding future interest not susceptible of reliable appraisal, the donor will not be entitled to any annual exclusion.

A mandatory accumulation trust will not qualify for an annual exclusion, since even the right to income is limited to commence in use, possession or enjoyment at a future date or time. United States v. Pelzer, 312 U.S. 399 (1941). The same result follows if the trustee is authorized but not required to accumulate income, since the beneficiary is not assured of receiving immediate enjoyment of any of the income from the trust. Reg. § 25.2503–3(c)

(Example 1). Even if the trustee is required to distribute all of the net income each year, no annual exclusion is allowed if the trustee has absolute discretion to allocate the income among several beneficiaries, since the amount of income to be received by each beneficiary rests entirely within the trustee's discretion and cannot be ascertained at the time of the gift. Reg. § 25.2503–3(c) (Example 3).

If the donor makes a gift in trust to pay income to A for life, with remainder at A's death to B, and the trustee has a discretionary power to invade corpus for the benefit of B but that power is limited to a fixed dollar amount or a specific portion of the corpus, A's income interest should be treated as a present interest to the extent it cannot be reduced by an exercise of the trustee's power of invasion. Kniep v. Commissioner, 172 F.2d 755 (8th Cir. 1949).

If the beneficiary of a trust has a power to compel the trustee to pay a fixed sum to him from corpus upon demand, such a power makes the gift a gift of a present interest, even if the beneficiary has no other immediate right to receive income or corpus. Crummey v. Commissioner, 397 F.2d 82 (9th Cir. 1968). Also, the Service concedes that a spendthrift clause which prohibits the income beneficiary from alienating, assigning or otherwise anticipating the income will not in and of itself cause the present right to income to be considered a future interest. Rev. Rul. 54–344, 1954–2 C.B. 319.

A gift of property to a corporation, which is treated as an indirect gift to the shareholders of the corporation, is a gift of future interests. Heringer v.

Commissioner, 235 F.2d 149 (9th Cir. 1956), cert. den., 352 U.S. 927 (1956). In contrast, a gift to another person of shares in an existing corporation generally will be considered a gift of a present interest, in the absence of extraordinary terms restricting the donee's rights as a shareholder. Problems may arise, however, in connection with gifts of interests in a family owned business entity. In one case, gifts made by parents to their children of shares in a limited liability company were held to be gifts of future interests, even though the donees received all of the legal rights originally possessed by the donors, where the donees could not receive any distributions, sell their shares, or withdraw from the company without the consent of the company's manager. The court concluded that the terms of the company's operating agreement foreclosed the donees' ability to realize any substantial present economic benefit from their ownership of the shares. Hackl v. Commissioner, 335 F.3d 664 (7th Cir. 2003).

As these cases and regulations make clear, the focus is upon the certainty of receiving an immediate benefit that is ascertainable in value. If either the fact of receipt or the value of the immediate benefit is uncertain, the gift is of a future interest. Additionally, it is helpful to distinguish the requirements for a completed transfer by gift (i.e., relinquishment by the donor of dominion and control) from the requirements for a present interest (i.e., immediate benefit to the donee). A gift that is incomplete because the donor retained too much power over its enjoyment (see § 39, *supra*) is not subject to gift tax at all. On the other hand, if the very same powers are given to an independent trustee and the donor retains no dominion or control, the trustee's powers will make the gift ineligible for the annual exclusion and hence fully taxable. Therefore, it is necessary to determine whether the donor has made a completed gift before testing to see whether the gift is of a present interest.

The future interest rule is especially troublesome in the case of a gift made to or for the benefit of a minor beneficiary. This problem has been addressed in part by the statute in § 2503(c), to be discussed in the next section. Since § 2503(c) is not exclusive, however, some of the general principles discussed in this section can also apply in the case of a gift to a minor.

§ 57 GIFTS TO MINORS, CRUMMEY TRUSTS, AND § 2503(c)

The future interest rule raises special problems when a gift to a minor is involved. Because of legal disabilities imposed by state law, a minor cannot personally exercise all the rights of property ownership in the same way that an adult donee can.

Because of such disabilities, there was, for a time, concern that even an outright gift to a minor might be treated as a gift of a future interest, and hence be ineligible for the annual exclusion, because of the minor's legal disability to deal fully with his property. This concern was dispelled by the Service in Rev. Rul. 54–400, 1954–2 C.B. 319. So, the annual exclusion is generally available for an outright gift to a minor. (Of course, if the gift is in trust and so limited as to grant a future interest, the exclusion will be unavailable as dictated by the general principles set forth in § 56, *supra*.)

Often, however, a donor may find it convenient or prudent to make a gift to or for the benefit of a minor in the form of a custodianship or trust arrangement, rather than as a direct gift. Before the enactment of I.R.C. § 2503(c) (discussed below), and even thereafter in cases not covered by that provision, there was some uncertainty about whether a gift of property to a trustee for a minor could be regarded as a gift of a present interest. Some courts held that the gift was a transfer of a present interest if the trustee did not have any discretion to withhold payment or if a guardian could demand payment of the income or property on behalf of the minor. See Crummey v. Commissioner, 397 F.2d 82 (9th Cir. 1968); Kieckhefer v. Commissioner, 189 F.2d 118 (7th Cir. 1951). Other courts, however, refused to find a gift of a present interest if no guardian was actually appointed and authorized to act for the minor at the time of the gift. Stifel v. Commissioner, 197 F.2d 107 (2d Cir. 1952).

The Service now accepts the *Crummey* approach. A withdrawal power given to a minor will qualify a transfer in trust as a present interest so long as there is no impediment to the appointment of a guardian who could exercise the withdrawal power on the minor's behalf. Rev. Rul. 73–405, 1973–2 C.B. 321. The beneficiary must be informed of the existence of the withdrawal power and must be given a reasonable opportunity to exercise that power.

Frequently the beneficiary is given a limited period of time in which to exercise the withdrawal power, which will automatically lapse if the beneficiary fails to act. The Service has ruled that a power that lapsed after only two days was "illusory," but has allowed an exclusion for a power that lapsed after 45 days. See Rev. Rul. 81–7, 1981–1 C.B. 474; Rev. Rul. 83–108, 1983–2 C.B. 167.

The uncertainty of the case law led to the enactment in 1954 of § 2503(c). This provision provides a way to obtain an annual exclusion even if the gift is not outright and does not require an immediate payment to or for the benefit of the minor beneficiary.

Section 2503(c) provides that, for purposes of the future interest rule of § 2503(b), no part of a gift to an individual who has not reached the age of 21 years on the date of the transfer shall be considered to be a gift of a future interest in property if the property and the income therefrom may be expended by or for the benefit of the donee before he reaches the age of 21 years and, to the extent not so expended, will pass to the donee when he reaches age 21 or, if he dies before that age, will be payable to the donee's estate or as he may appoint under a general power of appointment. Thus, for example, a gift in trust for a minor child will be eligible for the annual exclusion, even though the child is not immediately entitled to any distributions of income or corpus, if the trustee has unlimited discretion to expend income and corpus for the benefit of the child and all unexpended income and corpus is required to be paid to the child at age 21 (or to the child's estate if the child dies before reaching age 21). Indeed, the income and corpus need not actually be paid to the child at age 21, if the child has a power to demand payment at that time or to extend the trust. Reg. § 25.2503–4. (Note that a properly designed withdrawal power, whether held by a minor or an adult, will make the annual exclusion available under § 2503(b), even if the requirements of § 2503(c) are not met.)

If the requirements of § 2503(c) are fully satisfied, both the income interest and the gift of corpus will qualify for the annual exclusion. It is also possible that some (but not all) of the interests will qualify. For example, suppose the trustee has discretion to distribute or accumulate income until the beneficiary reaches age 21, at which time any undistributed income must be paid to the beneficiary. Thereafter, the trust will continue, with the beneficiary to receive all of the income annually and corpus at age 30. On similar facts, it has been held that the income interest until age 21 (but not the interest in income after age 21 or in corpus) is a present interest which qualifies for the annual exclusion. Commissioner v. Herr, 303 F.2d 780 (3d Cir. 1962). Thus, for purposes of § 2503(c), "property" does not necessarily mean "corpus," but can also refer to a more limited interest such as income during minority. The income interest after age 21 is treated as a future interest under § 2503(b), even though the interest immediately preceding it qualifies as a present interest by virtue of § 2503(c). In other words, the safe harbor of § 2503(c) cannot be stretched to cover an income interest extending beyond age 21. Estate of Levine v. Commissioner, 526 F.2d 717 (2d Cir. 1975).

If the requirements of § 2503(c) are not met, and the donee has no presently exercisable power of withdrawal, a gift in trust for a minor beneficiary may nevertheless qualify as a present interest under the general rules of § 2503(b). For example, if the donor transfers property in trust, with income to be paid annually to a minor beneficiary and corpus to be distributed to the beneficiary at age 25, the beneficiary's right to receive income until age 25 qualifies as a present interest under § 2503(b) but the right to receive corpus at age 25 does not. As a result, the annual exclusion will be available only for the income interest in the year the gift is made. Reg. § 25.2503–4(c). So, if the donor is reluctant to comply with the rules of § 2503(c)—for example, because he is unwilling to give the donee unfettered access to the property at the tender age of 21 or to give the donee a presently exercisable power of withdrawal—it may be possible for at least some interest that does not satisfy the requirements of § 2503(c) to qualify for the annual exclusion under § 2503(b).

All of the states have enacted some version of the Uniform Transfers to Minors Act (or its predecessor, the Uniform Gifts to Minors Act), which authorizes gifts of stocks, bonds, and other property to be made to a minor donee in custodianship form. The Service has ruled that gifts made pursuant to such a statute will qualify for the annual exclusion. Rev. Rul. 59–357, 1959–2 C.B. 212.

§ 58 ESTATE TAX EXCLUSION FOR QUALIFIED CONSERVATION EASEMENTS: § 2031(c)

Section 2031(c), enacted in 1997, allows the decedent's executor to elect to exclude from the gross estate a portion of the value of land that is subject to a "qualified conservation easement." To be eligible for the exclusion, the land must be located in the United States (or a U.S. possession) and must have been owned by the decedent or by a family member at all times during the three-year period ending at the date of the decedent's death. The easement must impose a perpetual restriction on the use of the land and must be granted to a qualified organization "exclusively for conservation purposes" by the decedent, by a family member, or by the decedent's executor or trustee. Eligible "conservation purposes" include the preservation of land areas for outdoor recreation or education of the general public, protection of a natural habitat or ecosystem, and preservation of open space for scenic enjoyment or pursuant to a governmental conservation policy. I.R.C. §§ 170(h)(4) and 2031(c)(8).

The election to claim the § 2031(c) exclusion must be made by the executor on a timely-filed estate tax return. I.R.C. § 2031(c)(6).

The amount of the § 2031(c) exclusion is based on the value of the land, after any estate tax charitable deduction allowable for the grant of the qualified conservation easement. In general, the amount of the exclusion is equal to 40% of the net value of the land, subject to a ceiling of $500,000. The full benefit of the

40% exclusion is available only if the qualified conservation easement reduces the value of the land by at least 30%; for each percentage point below the 30% threshold, the exclusion must be reduced by two percentage points. Thus, the easement must reduce the value of the land by more than 10% to produce even a partial exclusion. I.R.C. § 2031(c)(1) through (c)(3). The statute contains special rules governing the treatment of debt-financed property and retained development rights. I.R.C. § 2031(c)(4) and (c)(5).

The estate tax exclusion under § 2031(c) involves an income tax tradeoff. To the extent the § 2031(c) exclusion is allowed in determining the gross estate, the decedent's successors will take a carryover basis (rather than a fresh-start basis) in the land for income tax purposes. I.R.C. § 1014(a)(4).

CHAPTER 12

DEDUCTIONS: ESTATE AND GIFT TAX

§ 59 ESTATE TAX DEDUCTIONS FOR EXPENSES, DEBTS, TAXES, LOSSES: §§ 2053 AND 2054

I.R.C. § 2051 provides that the value of the *taxable estate* shall be determined by deducting from the value of the *gross estate* the *deductions* provided for in the statute. The taxable estate, thus determined, is the base against which the tax rates of I.R.C. § 2001 are applied. (The rates themselves are, of course, a function of all the post-1976 gratuitous transfers of the decedent, including inter vivos gifts. See § 13, *supra.*)

In determining the taxable estate, I.R.C. § 2053(a) grants a *deduction* from the gross estate for several items, including funeral expenses, administration expenses, claims against the estate and unpaid mortgages on, or indebtedness in respect of, property whose value is included in the decedent's gross estate undiminished by such mortgage or indebtedness. These deductions are allowed for such expenses or claims only to the extent that they are "allowable by the laws of the jurisdiction" under which the estate is being administered. The regulations provide detailed guidance about the scope and terms of the particular items for which deductions are allowable under § 2053(a). See Reg. §§ 20.2053–1 through 20.2053–10.

At first glance, the statutory language of § 2053(a)(2) might appear to allow a deduction for any item that is allowable as an administration expense under the local law governing the administration of the estate. Nevertheless, the regulations impose a considerably more stringent test. According to the regulations, the deduction under § 2053(a)(2) is limited to such expenses as are actually and necessarily incurred in the administration of the decedent's estate, i.e., in the collection of assets, payment of debts, and distribution of the property to the persons entitled to it. As a result, no deduction is allowed for expenditures that are not essential to the proper settlement of the estate but are incurred for the individual benefit of the heirs, legatees, or devisees. Reg. § 20.2053–3(a). In effect, the regulations set forth an independent federal tax law definition of "administration expenses" which must be met in addition to the requirements of applicable state law for the deduction to be allowed. The regulations are of long standing and have repeatedly been upheld against challenges in the courts. See Hibernia Bank v. United States, 581 F.2d 741 (9th Cir. 1978).

Items deductible under the general rule of § 2053(a) will not be allowed to the extent they exceed the value of property subject to claims, except to the extent the amounts have actually been paid before the due date for filing the estate tax return. I.R.C. § 2053(c)(2). For this purpose, "property subject to claims" refers to property which is includable in the gross estate and which would bear the burden of payment for such items under applicable state law (e.g., probate assets). Under this rule, the deduction for items described in § 2053(a) is ordinarily limited to the value of property subject to claims. However, even amounts in excess of the value of property subject to claims may be deducted if they are in fact paid from other property within the specified time period. Reg. § 20.2053–1(c).

Section 2053(b) allows, in addition, a deduction for amounts representing expenses incurred in administering property that is included in the gross estate but is "not subject to claims" (i.e., property passing outside the probate estate), to the same extent that such amounts would be allowable as a deduction under § 2053(a) if such property were subject to claims, but only if those amounts are actually paid before the expiration of the limitation period for assessment of tax (ordinarily three years from the filing of the return). For example, this provision would allow a deduction for expenses involved in winding up an irrevocable trust which the decedent created during life and which terminated at his death. See Reg. § 20.2053–8.

Section 2053(c) imposes several limitations on the deductions available under § 2053(a) and (b). One of the most important is set forth in § 2053(c)(1)(A), which provides that the deduction allowed in the case of claims against the estate, unpaid mortgages or any indebtedness shall, when founded on a promise or agreement, be limited to the extent that they were contracted bona fide and for an adequate and full consideration in money or money's worth. This provision prevents a taxpayer from converting a nondeductible bequest into a deductible payment of a claim merely by making an enforceable promise to transfer property at death. For example, if a husband and wife agree, pursuant to a common testamentary plan, to leave their collective property to the survivor at the death of the first spouse and then to another beneficiary at the death of the survivor, the payment to the last beneficiary cannot be deducted as a claim against the estate, even though it is enforceable as a contractual obligation under applicable state law. Bank of New York v. United States, 526 F.2d 1012 (3d Cir. 1975).

In the event of a promise of a gift to charity, the limitation for consideration in money or money's worth does not apply, but the deduction will be allowed only to the extent that the promise would qualify for a charitable deduction under § 2055 if it constituted a bequest. I.R.C. § 2053(c)(1)(A). The requirement of consideration in money or money's worth is also inapplicable to liabilities imposed by law or arising out of torts, since these claims are not founded on a promise or agreement. In any event, amounts that may be deducted as claims against the estate are limited to personal obligations of the decedent existing at his death, plus interest accrued to the date of death. Reg. § 20.2053–4.

Any income taxes on income received after the death of the decedent, or property taxes not accrued before his death, or any estate, succession, legacy or inheritance taxes, are not deductible under § 2053. I.R.C. § 2053(c)(1)(B). On the deductibility of taxes in general, see Reg. § 20.2053–6.

Notwithstanding the rule of § 2053(c)(1)(B), the executor may elect to deduct certain foreign death taxes imposed on a charitable bequest, if the resulting decrease in the federal estate tax will inure solely for the benefit of the charitable organization. I.R.C. § 2053(d). If the executor elects to claim a deduction for such taxes under § 2053(d), the credit that would otherwise be allowable under § 2014 will be correspondingly reduced. The credit under § 2014 is discussed in § 73, *infra.*

To qualify for a deduction under § 2053, a claim or expense must represent an enforceable obligation of the decedent or of his or her estate. The rights and obligations of the decedent under applicable state law bear heavily on the allowability of the deduction. In a community property state, for example, the decedent may be personally liable for the full amount of a community debt but may also be entitled to contribution from the surviving spouse for one-half of the debt. In such a case, the deduction under § 2053 will be limited to one-half of the debt, corresponding to the decedent's net personal liability. Similarly, a mortgage indebtedness on community property can be deducted only to the extent of one-half. If only half of the community property is includable in the decedent's gross estate for tax purposes, even though all of it comes under the control of the executor for purposes of administration, only one-half of the expenses incurred in administering the community property can be deducted, unless the expense is specifically allocable to the decedent's share of the community property.

These principles and the complexities that community property law introduces are illustrated by United States v. Stapf, 375 U.S. 118 (1963). In that case, the will of a decedent in a community property state directed his executors to pay all of the community debts and administration expenses if his wife elected to take under the will and forego her interest in the community property. (Under applicable state law, the decedent was personally liable for the full amount of the community debts, with a right to proceed against the wife's share of the community property for half of that amount.) Although the wife accepted the terms of the will, the Supreme Court held that the estate was entitled to deduct only half of the debts and an allocable portion of the expenses because the amounts chargeable against the wife's share of the community property could not realistically be deemed personal obligations of the decedent or claims against his estate. The Court characterized the payment by the estate of more than the decedent's share of the debts and expenses as a bequest to the surviving spouse, rather than the payment of a deductible claim or expense.

The regulations under § 2053 limit the deduction to amounts actually paid in settlement or satisfaction of a claim or expense. Reg. § 20.2053–1(d)(1). Under this general rule, an otherwise eligible claim or expense may be deducted on the estate tax return if the item has already been paid or if the amount to be paid "is ascertainable with reasonable certainty and will be paid"; however, no deduction is allowed based on a vague or uncertain estimate. Reg. § 20.2053–1(d)(4). The regulations further provide that, in determining the amount of the deduction, events occurring after death and before the expiration of the limitation period for assessment of tax (ordinarily three years from the filing of the return) shall be taken into account. Reg. § 20.2053–1(d)(2). Consequently, no deduction is allowed for items that are contested or contingent as to the amount or the certainty of future payment at the time the estate tax return is filed. To preserve the ability to claim a deduction upon subsequent payment of such items, the executor should file a protective claim for refund. Reg. § 20.2053–1(d)(5). For a more detailed exposition of these requirements as well as special rules for certain types of claims, with illustrative examples, see Reg. § 20.2053–4.

I.R.C. § 2054 allows a deduction for losses incurred during the settlement of the estate if the loss arises from fire, storm, shipwreck or other casualty or from theft, when the loss is not compensated for by insurance or otherwise. If the loss is partly compensated, the excess over the compensation may be deducted. Reg. § 20.2054–1.

In general, the items allowed by §§ 2053 and 2054 operate as deductions from the gross estate in arriving at the amount of the taxable estate. Broadly speaking, these items represent costs of transferring property at death, which reduce the net value of property passing from the decedent to the beneficiaries. The net value transferred is the base used for determining the amount of tax in a system based on "ability to pay." The correct determination of the taxable base is essential to horizontal equity and vertical equity in the tax law.

In a system with graduated tax rates, a deduction (or an exemption or an exclusion, but not a credit) serves to reduce the *marginal* rate of tax and thus it has a "wealth-variant" quality. For example, a funeral expense deduction of $1,000 will have a different tax effect in the case of a decedent with a large gross estate than it will in the case of a decedent with a small gross estate. The $1,000 deduction will reduce the tax liability of the estate by an amount equal to $1,000 times the marginal rate of tax payable "at the top" by the estate. Thus, a $1,000 deduction for an estate in the 40% bracket would save $400 in tax, but a deduction of the same amount for a smaller estate in the 20% bracket (i.e., a taxable estate over $10,000 but not over $20,000) would save only $200 in tax. This "wealth-variant" (or more properly, "estate-size-variant") effect of the deduction is perfectly proper in a tax system with a graduated rate schedule. A larger net estate pays tax at a higher rate and hence should be relieved of more tax than a smaller net estate when it incurs a deductible expense. In recent years the wealth-variant effect has largely disappeared from the transfer tax area as a result of changes in the unified tax rate schedule and the unified credit. Since 2013, the top marginal rate has been set at 40% on taxable transfers in excess of $1 million, and beginning in 2026 the unified credit is functionally equivalent to an exemption from tax for the first $15 million (indexed for inflation) of taxable transfers; in effect, the gift and estate taxes are imposed at a flat rate of 40% on taxable transfers above the inflation-indexed $15 million exemption equivalent. Nevertheless, the lower rate brackets for estates of $1 million or less retain some residual significance. For instance, the lower rate brackets may apply to the estate of a nonresident decedent who was not a U.S. citizen, as a result of the limited unified credit allowable under I.R.C. § 2102(b) in such cases.

I.R.C. § 642(g) provides that an estate may not claim deductions for the items described in §§ 2053 or 2054 both on its estate tax return and on its income tax return. No double deduction is permitted; in order to obtain an income tax deduction for such items (or to offset expenses of selling property against the sales price in determining gain or loss for income tax purposes), the executor must waive the right to claim an estate tax deduction under §§ 2053 or 2054. As a result, the executor often has a choice to deduct all or part of an item (e.g., an administration expense or a casualty loss) against either the estate tax or the income tax, whichever will produce the greatest tax saving, but not against both. A similar rule applies to deductions for items described in §§ 2621(a)(2) and 2622(b) of the generation-skipping transfer tax. The rule against double deductions does not apply, however, to deductions in respect of a decedent described in I.R.C. § 691(b).

At one time a deduction was allowed for amounts expended from the estate for the support of dependents of the decedent during the period of estate administration. This deduction was removed from the Code in 1950, shortly after the introduction of the marital deduction. Therefore, even though the executor may be authorized by state law to expend funds for the support of a surviving spouse or other dependents, such expenditures cannot be deducted from the gross estate in arriving at the taxable estate, unless they qualify for the marital deduction.

§ 60 ESTATE TAX CHARITABLE CONTRIBUTION DEDUCTION: § 2055

I.R.C. § 2055 allows a deduction, in determining the taxable estate, for the amount of all bequests, legacies, devises, or transfers to a governmental entity for exclusively public purposes, or to a corporation, trust or association organized and operated exclusively for religious, charitable, scientific, or educational purposes, or to a veterans' organization, as described in the statute. Like its counterparts in the income and gift taxes, the estate tax charitable deduction serves to encourage charitable contributions and to provide an incentive for such socially desirable activity. To the extent the activity supported by deduction-induced contributions provides benefits and services that otherwise would have to be financed by government, the charitable deduction serves to reduce the cost of government at the same time that government foregoes some tax revenue. The estate and gift tax charitable deductions are unlimited in amount; they include no percentage limitations comparable to those found in the income tax. Consequently, even a very wealthy taxpayer can avoid incurring any estate tax liability by arranging to make charitable bequests or gifts, in qualifying form, of any property that would otherwise be exposed to estate or gift tax.

Section 2055 and its accompanying regulations specify in some detail the kinds of organizations that qualify for deductible bequests. In general, the recipient must be organized and operated exclusively for charitable purposes, no part of its net earnings may inure to the benefit of private stockholders or individuals (other than as a legitimate object of its charitable purposes), no substantial part of its activities may consist of attempting to influence legislation, and it must not participate in political campaigns. (There is no provision in the estate tax comparable to the statutory exemptions in the gift tax for contributions to political organizations and to tax-exempt social welfare organizations, labor organizations, and trade associations, discussed in § 23, *supra.*)

If the decedent possessed a power of appointment as a result of which the property subject to the power was included in the gross estate, the estate is entitled to a charitable deduction for amounts actually received by a qualifying organization as a result of the exercise, failure to exercise, release, or lapse of the power. I.R.C. § 2055(b).

The regulations have long imposed restrictions on the availability of the charitable deduction, in order to ensure that amounts for which a charitable deduction is allowed will in fact be used for charitable purposes and not diverted to other uses. If property is transferred for both a charitable and a private purpose, the deduction is allowed for the charitable interest only insofar as that interest is presently ascertainable, and hence severable from the noncharitable interest. Reg. § 20.2055–2(a). If, at the date of the decedent's death, a transfer for charitable purposes is conditioned to become effective upon the performance of some act or the happening of some event, no deduction is allowable unless the possibility of the charitable transfer not taking effect is so remote as to be negligible. Moreover, if the recipient or trustee is empowered to invade or consume the property or otherwise divert it from charitable purposes, the deduction is limited to that portion, if any, of the property or fund which is exempt from an exercise of the power. Reg. § 20.2055–2(b)(1).

Prior to the enactment of § 2055(e)(2) in 1969, a much-litigated question was whether a charitable deduction was allowable if property was transferred in trust to pay income to an individual for life and at his or her death to pay the remainder to a charity. The courts held that the present value of the charitable remainder interest could be deducted to the extent that the interest was presently ascertainable and substantially certain to take effect. However, the deduction was not allowed if the remainder was subject to a condition precedent such as the deaths of the decedent's wife and of his unmarried, childless 27-year-old daughter without surviving issue, since there was a more than negligible chance that the charity would not receive anything at all. Commissioner v. Estate of Sternberger, 348 U.S. 187 (1955). Similarly, the deduction was denied where a trustee was given such broad discretion to invade corpus for the income beneficiaries that the value of the charitable remainder interest could not be readily ascertained. Merchants National Bank v. Commissioner, 320 U.S. 256 (1943). Given the innumerable variations in the drafting of powers of invasion and in the personal and financial circumstances of individual income beneficiaries, courts encountered considerable difficulty in applying the general principles set forth in the regulations. Congress finally intervened in 1969 by enacting § 2055(e)(2), which imposes strict limitations on the deductibility of split-interest charitable bequests. The split-interest rules of § 2055(e)(2) are discussed in § 62, *infra*.

As government faces ever-increasing budgetary constraints, the efficiency of the charitable contribution deduction as a way of providing support to charitable organizations or relieving government of some burdens of providing social benefits deserves closer scrutiny. In particular, the "wealth-variant" effect of the charitable deduction raises difficult questions of policy. A deduction for a contribution of, say, $1,000 to charity will have a very different impact in a very large estate than in a small estate. The after-tax cost for a very wealthy decedent to make a gift of $1,000 to his favorite charity can be as little as $600 ($1,000 contribution minus $400 saved in taxes by the deduction for an estate in the 40% bracket yields a net cost of $600 to the taxpayer). For a taxpayer who, as a result of other deductions, credits or exemptions, would have no taxable estate, the charitable contribution deduction afforded by § 2055 provides no benefit at all. The after-tax cost of his gift is equal to the amount of the gift—$1,000 in the example. This wealth-variant effect may appear unjust, but it must be remembered that in the case of the high-bracket estate the deduction merely relieves the estate of the relatively high tax it would have had to pay if the gift had gone to a private beneficiary instead of a charitable organization. Moreover, as an incentive, the deduction may stimulate more charitable giving by giving proportionally greater tax benefits to larger estates for each dollar contributed.

It would be possible to construct an allowance for charitable contributions that would not be "wealth-variant." For example, each taxpayer might be given a *credit* against his tax of some percentage of the amount he contributed to charity. Then, the dollar-for-dollar benefit of a charitable contribution would be the same for very wealthy decedents and for not-so-wealthy decedents. (Such a credit could even be made to be refundable to the extent it exceeded the tax payable.) Or, the deduction might be geared to a percentage formula so as to provide a tax benefit that did not vary with the size of the estate. More radically, the tax benefit could be made to vary *inversely* or to phase-out with the size of the estate, so that a greater tax saving per dollar of contribution would be afforded to poorer taxpayers than to richer ones. All in all, whether the deduction should remain in the Code or should be repealed or should be converted to some other form of tax allowance is a question that merits further analysis; the existing structure need not be taken for granted. Similar rethinking led to the unification of gift and estate tax rates and the enactment of the unified credit in 1976.

Racial and Other Discrimination. Whether an educational or other charitable organization remains eligible to receive tax-deductible contributions (and tax-exempt income) if it practices racial discrimination has been a controversial issue. In the late 1960s and early 1970s, the Service ruled that racial discrimination would disqualify a nonprofit recreational or educational institution as a tax-exempt organization eligible to receive tax-deductible contributions. Rev. Rul. 67–325, 1967–2 C.B. 113; Rev. Rul. 71–447, 1971–2 C.B. 230. Eventually, the Supreme Court upheld the validity of Rev. Rul. 71–447 and concluded that a nonprofit private school's tax-exempt status was properly revoked by reason of its racially discriminatory policies, in a case that surely stands for the same principle for estate and gift tax purposes. Bob Jones University v. United States, 461 U.S. 574 (1983).

§ 61 GIFT TAX CHARITABLE CONTRIBUTION DEDUCTION: § 2522

I.R.C. § 2522 allows a gift tax deduction for transfers to charities parallel to the deduction in the estate tax. As a result, contributions to charities are not treated as taxable gifts, largely in order to encourage (or to avoid discouraging) such donations. See generally Reg. §§ 25.2522(a)–1 through 25.2522(d)–1. This deduction, like the charitable deduction in the estate tax, has a "wealth-variant" or "gift-variant" quality. That is to say, a taxpayer who has considerable wealth and who has made substantial gifts in the past will save more in gift taxes by making a deductible gift to a charity in lieu of a taxable gift to some other recipient than will a poorer taxpayer. The basis for this effect is revealed by a glance at the graduated transfer tax rates set forth in § 2001(c) and incorporated by reference in § 2502. A "limiting case" of the wealth-variant effect of the charitable gift deduction is that of the taxpayer who has not sufficiently used up his or her annual exclusions to have to pay any tax on a non-charitable contribution. For such a taxpayer, no tax is saved by making a charitable rather than a non-deductible gift. As a result, no incentive is provided to make a deductible charitable contribution rather than a non-deductible gift.

§ 62 DISALLOWANCE OF CHARITABLE DEDUCTIONS—ESTATE TAX AND GIFT TAX: §§ 2055(e)(2) AND 2522(c)(2)

The Tax Reform Act of 1969 imposed significant restrictions on the availability of charitable deductions for contributions of partial interests in property. The estate and gift tax provisions are found in I.R.C. §§ 2055(e)(2) and 2522(c)(2), respectively. (For a parallel set of provisions in the income tax area, see I.R.C. § 170(f).) These provisions were added to prevent taxpayers from obtaining deductions for the present value of interests given to charity which were calculated according to general valuation principles but often turned out to be much larger than the amount eventually received by the charity. For example, under prior law a transferor could create a trust to pay income to a private beneficiary for life, with a power in the trustee to invade corpus for the support of the income beneficiary; at the death of the beneficiary, the remaining trust property would go to charity. Under the general rules discussed in § 60, *supra,* a deduction would be allowed for the present value of the charitable remainder if that interest was presently ascertainable and substantially certain to take effect. However, the amount actually received by the charity might turn out to be much less than initially estimated, if the trust corpus were depleted through invasions for the income beneficiary or through investment policies skewed in favor of the income beneficiary.

The split-interest rules of §§ 2055(e)(2) and 2522(c)(2) are highly technical. In general, these provisions deny a charitable deduction where an interest in property is transferred to charity and another interest in the same property passes to a non-charitable beneficiary (or is retained by the transferor, in the case of an inter vivos transfer). The statute then carves out exceptions for certain types of interests that can be valued relatively easily and accurately: a charitable remainder interest in trust following an annuity or a unitrust interest; a charitable remainder interest in a pooled income fund; or a charitable lead interest in the form of an annuity or a unitrust interest. (Conceptually, the provisions for annuity and unitrust interests are quite similar to the safe harbor provisions of § 2702 which permit certain retained interests to be valued under general valuation principles, as discussed in § 49, *supra.*) A deduction is still allowed for the present value of a charitable interest that falls within one of the statutory exceptions, but no deduction is allowed for other interests, whether passing to charity or to private beneficiaries.

Thus, § 2055(e)(2) disallows a deduction for a bequest of a remainder interest to charity unless it is in the form of a charitable remainder annuity trust or unitrust (described in I.R.C. § 664) or a pooled income fund (described in I.R.C. § 642(c)(5)). Section 2522(c)(2) does the same in the gift tax context. A charitable remainder trust is one which provides for payments, at least annually, to one or more non-charitable beneficiaries for life or for a term of not more than 20 years, followed by a remainder to charity. The trust must be irrevocable and must not be subject to invasion for any non-charitable beneficiary (other than the required annual payments). The value of the charitable remainder interest must be at least 10% of the net fair market value of the trust property at inception. In a charitable remainder annuity trust, the annual payments must be in the form of a fixed dollar annuity which is not less than 5% nor more than 50% of the net fair market value of the trust property at inception. In a charitable remainder unitrust, the annual payments must be in the form of a fixed percentage—not less than 5% nor more than 50%—of the net fair market value of the trust property, valued annually. A pooled income fund is a fund maintained by the charitable recipient, which receives funds from a number of contributors and pays income from the commingled funds in ratable shares to the contributors or other beneficiaries for life with the remainder payable at death to the charity.

The restrictions of §§ 2055(e)(2) and 2522(c)(2) on split-interest transfers do not apply to a contribution of a remainder interest in a personal residence or farm, a contribution of an undivided portion of the transferor's entire interest in property, or a qualified conservation contribution. Thus, the present value of such contributions remains eligible for the charitable deduction.

Under a special rule enacted in 1981, a work of art and the copyright thereon are treated as two separate properties. The charitable deduction is allowed for a transfer of *either* the work *or* the copyright to a § 501(c)(3) organization (other than a private non-operating foundation), if the organization's use of the property is related to its exempt purpose. I.R.C. §§ 2055(e)(4) and 2522(c)(3). This rule allows a taxpayer to deduct a charitable bequest or gift of tangible art works while retaining private ownership of the copyright therein, or vice versa.

§ 63 ESTATE TAX DEDUCTION FOR QUALIFIED FAMILY-OWNED BUSINESS INTERESTS: § 2057

I.R.C. § 2057 has had a checkered history. In 1976 Congress added former § 2057, which authorized an estate tax deduction for property passing from the decedent to a minor child if the decedent left no surviving spouse and the child had no known living parent. The purpose of this so-called "orphan's deduction" was to relieve the estate tax burden and provide greater support for the decedent's immediate family in cases where the marital deduction was not available because there was no surviving spouse. The deduction was limited in amount to $5,000 per minor child, times the difference between 21 and the minor's age at the date of the decedent's death. This provision was repealed in 1981, at the same time that the amount of the unified credit was significantly increased.

In 1986 Congress enacted a completely different version of former § 2057. This provision allowed a deduction for half of the proceeds from certain sales of "qualified employer securities" to an employee stock ownership plan or an eligible worker-owned cooperative. This deduction was intended to promote the formation of qualified employee benefit plans which would provide retirement benefits and give employees an equity interest in their corporate employers. This provision was repealed in 1989.

In 1998 Congress enacted still another version of § 2057 which allowed an estate tax deduction of up to $675,000 for the adjusted value of "qualified family-owned business interests" that were included in the gross estate. (This version of § 2057 replaced a similar provision originally enacted in 1997 as former § 2033A.) This deduction was aimed at active, closely held businesses in which the decedent and members of his family had a substantial and continuing role and which constituted a substantial portion of the decedent's property. The deduction was available, at the election of the executor, if the detailed technical requirements of the statute were met, including the filing of a recapture agreement in which all persons who had an interest in specified qualified family-owned business interests agreed to pay an additional estate tax in the event of cessation of material participation, disposition of an interest, or expatriation. This version of § 2057 was repealed by the 2001 Act, effective for estates of decedents dying after 2003. Thus, under current law § 2057 has no operative effect.

§ 64 ESTATE TAX DEDUCTION FOR STATE DEATH TAXES: § 2058

I.R.C. § 2058, added by the 2001 Act, allows an estate tax deduction for the amount of any estate, inheritance, legacy or succession taxes actually paid within a specified period to a state with respect to property included in the gross estate. This deduction replaces the similar allowance made in the form of a credit under former § 2011, discussed in § 73, *infra*. Section 2058 is effective for estates of decedents dying after 2004.

§ 65 DEDUCTIONS IN THE GENERATION-SKIPPING TRANSFER TAX

Deductions found in the generation-skipping transfer tax were described in earlier sections of this book outlining the federal transfer taxes, and will not be repeated here. See §§ 6 and 15, *supra*.

CHAPTER 13

THE MARITAL DEDUCTION AND SPLIT GIFTS

§ 66 INTRODUCTION TO THE MARITAL DEDUCTION AND SPLIT GIFTS

I.R.C. § 2056 allows a marital deduction in the estate tax for the value of property passing from the decedent to his or her surviving spouse. I.R.C. § 2523 grants a similar marital deduction in the gift tax for gifts made by a donor during life to his or her spouse. I.R.C. § 2513 permits gifts by a husband or wife to a third party to be treated as if made one-half by each spouse. These statutory rules, to be explored in greater detail in the following sections, first entered the Code in 1948 and presently provide important opportunities as well as obstacles for the estate planner.

The primary purpose of the marital deduction, as originally enacted in 1948, was to allow a spouse to pass non-community property to his or her surviving spouse with the same tax consequences that would have obtained if the spouses had lived and saved and transferred property in a community property system, so long as the separate property taxpayers were in fact in roughly the same economic position as community property taxpayers. Thus, the marital deduction rules have their roots in community property laws, whose tax advantages the marital deduction is designed to neutralize.

Early in the development of the modern federal tax system, the Supreme Court held that income earned by a married taxpayer in a community property state was taxable only half to him; the other half was taxable to his or her spouse, since the non-earning spouse was entitled to half the income as a matter of state law. By the same token, half the income from property owned as community property was taxable to each spouse. Similarly, at the death of one spouse, only half the couple's community property was regarded as owned by the decedent and hence includable in his or her gross estate, even if all the property had originated with the decedent's efforts or other sources. Under a parallel rule, if one spouse made a gift of community property, the gift was considered to be made one-half by each spouse. These income, estate and gift tax rules, which mirrored state property law, provided very substantial tax savings for spouses living in community property states compared to spouses living in separate property states.

To remove the difference in tax consequences between community property and separate property systems, Congress first attempted to eliminate the estate and gift tax advantages formerly enjoyed by spouses living in community property states. Legislation in 1942 was directed toward this end. The income tax advantages of community property law, however, remained untouched, and several states that historically had operated under the common-law, separate property system changed or attempted to change to community property law, solely because of its federal tax advantages.

In 1948 Congress enacted the income tax joint-return and split-income rules in order to give essentially the same income tax treatment to separate property spouses as was available to community property spouses. At the same time, amendments were made in the estate and gift tax laws in order to remove the discrepancies in treatment between separate property and community property states. The marital deduction and split-gift provisions originally were enacted in order to grant to separate property spouses the transfer tax advantages that only community property spouses had enjoyed before the 1942 legislation. The starting point for understanding the marital deduction and split-gift provisions is § 2056, the marital deduction provision of the estate tax.

§ 67 THE ESTATE TAX MARITAL DEDUCTION: § 2056

Prior to the 1976 Act, § 2056 allowed a deduction from the gross estate, in determining the taxable estate, of an amount equal to the value of property passing to the surviving spouse to the extent that the property transferred did not exceed *one half* of the decedent's *adjusted gross estate,* and so long as other conditions were met. (The "adjusted gross estate" was generally defined as the decedent's gross estate minus the deductions allowed under §§ 2053 and 2054.) The marital deduction was generally denied with respect to community property, however, because even without the deduction the surviving spouse took one half of the community property held at death without any inclusion in the decedent's gross estate. If the estate consisted entirely of community property and the decedent left his or her share of that property to the surviving spouse, the marital bequest was subject to estate tax. The 50% marital deduction produced a similar tax result for a marital bequest of the decedent's own separate property. The surviving spouse could take up to one half of the separate property tax-free, but a marital bequest of separate property in excess of the 50% limitation was subject to estate tax.

In the years leading up to the 1976 Act, several proposals (including an influential 1969 Treasury proposal) had suggested that interspousal transfers should not be subject to the transfer taxes at all. The theory was that, as between husband and wife, such transfers should be regarded as nontaxable arrangements for the technical title holding of shared marital wealth; in other words, for transfer tax purposes, the married couple should be treated as a unit, with transfer tax consequences to follow only upon the transfer of property outside the marital unit to younger generations or other beneficiaries. This idea—a complete interspousal exemption or "unlimited marital deduction"—was not fully embraced by Congress in 1976, but did eventually prevail in the 1981 Act.

The 1976 Act did introduce what can be characterized as a "limited 100% marital deduction" in both the estate and gift tax contexts. This was accomplished by allowing a marital deduction in the estate tax equal to the greater of $250,000 or the old 50% limit, thus providing a 100% deduction for transfers of amounts up to $250,000. (The $250,000 amount was subject to complex adjustments in cases involving community property.) For smaller estates, this did indeed amount to a 100% deduction and it sometimes was referred to as the "small estate" marital deduction.

The 1981 Act removed all quantitative limits on the marital deduction, for the estates of decedents dying after 1981. As a result, the original purpose of the marital deduction, to eliminate disparate treatment of married couples in community property and separate property states, was superseded by the more sweeping goal of allowing unlimited tax-free transfers between spouses during marriage and at the death of the first spouse. The gift tax marital deduction is described in § 70, *infra*.

In allowing a marital deduction for transfers from the decedent to his or her surviving spouse, § 2056 requires that the transfer be of an *interest in property* which is included in the gross estate and which *passes* from the decedent to the surviving spouse. The requirement that the interest be included in the decedent's gross estate modifies the broad language of § 2056(a) allowing the deduction for any interest in property which "passes or has passed from the decedent to his surviving spouse," and ensures that the deduction is available only for transfers that would otherwise be subject to estate tax. Also, if the interest is to be paid out of assets some of which would not qualify for the marital deduction, the value of the otherwise eligible interest must be reduced by the value of the ineligible assets. To prevent the possibility of a double deduction, the regulations provide that no marital deduction is allowed for an interest passing to the surviving spouse to the extent that another deduction is allowed for the same interest under §§ 2053 or 2054. Reg. § 20.2056(a)–2(b).

For purposes of the marital deduction, property is considered as passing from the decedent to a recipient who takes the property by bequest, devise, or inheritance, by right of survivorship, pursuant to a life insurance beneficiary designation, under a power of appointment, or indeed by transfer from the decedent at any time. I.R.C. § 2056(c). The regulations confirm that property received by the surviving spouse by reason of an election against the decedent's will is treated as passing from the decedent to the spouse for purposes of the marital deduction. Reg. § 20.2056(c)–2(c); see also Reg. § 20.2056(c)–2(d), concerning property received pursuant to a will contest.

Qualified disclaimers are to be taken into account in determining whether particular property passes from a decedent to a surviving spouse. For example, if a child makes a qualified disclaimer of an intestate share of a deceased parent's estate, causing the disclaimed share to pass to the decedent's surviving spouse, that share will be treated as passing directly to the spouse and will qualify for the marital deduction. The converse is also true: if an interest passes to another person as a result of a qualified disclaimer by the surviving spouse, no marital deduction will be allowed for the disclaimed interest.

Whether a person is recognized as the "surviving spouse" of the decedent for federal tax purposes is generally a function of the decedent's marital status as determined under applicable state law. For estate tax purposes, the relevant law is normally that of the state where the decedent was domiciled at death, which has primary jurisdiction over the administration of the estate. Problems can arise where the validity of a marriage is called in question because, for example, one of the parties was previously married and obtained a divorce in another jurisdiction on grounds that are not recognized under the law of the decedent's state of domicile.

The legal status of same-sex couples has changed dramatically in recent years. In United States v. Windsor, 570 U.S. 744 (2013), the Supreme Court held that a decedent's bequests to her same-sex spouse were eligible for an estate tax marital deduction, and struck down on constitutional grounds a federal statute that defined marriage to mean the legal union of one man and one woman as husband and wife for purposes of federal law. Two years later, in Obergefell v. Hodges, 576 U.S. 644 (2015), the Court held that state laws defining marriage to exclude same-sex couples violate federal constitutional guarantees of due process and equal protection. As a result, "same-sex couples may exercise the fundamental right to marry in all States," and "there is no lawful basis for a State to refuse to recognize a lawful same-sex marriage performed in another State on the ground of its same-sex character." In 2016 the Treasury promulgated regulations to reflect the holdings in *Windsor* and

Obergefell. For federal tax purposes, the terms "spouse," "husband," and "wife" mean "an individual lawfully married to another individual," and the phrase "husband and wife" means "two individuals lawfully married to each other." Reg. § 301.7701–18(a). Further, a marriage between two individuals is recognized for federal tax purposes if the marriage is recognized by the state where the marriage was entered into, regardless of the couple's domicile; in the case of a foreign marriage, the couple is deemed married if their relationship would be recognized as a marriage under the laws of any U.S. state. Reg. § 301.7701–18(b). However, the federal tax definition of marriage excludes "a registered domestic partnership, civil union, or other similar formal relationship not denominated as a marriage" under applicable state law. Reg. § 301.7701–18(c).

In addition to the threshold requirements of § 2056(a), the transfer must comply with the highly technical requirements of the "terminable interest rule" set forth in § 2056(b); the deduction may be lost entirely if the interest passing to the surviving spouse constitutes a prohibited terminable interest. The terminable interest rule and its several exceptions are designed to make sure that any property that is sheltered from estate tax at the death of the first spouse will eventually be subject to gift or estate tax upon a subsequent transfer by the surviving spouse during life or at death. The terminable interest rule is discussed in § 68, *infra.* The regulations under § 2056 provide extensive guidance in explaining the meaning and operation of the marital deduction. See Reg. §§ 20.2056(a)–1 through 20.2056(d)–3.

In sum, the marital deduction offers enormous flexibility to married couples in arranging their financial affairs. Because there is no longer any quantitative limit on the amount of property that can pass tax-free between spouses during the marriage or at death, a married couple can decide whether to hold their combined property in equal shares or in some other ratio without incurring adverse tax consequences. Moreover, with a bit of basic planning, the couple can arrange to avoid incurring any estate tax liability at the death of the first spouse. However, it should be kept in mind that the basic function of the marital deduction is to provide temporary deferral, not permanent forgiveness, of gift and estate taxes. Accordingly, to the extent that a transfer from one spouse to the other qualifies for a marital deduction, the transferred property will eventually be subject to gift or estate tax in the hands of the transferee spouse.

To illustrate the operation of the marital deduction, consider the situation of a husband and wife who live in a community property state and have combined wealth in the amount of $39 million, consisting of community property worth $30 million in which each spouse has an equal, present, vested interest, and $9 million of the husband's separate property which he inherited from his parents. Assume that the husband dies first and in his will leaves everything to his wife. Therefore, the wife will receive the husband's half of the community property plus all of the husband's separate property and will own that in addition to her own half of the community property in which she already had a present, vested interest before the husband's death. Assume also that deductions totaling $3 million are allowed for expenses and claims in computing the husband's taxable estate. The husband's *gross estate* includes his half of the community property (worth $15 million) and all of his separate property (worth $9 million), for a total of $24 million. (The wife's half of the community property is not included in the husband's gross estate under § 2033 because it is not property owned by him at his death, nor is it includable under any other provision.) From the gross estate of $24 million, a deduction of $3 million is allowable under § 2053 for expenses and claims, and a marital deduction is allowed under § 2056 for $21 million, the value of the property passing to the wife. As a result, the husband's *taxable estate* is zero, and no tax is payable at his death. The wife will become the owner of all of the couple's property remaining after payment of expenses and claims, and that property will be subject to gift or estate tax upon a subsequent transfer by the wife during life or at death.

The estate tax result in the preceding example would be similar if the couple lived in a separate property state, regardless of how ownership of their combined property was allocated between husband and wife. At the husband's death, a deduction of $3 million would be allowed under § 2053 for expenses and claims, and a marital deduction would be allowed under § 2056 for the value of all of the property that was includable in the husband's gross estate and that passed to the wife, leaving a taxable estate of zero. Also, the wife would end up owning all of the couple's remaining property and would incur gift or estate tax liability upon a subsequent transfer during life or at death.

In 1988 Congress added § 2056(d), which disallows the marital deduction if the decedent's surviving spouse is not a U.S. citizen, unless the property passes to the spouse in a "qualified domestic trust" (QDOT). Section 2056A sets forth the definition of a QDOT, and provides for a deferred estate tax to be imposed on distributions from the QDOT during the spouse's lifetime (other than distributions of income to the spouse) and on the value of the property remaining in the QDOT at the spouse's death. In addition to the usual requirements of § 2056, a QDOT must have at least one trustee who is an individual U.S. citizen or a domestic corporation, with the right to withhold the deferred estate tax from any distribution. A trust will qualify as a QDOT only if the decedent's executor so elects. See generally I.R.C. § 2056A and the regulations thereunder. Section 2056(d) does not apply if a noncitizen spouse becomes a U.S. citizen before the estate tax return is filed, as long as the spouse was a U.S. resident at all times after the decedent's date of death and before becoming a U.S. citizen. I.R.C. § 2056(d)(4).

The purpose of § 2056(d) is to ensure that property passing to a noncitizen surviving spouse will eventually be subject to estate tax. Without such a provision, such property might escape tax completely, for example, if a U.S. husband left property to his foreign wife and she removed the property to her home country and died there. Section 2056(d) ensures that the property will be taxed either upon the husband's death, at the time of distribution from a QDOT, or at the death of the noncitizen surviving spouse. For gift tax purposes, a parallel provision disallows the marital deduction for gifts to a spouse who is not a U.S. citizen, but allows an increased annual exclusion for such gifts. I.R.C. § 2523(i).

§ 68 THE TERMINABLE INTEREST RULE: § 2056(b)

The general marital deduction rule set forth in I.R.C. § 2056(a) is qualified by several limitations imposed by succeeding subsections, the most important of which is the *terminable interest rule* of § 2056(b). The terminable interest rule arises from the basic premise of the marital deduction that property which qualifies for the deduction in the estate of the first spouse to die will eventually be taxed in the estate of the surviving spouse (if not disposed of before death). In the early days of the limited marital deduction, this premise followed from the attempt to correlate the treatment of property transferred tax-free under the marital deduction with treatment of property enjoyed by the surviving spouse tax-free under community property law; with the removal of the quantitative limits on the marital deduction, the same premise can be viewed as implementing the policy objective of treating the married couple as a single taxable unit. Accordingly, no marital deduction should be allowed if an interest in property given to the surviving spouse might, after the termination of that spouse's interest, pass to someone else without being included in the surviving spouse's gift or estate tax base. A terminable interest, such as a life estate in the surviving spouse, with remainder to children or other beneficiaries, would ordinarily avoid taxation in the estate of such surviving spouse because § 2033 does not reach interests in property terminating at death. (See § 17, *supra.*) Therefore, a disposition of this sort should not be sheltered from taxation by the marital deduction in the first spouse's estate. See Reg. § 20.2056(b)–1(g) (Example 1). In other words, the value of the terminable interest should not escape transfer tax both at the time it is created and at the time it terminates.

Specifically, § 2056(b)(1) states that the marital deduction shall not be allowed with respect to an interest in property if the interest passing to the surviving spouse will fail or terminate on the lapse of time or on the occurrence or non-occurrence of an event or contingency, if another interest in the same property passes or has passed (for less than adequate and full consideration in money or money's worth) from the decedent to a third person, and if such third person may possess or enjoy any part of the property after termination or failure of the spouse's interest. Also, the deduction is not allowed for a terminable interest which is to be acquired for the surviving spouse, pursuant to directions of the decedent, by his executor or by the trustee of a trust. Notice that the mere termination of the surviving spouse's interest *alone* or the passing of an interest to a third person *alone* will not disqualify the bequest for the marital deduction. Rather, the terminable interest rule is designed to reach situations where the surviving spouse is given a temporary or contingent interest that may expire or be cut off at some point (such as a life estate), after which the property will go to another beneficiary (such as a remainder taker). The purpose of the rule is to ensure that no transfer to a surviving spouse will qualify for the marital deduction if the interest transferred might escape taxation at the spouse's death.

The statute now makes five exceptions to the terminable interest rule. The first, set forth in § 2056(b)(3), applies when the only way in which the surviving spouse's interest can terminate or fail is upon her death within six months after the death of the decedent (or in a common disaster) and when her death does *not* in fact so occur. The purpose of this rule is simply to permit a will or trust to provide for a gift over in the event of the spouse's early death (or death in a common disaster) without running afoul of the terminable interest rule. The exception allows the marital bequest to qualify for the marital deduction if the spouse actually survives for the required period; if the spouse fails to survive and the property passes to an alternative taker, of course, no marital deduction is allowed. See Reg. § 20.2056(b)–3.

The second exception, under § 2056(b)(5), applies if the surviving spouse is given a life estate in property and a general power of appointment with respect to that property. The general power of appointment must be exercisable by the spouse alone and in all events, by will or during life, in favor of herself or her estate. See Reg. § 20.2056(b)–5. Since the general power of appointment will cause the property subject to the power to be included in the gross estate of the surviving spouse at her death under § 2041, there is no reason not to permit the transfer to qualify for the marital deduction even though the spouse's life estate is a terminable interest. The spouse's rights will be regarded as the equivalent of outright ownership of the property at her death for purposes of inclusion in her estate, since she could have appointed the entire interest in favor of herself or her estate. A third exception is provided by § 2056(b)(6) for life insurance, endowment or annuity contracts payable in installments where the surviving spouse has rights in the contract similar to those described in the preceding exception, § 2056(b)(5). See Reg. § 20.2056(b)–6.

The fourth (and exceedingly important) exception to the terminable interest rule appears in § 2056(b)(7), which was added to the Code in 1981. Under this exception, a marital deduction *will* be allowed for "qualified terminable interest property" (QTIP) in which the spouse receives a simple life estate, if the decedent's executor so elects on the estate tax return. The entire property subject to such a life estate is treated as passing to the surviving spouse, and hence the full value of the property (not merely the life estate) qualifies for the marital deduction. "Qualified terminable interest property" is defined as property passing from the decedent, in which the surviving spouse has a qualifying income interest for life, and with respect to which a proper election is made. The spouse must be entitled to all the income from the property, payable at least annually, for life, and no person, including the spouse, may have a power to appoint any part of the property to any person other than the spouse during the spouse's life. See Reg. § 20.2056(b)–7. The underlying property may be held in trust to pay income to the spouse for life, but a trust is not required; a legal life estate can also qualify. Powers to appoint the property to a person other than the spouse are permitted, so long as they are exercisable only at or after the death of the spouse. Income interests for a term of years, or a life interest subject to termination upon the occurrence of a condition (e.g., upon the spouse's remarriage), do not qualify.

The fact that this exception necessarily involves an election provides an interesting opportunity for "post-mortem estate planning," depending on conditions arising at or after the decedent's death.

This important and widely-used exception to the terminable interest rule allows a decedent to qualify property for the marital deduction while at the same time keeping complete control over the ultimate disposition of the property following the surviving spouse's life estate. By contrast, the exceptions under § 2056(b)(5) and (b)(6) require that the surviving spouse be given control over the ultimate disposition.

Eligible property for which an election is made will qualify in its entirety for the estate tax marital deduction, and thus will not be taxed in the decedent's estate. Since the property *need* not be subject to a testamentary power of appointment in the surviving spouse (although it *may* be subject to such a power), special rules govern the taxation of the property in the spouse's hands. In the absence of these special rules, the property could pass to the remainder beneficiaries without being taxed in the spouse's estate, since the spouse owns only a life income interest which expires upon her death. Therefore, qualified terminable interest property will be subject to transfer taxation in the spouse's hands at the earlier of (1) the date on which the spouse disposes of all or part of the qualifying income interest (by gift, sale, or otherwise), in which case the spouse will be treated for gift tax purposes as making a transfer of the underlying property (see I.R.C. § 2519), or (2) the date of the spouse's death, when the value of the underlying property will be included in the spouse's gross estate (see I.R.C. § 2044). Upon such a taxable event, the spouse (or her estate) has a statutory right to recover the resulting gift or estate tax from the recipient of the property. See I.R.C. § 2207A.

The fifth and final exception to the terminable interest rule is set forth in § 2056(b)(8), which allows a marital deduction for the value of an annuity or unitrust interest passing from the decedent to the surviving spouse, if the spouse is the only noncharitable beneficiary of a qualified charitable remainder trust. I.R.C. § 2056(b)(8). (Charitable remainder trusts are discussed in § 62, *supra*.)

Whenever the marital deduction is placed in issue because the surviving spouse receives a terminable interest, the question must be asked whether that interest is *nondeductible*. Some examples may help to illustrate the scope of the terminable interest rule. Suppose, for example, that the husband is the first to die and his will creates a trust providing discretionary distributions of income or corpus to his wife during her life, with the remaining trust property and any accumulated income to be paid at her death to her estate. This arrangement, a so-called "estate trust," does *not* run afoul of the terminable interest rule because no interest in the property passes to any person other than the spouse or her estate. Rev. Rul. 68–554, 1968–2 C.B. 412. Suppose instead that the husband has purchased a self-and-survivor annuity which will pay an annual amount to the husband for life and then to his wife for life if she survives him, with no payment to any other beneficiary. If the husband dies first, the value of the wife's survivor annuity qualifies for the marital deduction. It is a terminable interest, but it is *not* nondeductible, since the annuity payments will simply terminate at the wife's death; no interest passes to any other beneficiary. Reg. § 20.2056(b)–1(g) (Example 3). In other words, even if the spouse receives a terminable interest, that interest may still qualify for the marital deduction as long as no other person can possess or enjoy the property after the termination of the spouse's interest. If the surviving spouse is the sole beneficiary of the transfer, there is no gift to any other person and hence no reason not to allow the marital deduction for the value of the interest passing to the spouse.

Some of the *exceptions* to the terminable interest rule may also be illustrated by examples. Suppose the husband leaves all of his property by will to his wife if she survives him by 90 days, or to his children if she does not so survive him. (A clause to this effect might be inserted to avoid double probate costs in the event of simultaneous or near simultaneous deaths of both spouses.) Also, suppose that the wife does in fact survive the husband for more than the required 90-day period. At the husband's death, the wife's interest appears to be a nondeductible terminable interest because it is subject to a condition of survival. However, the exception in § 2056(b)(3) makes this interest deductible since the survival requirement does not exceed the six-month period permitted by the statute. In contrast, if the bequest to the wife is conditioned on her survival until the date of distribution of the husband's estate, her interest will be a nondeductible terminable interest, even if distribution takes place within six months after the husband's death and the wife in fact survives until that date. The exception in § 2056(b)(3) does not apply if at the time of the husband's death there is a possibility that distribution might be delayed for more than six months. See Reg. § 20.2056(b)–3(d) (Example 4).

The terminable interest rule can apply in rather unexpected situations. For example, in Jackson v. United States, 376 U.S. 503 (1964), the Supreme Court held that the support allowance payable to the decedent's widow during the settlement of his estate did not qualify for the marital deduction. The support allowance was deemed to be a terminable interest because it would automatically terminate upon the widow's death or remarriage before the final settlement of the estate. Moreover, the widow's interest was nondeductible because it was payable from funds which would go to another beneficiary in the event of an early termination. Viewing the situation as of the time of the decedent's death, the Court held that the mere possibility of an early termination (even though it did not in fact occur) was sufficient to defeat the marital deduction. It should be added that the result would be different if the widow were the sole beneficiary of the husband's estate, since in that case no other beneficiary would be entitled to possession or enjoyment upon the early termination of the widow's interest. See Reg. § 20.2056(b)–1(g) (Example 8).

Due to the highly technical and intricate nature of the terminable interest rule, it is important to consult the provisions of the statute and the regulations as well as administrative rulings and judicial decisions with great care before approving a specific plan of disposition. Although the policy underpinnings of the statute have been invoked from time to time to explain the scope and operation of the rule, it is risky to reason from the general logic of the statute to a particular prediction about the outcome of a disputed or undecided point.

§ 69 THE ESTATE TAX MARITAL DEDUCTION IN REVIEW

The marital deduction provides a way of postponing the federal estate tax that otherwise would have to be paid on a married person's estate, as well as potentially reducing the aggregate tax that ultimately will have to be paid. The marital deduction does this by making it possible for the spouse who dies first to leave some or all of his estate in a manner that makes it deductible for federal estate tax purposes and thus reduces or eliminates the estate tax that must be paid at the decedent's death. Of course, any property that qualifies for the marital deduction in the estate of one spouse will, if retained by the surviving spouse until death, be taxed in the survivor's estate.

In addition to postponing the payment of tax on some or all of the family wealth, the marital deduction may result in payment of a lower aggregate tax on the combined estates of both spouses. By splitting their combined wealth between their respective estates, the spouses can ensure that each of them can make full use of his or her unified credit (and low rate brackets, in a system with graduated marginal tax rates). The advantage of "estate splitting" is greatest for couples whose aggregate wealth does not exceed the spouses' combined exemption equivalents; for couples with substantially larger estates, the potential tax benefit is less compelling because, under the current compressed rate schedule, once each spouse has exhausted his or her unified credit, any further taxable transfers will be subject to tax at a flat 40% rate.

The ultimate saving is more difficult to calculate, because it will depend on the intervention of unpredictable facts. In particular, the property qualifying for the marital deduction in the estate of the first spouse to die, when taxed in the survivor's estate to the extent it has been retained, will be valued at the time of the survivor's death rather than at the death of the first spouse. It is even possible that if the surviving spouse owns substantial separate property and the deceased spouse makes use of the marital deduction to the fullest extent allowable, the total taxes may be *increased,* even though there is a saving in the estate tax payable at the first spouse's death. This possibility was made much more likely by the passage of the unlimited marital deduction. So it frequently will be advisable not to use the marital deduction in full. Some couples, however, may view the additional future tax burden as a small price to pay for the financial and psychological advantages of postponing the payment of taxes and having the use of the interim tax saving for the lifetime of the surviving spouse.

In general, the task is to balance the advantage of having the use of the taxes saved at the first spouse's death during the surviving spouse's remaining lifetime against the additional tax liability that will be incurred at the death of the survivor.

In planning for the marital deduction, the tax counselor should keep three factors particularly in mind. The first is that except in small estates, where the surviving spouse will need unfettered access to all the family wealth to meet future needs, it often makes sense to use less than the maximum available marital deduction, at least to the extent of the decedent's exemption equivalent, currently $15 million (indexed for inflation). In a system with steeply progressive marginal rates, maximizing the deferral of estate taxes is often undesirable because the pyramiding of wealth in the survivor's estate may increase the total estate tax burden, but this concern has lost much of its urgency under the compressed rate schedule of current law. In large estates, the best result often can be achieved by limiting the marital bequest to the amount that would otherwise be subject to tax at the highest marginal rate (e.g., the amount in excess of the inflation-indexed $15 million exemption equivalent, after expenses and claims), and leaving the rest of the estate in a trust that will not be taxed in the survivor's estate at all. This plan takes full advantage of the unified credit for both spouses and also minimizes the estate tax payable at the first spouse's death.

Secondly, the use of growth assets (i.e., assets that are likely to appreciate in value) to fund the marital bequest is likely to prove disadvantageous. Since property qualifying for the marital deduction will be taxed in the survivor's estate at its value at the survivor's death, the use of growth assets will increase the tax on the survivor's estate and thus undermine the benefit of tax deferral. Therefore, planners sometimes recommend including a clause in the will directing that certain assets, ones that are likely to increase in value such as a parcel of real estate or common stock in a closely held corporation, will not be used to fund the marital bequest as long as other assets are available for that purpose.

Thirdly, it is often desirable to take advantage of the marital deduction by the use of a trust for the surviving spouse's benefit. The trust may have substantial non-tax advantages, in terms of management and conservation of the property. The trustee can be given broad powers over the property for the benefit of the surviving spouse. In fact, since the property qualifying for the marital deduction in the estate of the first spouse to die will eventually be taxed in the survivor's estate, the surviving spouse can be given an unrestricted power to withdraw corpus from the trust without thereby creating any additional estate tax liability.

Often, two trusts are used, one that qualifies for the marital deduction (the so-called "marital" trust) and a separate, nondeductible trust (the so-called "credit shelter" or "bypass" trust) which will not be taxed in the survivor's estate. The marital trust must be drafted with one eye on the Code in order to make sure that all the requirements for the marital deduction are satisfied. For example, all the income must be payable to the spouse each year. If necessary for her support and maintenance, the income from the credit shelter trust can also be paid to the spouse. If not needed for this purpose, the income from the credit shelter trust can be paid to the children or accumulated for their benefit. If trust corpus may have to be invaded for the benefit of the spouse, estate tax can be saved in the spouse's estate by drawing down corpus from the marital trust before dipping into the credit shelter trust. In point of fact, every dollar of corpus that is consumed from the marital trust will escape taxation in both spouses' estates. Therefore, plans are sometimes laid for systematic use of corpus from the marital trust rather than to have any income from the credit shelter trust paid to the spouse. There is an income tax reason for this planning as well; amounts coming from trust corpus are generally sheltered from income tax by the exclusion for gifts and bequests in I.R.C. § 102, while amounts coming from trust income are generally subject to income tax.

In conclusion, the marital deduction is a very important tool in estate planning. It can provide substantial interim tax savings which will give the surviving spouse additional income and greater financial protection. In some cases, it can also produce an ultimate tax saving with the result that more capital is left for the children or other beneficiaries. The marital deduction may also relieve liquidity problems by making it possible to pay the combined tax in two installments, part at the death of the first spouse and the balance at the death of the survivor. Since the marital deduction thus shifts some estate tax burden from the first estate to the estate of the survivor, the need for liquidity in the survivor's estate must be remembered. Also, since the order of deaths is never certain, an estate should always be planned with regard for the possibility that the expected order of deaths may be reversed.

The role of the marital deduction has evolved significantly since it first entered the Code in 1948. In its original form, the marital deduction served to adjust the tax treatment of family property for married couples residing in separate property states, in order to equalize that treatment with the automatic "estate splitting" available to married couples residing in community property states. The 50% marital deduction permitted up to one-half of separate property to pass tax-free at the death of one spouse to the surviving spouse, to the extent the decedent left property to the survivor outright or in a form approximating the ownership rights of a surviving spouse in community property. The structure and purpose of the marital deduction have shifted dramatically as a result of the 1981 amendments which completely removed the quantitative limitations and introduced the concept of qualified terminable interest property. Under current law, the marital deduction serves to make possible unlimited tax-free transfers of wealth between spouses, while assuring that such wealth will eventually be taxed when it leaves the marital unit and passes to other beneficiaries. This goes well beyond providing tax parity for separate and community property spouses, and offers important tax planning opportunities for married couples across the board.

§ 70 THE GIFT TAX MARITAL DEDUCTION: § 2523

The availability of automatic estate splitting for married couples in community property states, and the consequent need to provide similar tax treatment for couples in separate property states, led Congress in 1948 to enact a marital deduction not only in the estate tax but also in the gift tax. The gift tax provisions set forth in I.R.C. § 2523 closely resemble the estate tax provisions of § 2056, including a terminable interest rule with enumerated exceptions to ensure that inter vivos gifts which qualify for a marital deduction in the hands of the donor spouse will eventually be subject to gift or estate tax in the hands of the donee spouse. The following discussion will deal mainly with the differences between the marital deduction provisions in the gift tax and those in the estate tax.

Prior to the 1976 Act, § 2523 allowed a gift tax marital deduction for an amount equal to one-half the value of any qualifying interest in non-community property transferred by a donor to his or her spouse. (Thus, for gift tax purposes the marital deduction was allowed for half of the amount of the property transferred, whereas for estate tax purposes the deduction could apply to the entire value of transferred property up to the aggregate limitation of 50% of the adjusted gross estate.) In 1976 Congress relaxed the 50% limitation and allowed a 100% deduction for the first $100,000 of interspousal gifts, no deduction for the next $100,000 of such gifts, and a 50% deduction for all interspousal gifts over $200,000. The 1981 amendments introducing the unlimited marital deduction and the special treatment of qualified terminable interest property for estate tax purposes were accompanied by parallel provisions in § 2523 for gift tax purposes.

The terminable interest rule in the gift tax marital deduction is broader than its counterpart in the estate tax, reflecting the possibility that the donor may retain an interest or a power with respect to property transferred during life. In particular, the statute disallows the marital deduction for a transfer if the donee spouse receives a terminable interest and the donor retains or transfers (for less than adequate and full consideration in money or money's worth) an interest or a power that may ripen into possession or enjoyment at the termination of the spouse's interest. I.R.C. § 2523(b). Nevertheless, the marital deduction is not disallowed if the donor's retained interest consists of a right of survivorship in a joint tenancy with the donee spouse as the only other joint tenant. I.R.C. § 2523(d). Additional exceptions to the terminable interest rule are found in § 2523(e), relating to a life estate with general power of appointment, § 2523(f), relating to qualified terminable interest property, and § 2523(g), relating to an annuity or unitrust interest in a qualified charitable remainder trust.

The gift tax marital deduction statute does not contain a specific exception to the terminable interest rule corresponding to § 2056(b)(6) with respect to proceeds of life insurance or annuity policies held by an insurance company; the same result follows, however, from § 2523(e) concerning a life estate with general power of appointment.

The marital deduction available under § 2523 is allowed only to the extent that the gifts there specified are included in the amount of gifts against which the deduction is applied. In other words, the marital deduction in the gift tax may not exceed the donor's total includable gifts for the taxable year. The deduction may not be used to obtain a double tax benefit for transfers that are excludable or deductible under another provision or are completed in another taxable year.

In connection with the gift tax marital deduction of § 2523, recall the general gift tax rules concerning transfers made pursuant to an enforceable contract or agreement without adequate and full consideration in money or money's worth, as is often the case with antenuptial or other marital agreements. Also, reference should be made again to § 2516, which treats certain marital property settlements as made for an adequate and full consideration in money or money's worth and hence not taxable under the gift tax, and to the *Harris* doctrine, which exempts certain transfers of property incident to divorce from gift tax.

In 1988 Congress added § 2523(i), which prohibits a marital deduction for gifts to a spouse who is not a U.S. citizen. There is no gift tax counterpart to the estate tax marital deduction allowed by § 2056(d) for a qualified domestic trust (discussed in § 67, *supra*). However, the statute raises the annual exclusion under § 2503(b) from $10,000 to $100,000 (indexed for inflation, $194,000 in 2026) for gifts to a noncitizen spouse. I.R.C. § 2523(i)(1) and (i)(2).

The regulations under § 2523 provide detailed additional guidance concerning the application of the gift tax marital deduction. See Reg. §§ 25.2523(a)–1 through 25.2523(i)–3.

§ 71 SPLIT GIFTS AND THE GIFT TAX

I.R.C. § 2513 contains a split-gift provision designed to give spouses in a separate property setting much the same gift tax treatment as that afforded by community property laws to a gift made by both spouses to a third person. Since each spouse is deemed to have an equal, present, vested interest in community property, a gift of such property by a husband and wife to their child, for example, would be treated as a gift of half the property by each spouse. Hence, two annual exclusions and two unified credits would be available to offset the gift tax. In the absence of § 2513, a gift by one spouse of his or her separate property would be eligible for only one annual exclusion and one unified credit.

To allow similar tax treatment for gifts of separate property, § 2513 provides that a gift by either a husband or a wife to a third person shall be considered as made one-half by each spouse if both spouses consent to such gift-splitting treatment for all gifts made during the calendar year by either spouse while married to the other.

A gift-splitting election under § 2513 does not amount to a joint gift tax return filed by the spouses, nor does it enable either spouse to apply the other spouse's unified credit to offset the tax on his or her own one-half share of the taxable gifts.

Ordinarily the donor is primarily liable for the gift tax imposed on his or her own gifts. If a gift-splitting election has been made under § 2513, however, both spouses are jointly and severally liable for the entire gift tax imposed on the split gifts. Reg. §§ 25.2502–2 and 25.2513–4.

It would seem that the practical significance of the gift-splitting election has diminished to some extent since the enactment of the unlimited marital deduction. It may now be possible to achieve a similar result if the husband, for example, transfers some property to the wife and both spouses then make gifts to a third-party donee. A possible barrier to this type of transaction, however, is the "indirect transfer" doctrine, which would collapse the two gifts and treat the wife's gift to the third-party donee as an indirect transfer by the husband, with the wife acting as a "mere conduit." See Reg. § 25.2511–1(h)(2). This doctrine could apply if the transfer to the wife were conditioned on her making the gift to the ultimate donee. Perhaps § 2513, which now allows gift splitting only in a rigid 50–50 ratio, should be amended to permit splitting in any ratio. Then it would allow the flexibility inherent in the above plan, without the risk of recharacterization under the "indirect transfer" doctrine.

A collateral effect of a gift-splitting election under § 2513 is that split-gift treatment applies not only for purposes of the gift tax but also for purposes of the generation-skipping transfer tax, thus making two GST exemptions available for gifts to skip persons. I.R.C. § 2652(a)(2). However, the gift-splitting election has no application to the estate tax. Thus, for example, if the husband makes a gift subject to a retained life estate and the gift is treated as made one-half by husband and one-half by wife pursuant to an election under § 2513, the full value of the property may nevertheless be drawn back into the husband's gross estate at his death. In this situation, any gift tax payable by the wife on the split gift will be attributed to the husband for estate tax purposes. I.R.C. § 2001(d); for the estate tax consequences to the wife, see I.R.C. § 2001(e).

CHAPTER 14

CREDITS AGAINST THE ESTATE AND GIFT TAXES: LIABILITY AND PAYMENT OF THE TAXES

§ 72 UNIFIED CREDIT—ESTATE AND GIFT TAX: §§ 2010 AND 2505

Prior Law. Prior to the 1976 Act, each citizen or resident taxpayer was allowed an *exemption* of $30,000 over his or her lifetime in computing taxable gifts. See former I.R.C. § 2521. This lifetime exemption, which operated as a deduction in computing the amount of taxable gifts, could be spread over any number of taxable periods. The difference between an exemption and a deduction largely consists of the fact that the exemption is a flat amount fixed by the law for every taxpayer, whereas deductions vary from person to person or estate to estate, according to the facts in each instance.

Similarly, the *exemption* available in the estate tax appeared in former I.R.C. § 2052, which provided that the value of the taxable estate was to be determined by deducting an exemption of $60,000 from the value of the gross estate. This $60,000 exemption, available to every estate, had the exceedingly important result of freeing from tax any estate if the gross estate did not exceed $60,000. (Recall that the "gross estate" as determined under I.R.C. § 2031 may well exceed the amount of property owned by the decedent at death, since the gross estate may also include some property transferred during life, joint tenancies, annuities, life insurance, and property subject to a power of appointment.) Even though the function and purpose of the $60,000 exemption was to free small estates from estate tax, the exemption was available in every estate, no matter how large. The exemption thus reduced the progressivity of the estate tax rates, since those rates applied only to the taxable estate remaining after the exemption was deducted from the gross estate.

The separate gift and estate tax exemptions under prior law were worth more to high-bracket taxpayers than to those in lower brackets. For example, under the old estate tax rate schedule, the $60,000 estate tax exemption resulted in a tax saving of $9,500 for a $60,000 estate at the bottom of the rate schedule, compared to a $46,200 tax saving for an estate in the top rate bracket. In other words, the exemptions, acting as deductions, came "off the top," and thus eliminated tax on $30,000 (gift tax) and $60,000 (estate tax) of taxable transfers at the taxpayer's *highest* marginal rates.

Another possible vertical inequity in prior law was that, as a practical matter, the entirely separate gift tax exemption could be exploited only by the wealthy, since taxpayers of more modest means could not afford to make large lifetime gifts and needed to keep their property available to meet other lifetime demands. This disparity was compounded by the fact that the gift tax rates were only around three-quarters of the corresponding estate tax rates, so that inter vivos gifts bore a considerably lighter tax burden than transfers at death.

Current Law. In order to remedy these inequities, the 1976 Act abolished the separate estate and gift tax rate schedules and replaced them with a *unified rate schedule* which is set forth in I.R.C. § 2001(c) for estate tax purposes and is adopted by reference in I.R.C. § 2502(a) for gift tax purposes. The 1976 Act also abolished the separate estate and gift tax exemptions and replaced them with a *unified credit* which is found in I.R.C. §§ 2010 and 2505. As its name implies, the unified credit functions as a single, cumulative allowance against both the estate and gift taxes, even though the estate and gift tax components are set forth in separate statutory provisions.

Section 2505 provides a credit against the gift tax imposed by § 2501 for each calendar year in an amount equal to the *applicable credit amount* in effect for such calendar year less the sum of the credits previously allowed under § 2505. The "applicable credit amount" is defined in § 2010(c) as the amount of tax that would be computed under the unified rate schedule of § 2001(c) with respect to a transfer of the *applicable exclusion amount*. The "applicable exclusion amount" generally is the same as the *basic exclusion amount* ($15 million, indexed for inflation), increased in some cases by a predeceased spouse's unused exclusion amount (as described below). As a result of these rather convoluted provisions, the unified credit automatically eliminates the gift tax that would otherwise be imposed on each taxable gift made by the donor after 1976, in chronological order, up to the applicable exclusion amount (also referred to as the *exemption equivalent*). The unified credit is not affected by amounts allowed for pre-1977 gifts under the specific exemption of former § 2521, except that the credit is reduced by 20% of any exemption allowed under prior law for gifts made after September 8, 1976, the date the 1976 Act was enacted, and before January 1, 1977, the effective date of the unified credit provisions. I.R.C. § 2505(b).

Since the unified credit was first enacted in 1976, the amount of the credit (as well as the corresponding exemption equivalent) has grown by fits and starts. In 1981 Congress increased the credit in annual increments which brought the exemption equivalent up to $600,000, where it remained for more than a decade. Subsequent legislation increased the credit still further, bringing the exemption equivalent up to $1 million in 2002, $3,500,000 in 2009, $5 million in 2010, $10 million in 2018, and $15 million in 2026.* Furthermore, the basic exclusion amount is subject to automatic annual adjustment for inflation.

If a married couple elects split-gift treatment under § 2513 for gifts to third persons, each spouse's unified credit is available to offset the gift tax on his or her one-half share of such gifts, but neither spouse can make direct use of the other's unified credit. In

---

* For gift tax purposes, the exemption equivalent was frozen at $1 million from 2002 through 2010; beginning in 2011, the exemption equivalent is the same for both gift and estate tax purposes.

other words, the unified credit is personal to the individual who is treated as the donor; it cannot be directly shared or assigned between spouses during their joint lifetime. Nevertheless, it would appear that a gift to a spouse, tax-free under the unlimited marital deduction, followed by a gift from the donee spouse to a third person, may allow the spouses some additional flexibility in making use of their respective unified credits, unless the steps are telescoped into a single gift. (See § 71, *supra.*)

The unified credit (unlike the former $30,000 exemption) not only is cumulative over the lifetime of the donor, but any amount left unused at his or her death is available as a credit against the estate tax.

The mechanics of the unified credit in the estate tax context are somewhat complicated, due to the cumulation of lifetime gifts into the estate tax base. Section 2010 allows the *full* unified credit (reduced only by 20% of any exemption allowed under prior law for post-September 8, 1976 gifts) to be applied against the estate tax liability, seemingly regardless of whether any or all of the available credit has already been taken against the gift tax during life. In spite of appearances, however, this does not amount to a double allowance of the credit, since the estate tax is computed under § 2001(b) as the excess of (1) a tentative tax on the sum of the taxable estate *plus* taxable gifts made after 1976 (other than those already includable in the gross estate), over (2) the gift tax "payable" with respect to gifts made after 1976. The unified credit is then applied against this amount. To the extent that the unified credit was used during life, the gift tax "payable" will have been reduced, resulting in a smaller offset against the tentative tax under § 2001(b). The net result is that the unified credit will reduce the estate tax liability only to the extent that the credit was not already used against the gift tax during life.

Note the effect on the estate tax computation under § 2001(b) of any changes in the unified rate schedule occurring between the time of a post-1976 taxable gift and the date of death. In determining the amount of the offset against the tentative estate tax under § 2001(b)(2), the gift tax "payable" with respect to a post-1976 gift is computed as if the rate schedule in effect at the date of death had been applicable at the time of the gift. This method of computation allows a consistent application of the estate tax rate schedule to a cumulative base including post-1976 taxable gifts, and avoids giving retroactive effect to interim rate changes.

Not only does the unified credit free estates of small and moderate size from tax, it also frees them in most cases of the need to file an estate tax return. Under I.R.C. § 6018(a), an estate tax return must be filed for a citizen or resident decedent only if the gross estate (plus any adjusted taxable gifts and any exemption allowed under prior law for post-September 8, 1976 gifts) exceeds the exemption equivalent. As a practical matter, however, a return must be filed, even for a smaller estate, if it is desired to pass on the decedent's unused unified credit to the surviving spouse, since the "portability" provision (described below) applies only if the executor makes an election on a timely filed estate tax return.

An exemption equivalent or basic exclusion amount of $15 million corresponds to a unified credit of $5,945,800. In other words, $5,945,800 is the amount of tax computed under the unified rate schedule with respect to a taxable transfer of $15 million, and that tax is completely offset by the credit. To the extent that the unified credit is used against the gift tax during life, there will be a corresponding reduction in the available exemption equivalent remaining at death. The basic exclusion amount is indexed for inflation.

In many instances, no tax will be payable even though an estate tax return must be filed; even if the *gross estate* is very large, the *taxable estate* may well be equal to or less than the exemption equivalent due to various deductions. (Moreover, any tax computed on the taxable estate may be offset in whole or in part by other credits against the estate tax. See § 73, *infra.*)

The unified credit is available to each individual transferor, and generally cannot be transferred or assigned. Thus, if a decedent fails to make full use of his or her available unified credit, the unused credit amount is lost. However, under a special statutory provision added in 2010, a surviving spouse may make use of a deceased spouse's unused unified credit if the executor so elects on a timely filed estate tax return. Technically, the surviving spouse's applicable exclusion amount consists of the basic exclusion amount ($15 million, indexed for inflation), increased by a "deceased spousal unused exclusion amount." § 2010(c). The additional amount available to the surviving spouse is computed by subtracting the deceased spouse's cumulative taxable transfers from his or her own basic exclusion amount. Consequently, the deceased spouse's unused unified credit need not be wasted but instead can be used to augment the surviving spouse's own unified credit. The statute includes an overall ceiling which limits the amount of unified credit that a surviving spouse can accumulate from multiple predeceased spouses. As a policy matter, it may be asked why the "portability" feature is available only for married couples, or, in other words, whether a decedent should be able to pass on his or her unused unified credit to an individual other than a surviving spouse.

§ 73 OTHER CREDITS AGAINST THE ESTATE TAX: I.R.C. §§ 2012–2014

Credits against the estate tax liability determined under I.R.C. § 2001 are allowed for gift taxes paid on pre-1977 gifts that are includable in the gross estate (I.R.C. § 2012), for estate taxes paid on certain prior transfers of property (I.R.C. § 2013), and for foreign death taxes (I.R.C. § 2014).

Credit for State Death Taxes. Prior to 2005, former I.R.C. § 2011 allowed a credit for *state death taxes.* The credit was allowed for any estate, inheritance, legacy or succession taxes actually paid to a state (or the District of Columbia) with respect to property included in the decedent's gross estate. The amount of the credit was limited to a percentage, determined under the graduated rate schedule in § 2011(b), of the decedent's "adjusted taxable estate" (i.e., the taxable estate reduced by $60,000). This limitation carried forward the rate brackets established in 1926, when the credit was set equal to 80% of the estate tax then in force. The credit for state death taxes provided a powerful incentive for the states to levy death taxes up to the creditable amount, sometimes called "pick-up" or "sponge" taxes, since doing so diverted a portion of the estate tax revenue to the states without increasing the overall estate tax burden. As a revenue-sharing mechanism, however, the § 2011 credit was open to criticism on the ground that it conferred disproportionate benefits on states with wealthy residents. Note that increases in the amount of the unified credit had the ancillary effect of reducing state pick-up tax revenue, due to the fact that the § 2011 credit could be taken only after the unified credit was applied. I.R.C. § 2011(f). Further guidance can be found in Reg. §§ 20.2011–1 and 20.2011–2.

Under the 2001 Act, the § 2011 credit was phased out and replaced in 2005 by a *deduction* for state death taxes, with no percentage limitation. (See I.R.C. § 2058, discussed in § 64, *supra*.) The switch from a credit to a deduction reflects the fact that state death taxes reduce the net value of the estate passing from a decedent to his or her heirs. Conceptually, such taxes are indistinguishable from other items, such as funeral and administration expenses and claims, for which a deduction is allowed under § 2053. The repeal of the § 2011 credit has shifted a substantial portion of estate tax revenue away from the states back to the federal government. Indeed, many state death taxes that formerly were geared exclusively to the amount of the credit have disappeared along with the credit, giving rise to increased fiscal and political pressures on government at the state level. In response, several states have enacted new free-standing estate or inheritance taxes to replace the lost revenue from the old pick-up taxes; in contrast, other states have completely abandoned their death taxes in an attempt to attract wealthy residents.

Credit for Gift Tax. I.R.C. § 2012 allows a credit against the estate tax for *gift taxes* imposed on gifts made before 1977 that are drawn back into the gross estate at death. In general, the credit is designed to prevent a single transfer from being subject to both a gift tax and an estate tax when the two taxes overlap. The amount of the credit is subject to two limitations: it cannot exceed the lesser of (1) the gift tax attributable to the gift, or (2) the estate tax attributable to the inclusion of the gift in the gross estate. The gift or estate tax attributable to the gift is generally calculated as an amount that bears the same ratio to the total tax payable as the amount of the gift bears to the total taxable transfers. For specific rules governing the computation of the credit, see I.R.C. § 2012 and Reg. § 20.2012–1.

The § 2012 credit does not apply to gifts made after 1976, since the gift tax payable with respect to such gifts is automatically allowed as an offset in computing the estate tax under § 2001(b).

Credit for Tax on Prior Transfers. I.R.C. § 2013 allows a credit for all or a part of the estate tax paid on *prior transfers* to the decedent. The purpose of this credit is to ameliorate the impact of transfer taxes imposed on successive deaths within a relatively short period of time. An estate is entitled to a credit for the estate tax paid on a prior transfer of property to the decedent if the property was transferred by another person who died within ten years before, or within two years after, the decedent. There is no requirement that the property be traced or identified in the estate of the present decedent or even that the same property be in existence at the time of the decedent's death. Reg. § 20.2013–1(a). The amount of the credit depends on the amount of the estate tax paid by the transferor's estate and also on the length of time between the deaths of the transferor and the decedent. The larger the estate tax and the shorter the interval of time, the larger the credit. No parallel credit is allowed either in the gift tax or in the generation-skipping transfer tax. For further limitations and qualifications on the availability and amount of the credit, see I.R.C. § 2013 and Reg. §§ 20.2013–1 through 20.2013–6.

Credit for Foreign Death Taxes. Under I.R.C. § 2014, a credit is allowed for *foreign death taxes* paid with respect to any property situated within a foreign country and included in the gross estate. Were it not for this credit, a double tax could arise because (1) all property included in the gross estate of a decedent who was a U.S. citizen or resident is subject to the U.S. estate tax, even if that property is located in another country, and (2) many foreign countries impose an estate or inheritance tax on part or all of the same property to the extent it is situated within their territorial jurisdictions. The credit is limited to the portion of the foreign death tax which is attributable to the property situated in the foreign country and included in the decedent's gross estate. It is also limited to the portion of the U.S. estate tax that is attributable to the foreign property included in the gross estate. The credit may be denied for the estate of a decedent who was a citizen of another country if that country fails to allow a similar tax credit for estates of U.S. citizens who are residents of that country. I.R.C. § 2014(h). If the United States has entered into a tax treaty or convention with the foreign country in question, the estate is entitled to the § 2014 credit or the credit allowed by the treaty, whichever is more advantageous. In limited circumstances, a death tax credit may be taken under both § 2014 and a treaty or convention. See Reg. § 20.2014–4. For a detailed explanation of the terms of the § 2014 credit and the method of its computation, see Reg. §§ 20.2014–1 through 20.2014–7.

§ 74 LIABILITY AND PAYMENT OF THE ESTATE TAX

The amount of estate tax liability is determined under I.R.C. § 2001 by applying the unified rate schedule to a base consisting of the taxable estate and adjusted taxable gifts, with an offset for the gift tax payable with respect to post-1976 gifts.

Section 2002 directs that the estate tax shall be paid by the executor. The term "executor," as defined in § 2203, means the executor or administrator of the decedent or, if there is no person appointed, qualified, and acting as such, then any person in actual or constructive possession of any property of the decedent. Section 2205 declares that if the tax or any part of it is paid by or collected out of any of the estate passing to someone other than the executor in his capacity as such, that person shall be entitled to reimbursement out of the undistributed estate, or by equitable contribution from other persons interested in the estate.

In general, the matter of estate tax apportionment, involving the question of whether the estate tax is to be charged against the residuary estate subject to administration, or equitably apportioned among the recipients of the property that generated the tax, or apportioned in some other manner, is governed by the terms of the decedent's will or trust instrument and by applicable state law. In a few instances, however, the Code authorizes the executor to recover the estate tax attributable to particular types of property from the recipients of such property. Thus, if proceeds of an insurance policy on the decedent's life are subject to estate tax, the executor has a right under § 2206 to recover from the beneficiary an amount that bears the same ratio to the total estate tax paid as the beneficiary's share of the proceeds bears to the taxable estate. Section 2207 grants the executor a similar right of recovery with respect to property over which the decedent held a general power of appointment. In the case of qualified terminable interest property, at the death of the life income beneficiary, § 2207A(a) authorizes the executor to recover any estate tax attributable to such property. Finally, under § 2207B the executor has a right to recover any estate tax attributable to property included in the decedent's gross estate under § 2036. In contrast to the pro rata recoveries allowed under §§ 2206, 2207, and 2207B, the § 2207A recovery is calculated at the estate's marginal rate. All of these statutory rights of recovery can be waived if the decedent directs a different apportionment of estate tax liability.

An estate tax return must be filed in the case of a citizen or resident decedent if the gross estate (plus any adjusted taxable gifts and any exemption allowed under prior law for post-September 8, 1976 gifts) exceeds the inflation-indexed $15 million basic exclusion amount. I.R.C. § 6018(a)(1). A return must also be filed, even for a smaller estate, if the executor wishes to make a valid election to pass on the decedent's unused unified credit to the surviving spouse (see § 72, *supra*). The estate tax return is due nine months after the date of the decedent's death, unless an extension is obtained. I.R.C. §§ 6075(a) and 6081. Payment of the tax is due at the same time as the return, unless an extension is obtained. I.R.C. §§ 6151(a) and 6161. An extension of up to fourteen years for payment of the estate tax attributable to an interest in a closely held business may be available in certain cases, if the executor so elects. I.R.C. § 6166.

If the estate tax is not paid when due, any person who, on the date of the decedent's death, receives or holds property included in the gross estate under I.R.C. §§ 2034 to 2042 is personally liable to the extent of the value of such property at the time of the decedent's death. I.R.C. § 6324(a)(2).

Under the general rule of I.R.C. § 6501(a), the period of limitations on assessment and collection of the tax is three years from the time an estate tax return was filed, but a longer period may apply under § 6501(c) in instances of false or fraudulent returns made with intent to evade tax, or failure to file a return. I.R.C. § 7403 sets forth the rules governing an action to enforce a lien or to subject property to the payment of tax.

§ 75 LIABILITY AND PAYMENT OF THE GIFT TAX

The gift tax is computed on an annual basis under I.R.C. § 2502. The tax on the donor's gifts for the current calendar year is equal to (1) a tentative tax, computed under the unified rate schedule set forth in § 2001(c), on the donor's aggregate taxable gifts for the current year and all preceding years, minus (2) a tentative tax, computed under the same rate schedule, on the donor's aggregate taxable gifts for all preceding years. (By its terms, the gift tax is prospective in application, so that only gifts made after June 6, 1932 are taken into account.) Thus the gift tax rates are applied on a cumulative, lifetime basis, with the taxable gifts made in each succeeding year potentially taxable at progressively higher rates.

In general, a gift tax return is required for any calendar year in which the donor makes a taxable gift. I.R.C. § 6019. A return is also required, as a practical matter, if the donor wishes to make a gift-splitting election under § 2513 or to make an election under § 2523(f) with respect to qualified terminable interest property. The gift tax return for a calendar year is generally due on April 15 of the following year. I.R.C. § 6075(b).

The primary liability for the gift tax imposed by § 2501 falls on the donor. I.R.C. § 2502(c). Under § 2207A(b), the gift tax attributable to a lifetime disposition of qualified terminable interest property under § 2519 may be recovered from the person receiving the property. But if the donor does not pay the tax when it is due, the donee becomes personally liable to the extent of the value of the gift—even if there has been no particular effort to collect the tax from the donor and even if he or she is perfectly able to pay it. I.R.C. § 6324(b).

The general period of limitations on assessment and collection of tax under I.R.C. § 6501(a) is three years from the time a gift tax return was filed, but a longer period may apply under § 6501(c) in instances of false or fraudulent returns made with intent to evade tax, failure to file a return, failure to disclose a gift on a return, or extension by agreement.

§ 76 LIABILITY AND PAYMENT OF THE GENERATION-SKIPPING TRANSFER TAX

Liability for, and payment of, the generation-skipping transfer tax is outlined in § 15, *supra*. See generally I.R.C. § 2662 and Reg. § 26.2662–1.

CHAPTER 15

A FEW FUNDAMENTALS OF ESTATE PLANNING

§ 77 INTRODUCTION

Estate planning is a specialty involving complicated techniques and sound legal judgment; it cannot be mastered merely by applying mechanical rules. Nevertheless, some general introduction to a few guiding principles of estate planning can serve to review the basic structure of the federal estate and gift and generation-skipping transfer taxes and also convey something about the nature of estate planning possibilities given the impact of these transfer taxes. (Income tax factors also form an important component of estate planning, but they will be considered only briefly here.)

In general, taxpayers contemplating transfers of substantial wealth probably should make at least some inter vivos gifts in order to take full advantage of the annual per-donee gift tax exclusion, which will be lost year by year if it is not used. Gifts that qualify for the annual exclusion or for the unlimited medical and educational exclusions can be made free of gift and estate taxes, and do not use up any of the donor's unified credit.

The unified credit applies automatically to offset the gift or estate tax liability on taxable transfers made during life or at death, up to the exemption equivalent. Although any amount of unified credit used against the gift tax will reduce the amount later available to the estate, there is some benefit in utilizing the unified credit during life, especially in the case of property that is likely to appreciate rapidly in value. After the unified credit has been exhausted, additional lifetime gifts may still be advantageous, despite the payment of an immediate gift tax, since they can generally be made on a "tax-exclusive" basis whereas the estate tax applies to transfers at death on a "tax-inclusive" basis.

The marital deduction and the gift-splitting election can be used by married couples to shift wealth tax-free from one spouse to the other and to make use of both spouses' annual exclusions and unified credits. However, tax considerations alone should not lead a taxpayer to make a transfer that is undesirable from a non-tax point of view.

§ 78 THE MARITAL DEDUCTION

For purposes of the estate tax, the marital deduction should be carefully considered whenever it makes sense for non-tax purposes. In employing the marital deduction, the taxpayer and the tax advisor must be knowledgeable and wary to avoid some of the traps that lie buried in its complicated provisions.

Because the unified credit is equivalent to an exemption of $15 million or more, an individual or a married couple can make substantial gifts of a testamentary nature without imposition of a transfer tax. For example, assuming no post-1976 taxable gifts were made during life, a husband with an estate of $21 million can use his unified credit to make a tax-free bequest of $15 million to children or other relatives; if he leaves the rest of his property to his surviving wife, that bequest will also pass free of tax due to the unlimited marital deduction. If the wife consumes all or part of what her husband left her and then dies with a taxable estate of $15 million, she will be able to transmit that property outright without a tax in her estate because a unified credit will be available to her also.

In general, the marital deduction offers considerable flexibility and should be considered when a transfer to the surviving spouse is desired. The marital deduction does not permanently eliminate gift or estate taxes, but it does postpone tax on the property left to the surviving spouse until she disposes of that property either by gift during life or by transfer at death. If the surviving spouse consumes or dissipates the property during her life and does not hold it at her death, it will escape transfer tax altogether. In any event, she will have the use of the taxes saved in the first estate.

Estate planning for married couples involves careful use of the marital deduction to maximize the planning goals of the family as a whole. Special attention should be paid to the various exceptions to the terminable interest rule where a marital bequest is to be made in trust or subject to special conditions or limitations, rather than as an outright bequest to the surviving spouse. For example, a survival requirement of up to six months is permitted, as are various arrangements that provide lifetime benefits for the surviving spouse short of outright ownership. In this regard, the "qualified terminable interest property" (QTIP) provisions of I.R.C. § 2056(b)(7) have become widely used because they allow a marital deduction for the full value of the property in the decedent's estate even though the surviving spouse receives only a life estate in the property; unlike the other exceptions to the terminable interest rule, the QTIP provisions permit the decedent to control the ultimate disposition of the property at the death of the surviving spouse. Moreover, the decedent's executor can elect to claim the marital deduction for all or a specific portion of qualified terminable interest property.

A common form of estate planning structure in a family with substantial wealth involves the creation of two trusts at the death of the first spouse. For example, if the husband dies first, he can leave his property to be divided between a marital deduction trust (the "A" trust) and a "credit shelter" or "bypass" trust (the "B" trust). The marital deduction trust, as its name implies, will be deductible in the husband's estate and eventually taxable in the wife's estate. It may take the form of a QTIP trust in which the wife has only a life estate, or an estate trust with remainder payable to her estate, or a trust in which the wife has a life estate and a general power of appointment. By contrast, the credit shelter trust is designed *not* to qualify for a marital deduction in the husband's estate, so that it will be taxable at his death but will subsequently escape tax in the wife's estate. This result can be achieved even if the credit shelter trust gives the wife substantial benefits, such as an income interest for life, a special power of appointment over corpus, and a noncumulative limited power to withdraw corpus for her support or health needs. The credit shelter trust is usually funded with just enough property to maximize the tax benefits of the husband's available unified credit, pursuant to a formula clause, and the rest of the property is used to fund the marital trust. If the wife is to receive discretionary distributions of corpus from either trust, it would make sense for such distributions to come first from the marital trust in order to minimize the amount subject to tax in her estate.

Tax planners often recommend structuring wills and trusts so that the share of property passing to a surviving spouse (and in a form qualifying for the unlimited marital deduction) will be of sufficient size to eliminate estate tax liability at the death of the first spouse. However, this approach may actually increase the amount of estate tax on the surviving spouse's estate by an amount that exceeds the tax saving in the first spouse's estate, if the credit shelter bequest is not adequately funded. (This might occur, for example, if the couple held all of their property in joint tenancy with a right of survivorship.) In a system with graduated tax rates, some tax planners have recommended an alternative approach of equalizing the taxable estates of the married couple in order to allow each spouse not only to use his or her unified credit but also to obtain a separate "ride" up the rate ladder. However, the advantages of splitting estates between spouses have been severely curtailed by recent legislation which provides for increases in the exemption equivalent and reductions in the top marginal estate and gift tax rates. Under current law, the estate and gift taxes are imposed at a flat rate of 40% on cumulative taxable transfers above the (inflation-indexed) $15 million exemption equivalent. Accordingly, it will still make sense to ensure that each spouse has enough property to make full use of his or her available unified credit; beyond that point, however, there will be no additional tax benefit from a separate "ride" up the rate schedule, since all property in excess of the exemption equivalent will be subject to tax at a flat 40% rate, regardless of how it is allocated between the respective spouses.

Traditionally there has been a risk that the first spouse to die may fail to use all of his or her unified credit, either because the decedent's estate is less than the exemption equivalent or possibly because the marital share is inadvertently overfunded. This risk has been significantly reduced by a statutory amendment to § 2010(c), enacted in 2010, which allows the surviving spouse to make use of the deceased spouse's unused exemption equivalent (in addition to the surviving spouse's own exemption equivalent) if the decedent's executor so elects on a timely filed estate tax return. (See § 72, *supra*.) This "portability" provision offers married couples considerable flexibility in tax planning. Since the deceased spouse's unused unified credit can be passed on to the surviving spouse, it has become far less important to make sure that the decedent makes full use of his or her unified credit. As a result, the need for a credit shelter bequest (or for lifetime gifts to ensure adequate funding of such a bequest) has become less pressing.

Marital deduction planning under the federal transfer taxes can occasionally be complicated by estate or inheritance taxes at the state level, if the state tax does not follow the federal model. For example, if the estate tax threshold under state law is less than the federal exemption equivalent, a credit shelter bequest may generate a state estate tax liability but be completely sheltered from federal estate tax. In that event, it may make sense to leave a portion of the credit shelter bequest in a form that qualifies for an elective marital deduction for state (but not federal) tax purposes, if this is permissible under state law.

Occasionally *post-mortem* estate planning can serve to reduce taxes and to tailor the disposition of property to the family situation. For example, a wife might take action after her husband's death, with the additional facts then known to her, to disclaim a bequest under her husband's will if doing so will cause the property to go to a child or someone else on whom she would like to confer a benefit. She may choose to do this if she does not need the property and if keeping it out of her hands will reduce transfer taxes because she has separate property that will make her taxable estate larger than her husband's and because she cannot make large lifetime gifts without incurring gift tax liability. She may do this even if the disclaimed property thereby passes to a trust of which she is a beneficiary. See I.R.C. § 2518(b)(4)(A).

§ 79 TRANSFER TAX ADVANTAGES OF LIFETIME GIFTS

For transfer tax purposes, it is usually desirable—for wealthy taxpayers who can afford it—to make substantial lifetime gifts, even if those gifts will be taxable when made. And substantial amounts of property may be given away even before giving does become taxable. For example, a married couple with two children and four grandchildren can give away more than $2 million over a ten-year period with no transfer tax consequences whatever, simply by conscientious use of the per-donee gift tax annual exclusion. In addition, large gifts in the form of direct payments of educational and medical costs can be made free of tax.

Prior to the 1976 Act, the advantages of making taxable lifetime gifts were plainly visible. The gift tax provided a separate graduated rate schedule which allowed a separate "ride" up the brackets for lifetime gifts. Moreover, the gift tax rates were around 25% lower than the estate tax rates, and a separate $30,000 exemption was available only for lifetime gifts. As explained in previous sections, the unification of the estate and gift taxes in the 1976 Act put an end to these advantages. However, the 1976 Act left untouched two less obvious advantages of lifetime gifts compared to transfers at death.

First, the property valuation dates are different under the gift tax and the estate tax. A gift is valued at the time it is made, while property included in a decedent's gross estate is valued at the date of death (or the alternate valuation date, if applicable). If a donor makes a completed gift of property and retains no powers or interests that will cause the transferred property to be drawn back into the gross estate at death, any future appreciation in the transferred property will escape inclusion in the donor's transfer tax base. Moreover, separate gifts of property made to several donees (or to a single donee at different times) may be eligible for valuation discounts that would not be available for an aggregate bequest of the same property at death. This creates an opportunity for what is called "estate freezing," a technique whereby a donor makes lifetime gifts of property interests which are expected to appreciate rapidly in value, while retaining property interests with little or no potential appreciation. The usefulness of this technique, however, like that of all inter vivos giving, must be weighed against the *income* tax advantages of a stepped-up basis available for property included in a decedent's gross estate. (See § 80, *infra.*)

The second general tax advantage of making lifetime gifts is that the "tax-exclusive" gift tax base includes only the value of the transferred property (not including any gift tax imposed on the transfer), while the "tax-inclusive" estate tax base includes the entire value of property transferred at death (including any funds used to pay the estate tax). Thus, if a donor makes a gift more than three years before death, the amount of the resulting gift tax will never be subject to transfer tax. (If the gift is made within three years of death, the amount of the gift tax will be subject to the gross-up provision of § 2035(b).) This difference may seem inconsequential in small estates, but it becomes significant in very large estates. For example, assuming a flat 40% tax rate, a person starting with $42 million can make a $30 million gift and pay the resulting gift tax of $12 million. In contrast, a transfer of $42 million at death will incur an estate tax of $16,800,000, leaving only $25,200,000 for the recipients after tax. Thus, the transferor can save $4,800,000 simply by making the transfer during life instead of at death.

It is mainly these two factors—the differing valuation dates, and the tax-exclusive gift tax base—which explain the continued importance of the complex rules of I.R.C. §§ 2035–2038, which require that certain lifetime transfers be drawn back into the gross estate at death, in order to prevent significant tax avoidance. Against both these factors, however, must be balanced the postponement in tax until death that can be accomplished by holding property until death, rather than paying tax on inter vivos gifts when made.

§ 80 FEDERAL INCOME TAX CONSEQUENCES OF CERTAIN PROPERTY DISPOSITIONS*

In planning transfers to effect the wishes of a donor and to minimize the transfer tax consequences, it should never be forgotten that various dispositions may have significant income tax consequences as

* For a more extensive introduction to federal income tax principles, see Lathrope, Yamamoto & McNulty, Federal Income Taxation of Individuals (9th ed. 2023), especially §§ 79 through 90, and McCouch, Federal Income Taxation of Estates, Trusts, and Beneficiaries (4th ed. 2026).

well. To take a simple example, an outright, no-strings inter vivos gift of corporate stock will not only remove that stock from the donor's gross estate, but will also cause any future dividends from it to be taxable to the donee for income tax purposes, and not to the donor. The interrelations between the gift, estate and income taxes are many and complicated, and in this chapter discussion will be confined principally to the effects of gifts or bequests on the sale or other disposition by the recipient of the gift property, i.e., to the question of the recipient's *basis* in the transferred property.

First, it must be remembered that a person who receives property by gift or bequest is not subject to income tax on the receipt of the property. I.R.C. § 102 excludes the transferred property from the recipient's gross income at the time of the transfer. Nevertheless, the recipient may have occasion to report income as a result of a subsequent sale of the property. For as a price of tax-free receipt, the donee of an inter vivos gift must take over the donor's basis as his own basis in the gift property for purposes of determining gain on a subsequent sale of that property (with an adjustment for any gift tax attributable to net appreciation in the value of the property). See I.R.C. § 1015(a) and (d). Consequently, if A owns Blackacre for which he paid $10,000 (his cost basis) and gives it to B when Blackacre is worth $15,000, and if B later sells Blackacre for $17,000, B will have taxable gain of $7,000. If Blackacre had been worth just $8,000 when A gave it to B, B would still have $7,000 gain when he sold it for $17,000 later. This is an entirely lawful and proper way to shift taxation of the gain in appreciated property to a donee.

Deductible loss, however, cannot be shifted in this way. For purposes of determining loss on a subsequent sale, the donee must take as his basis the lesser of (1) the donor's own basis or (2) the fair market value of the property at the time of the gift. Consequently, if A had a basis of $10,000 and Blackacre was worth $8,000 at the time of the gift, and B later sold Blackacre for $7,000, B would realize a loss of only $1,000; A's loss of $2,000 will never be recognized by A or B. If, perchance, B sold Blackacre for $9,000 (an amount in between A's basis of $10,000 and the value of $8,000 at the time of the gift), B would realize neither gain nor loss, a strange result that follows from selling the property in the "gray" area between the two basis rules of I.R.C. § 1015(a). (The rule for computing gain is irrelevant because the sale price is less than the basis of the property in the donor's hands; the rule for determining loss is also inapplicable because the sale price is higher than the value at the time of the gift.)

The potential loss deduction will have disappeared; no deduction will be available to anyone. Perhaps the policy justification for allowing gain and tax burden to be shifted is that the donee will be in a more liquid position than the donor when the gain is realized by sale; such policy, however, does not support shifting losses between taxpayers.

Very different rules apply to property passing from a decedent which is includable in the decedent's gross estate. The recipient's basis is the fair market value of the property at the date of death (or the alternate valuation date, if applicable). I.R.C. § 1014(a). Thus if A devises Blackacre, which he originally purchased for $10,000, to B, and if Blackacre is worth $12,000 at A's death, B's basis in Blackacre will be $12,000. If the value at death were $9,000, B's basis would be $9,000. Thus, in the *gift* situation, the donor's gain is later taxed to the donee, if the donee sells the property and realizes a price in excess of the donor's basis, but in the case of a transfer at death the decedent's gain (or loss) goes unrealized and the recipient begins with a fresh basis equal to the value of the property in the decedent's gross estate.

In the case of property acquired from a decedent, gain accrued before death often goes untaxed. Pre-death loss in property cannot be shifted, just as in the case of an inter vivos gift, because the recipient of property passing from the decedent takes a basis equal to value at death for purposes of computing gain or loss on a subsequent sale. Again, the reason for not taxing gain at death may be a concern over lack of liquidity. And the decedent's old basis is not carried over after death because of the heavy administrative burdens involved in tracing the decedent's basis. So potentially taxable gain escapes tax altogether, and potentially deductible loss disappears without a deduction.

Under these rules for transfers at death, an elderly taxpayer has a strong income tax incentive to sell property that has decreased in value below his basis, in order to realize and deduct the loss, and to retain property that has risen in value in order to avoid realizing the gain and to pass the property on to his heirs with a stepped-up basis—equal to fair market value—at death. Gift property with built-in appreciation can often be donated to a low-bracket (or tax-exempt) person and the gain shifted to that person; loss property is better sold, if the loss is deductible by the high-bracket original owner.

Traditionally, estate planners have weighed the benefits of a fresh-start income tax basis for inherited property against the burden of a countervailing estate tax liability. That calculus has shifted significantly in recent years, however, as a result of dramatic increases in the taxable threshold for estate taxation. In effect, estates below the inflation-indexed $15 million estate tax threshold face an effective estate tax rate of zero while obtaining a tax-free basis step-up for all appreciated property owned at death. With no countervailing estate tax liability, the advantages of eliminating potential capital gains tax by holding appreciated property until death will become irresistible as a basic planning strategy for many individuals of moderate or even substantial wealth.

Although § 1014(a) generally allows a fresh-start basis for property passing from a decedent, the general rule does not apply to appreciated property that was given to the decedent within one year of death and was then *reacquired* from the decedent by the original owner (or his spouse). In this instance, the basis of the reacquired property in the hands of the original owner will be the same as the decedent's basis immediately before death. I.R.C. § 1014(e). For example, suppose that A owns appreciated property which she cannot sell without realizing a large capital gain. A is the sole beneficiary under the will of her parent B, who is terminally ill. But for the special rule of § 1014(e), A might give the property to B with the expectation of getting it back with a stepped-up basis after it passed through B's estate. It is not clear that this sort of "basis laundering" was ever widely used, since it might well give rise to gift or estate tax liability exceeding the income tax saved, but § 1014(e) clearly requires that A take a carryover basis in the property. A similar rule also covers the case where the property is sold by B's estate and A is entitled to receive the proceeds. Note the possibility that this rule may easily be avoided if B leaves the property not to A or her spouse, but to another family member (e.g., A's child).

Over the years, the fresh-start basis rule of § 1014 has come under heavy criticism, largely on the grounds that it violates principles of horizontal and vertical equity and undermines economic efficiency. Allowing a permanent exemption from income taxation for built-in gain in property transferred at death is thought to be unacceptable as a matter of tax equity, both because it favors taxpayers who hold appreciated property at death over those who realize gain during life (a horizontal inequity) and because it favors wealthy taxpayers who can afford to retain appreciated property over long periods of time (a vertical inequity). Moreover, the resulting incentive to retain appreciated property until death (and to sell loss property in order to realize the tax deduction before death) is believed to create a "lock-in" effect with undesirable effects on investment behavior. To be sure, the *estate tax* already reaches the fair market value of property transferred at death, but that does not justify an *income tax* preference for unrealized appreciation. The main advantage of the fresh-start basis rule is that it avoids the difficulty of ascertaining the decedent's basis in property owned at death. Ascertaining the fair market value of property owned at death is relatively easy, especially if that value must be determined in any event for estate tax purposes.

It would be possible to maintain the fresh-start basis rule while closing the escape route for unrealized appreciation if death were to be treated as a realization event for income tax purposes. *Constructive realization,* however, raises potential liquidity problems; assets might have to be sold to pay income tax at a time when there was no voluntary disposition, such as a sale or exchange, to justify imposing a tax. This problem could be especially severe for small businesses, farms, and estates consisting mainly of a family residence or other illiquid assets.

In 1976 Congress repealed the longstanding fresh-start basis rule for property transferred at death and attempted to bring unrealized appreciation within reach of the income tax. The solution adopted, however, did not take the form of a constructive realization rule. Instead, Congress opted for a carryover basis rule somewhat similar to the existing rule for inter vivos gifts. In general, the recipient's basis in property acquired from a decedent was to be the same as the decedent's basis immediately before death, with an adjustment for transfer taxes paid. See former I.R.C. § 1023. The new rule gave rise to a host of problems involving administration and compliance. How is the decedent's basis to be determined after death, in an asset acquired years earlier, with adjustments for depreciation or capital improvements? And how is an executor to treat beneficiaries fairly and impartially in distributing assets that have bases different from their respective fair market values, especially if there are material differences in the tax brackets and other tax characteristics of the various recipients? A piece of property worth $100,000 with a basis of $90,000 might well be worth more than another property with the same fair market value but a lower basis. And the basis differential would matter more to a high-bracket recipient than to a low-bracket one, or to someone planning to sell the property soon or to use it in a trade or business where depreciation deductions would be a factor, than to someone planning to retain the property for personal use.

The carryover basis rule enacted in 1976 became the focus of much comment and criticism, both because of basic policy concerns and also as a consequence of the greatly increased burdens on fiduciaries administering decedents' estates. Opponents of the carryover basis rule persuaded Congress first to postpone its effective date and ultimately to repeal the rule in 1980 before it ever became generally effective.

Undaunted by the failure of the 1976 experiment, Congress in 2001 enacted a modified carryover basis rule to replace the longstanding fresh-start basis rule for property acquired from a decedent. The carryover basis rule, set forth in former I.R.C. § 1022, eventually took effect in 2010, in conjunction with repeal of the estate tax, but only on an optional basis and only for estates of decedents who died during that year. If the executor made a valid election, property passing from the decedent took a basis in the recipient's hands equal to the lesser of the decedent's basis or the value of the property at death. Nevertheless, the carryover basis rule was subject to two important exceptions which allowed a basis increase of up to $1,300,000 for appreciated property "owned" by the decedent at death (including revocable trust property) and a separate, additional basis increase of up to $3 million for appreciated property passing to a surviving spouse (either outright or in the form of qualified terminable interest property). The opportunity to opt out of the estate tax, even at the cost of foregoing a fresh-start basis for appreciated property, provided substantial tax savings, especially to very large estates, but that option is no longer available for estates of decedents dying after 2010.

§ 81 PLANNING AND THE GENERATION-SKIPPING TRANSFER TAX

The tail shouldn't wag the dog. Experienced estate planners understand that individuals should decide how to dispose of their wealth during life and at death without placing undue emphasis on the impact of taxes. Tax savings are one factor, to be sure, but they should not be the exclusive or even the primary consideration. This is a fundamental principle of family estate planning. Preferably the tax advisor's role is to analyze the tax consequences of the individual's plan, advise of tax savings that could be achieved with major or minor alterations to the plan, and then let the client decide whether the tax savings are worth the non-tax-related costs of deviations from the initial plan. Of course, in practice, many clients do not know what they want and will seek the estate planner's advice for both the tax and non-tax aspects (e.g., how much wealth is it prudent for an 18-year-old to control?) of estate and personal financial planning.*

Tax-Free Transmission of Wealth to Remote Generations. If a client wishes to transfer wealth to individuals who are removed from the client by two or more generations, it will be important to consider all the ways that such transfers can be accomplished without paying any generation-skipping transfer tax.

The most obvious planning tool is the $15 million GST exemption (indexed for inflation) provided by I.R.C. § 2631. As was discussed in the outline at § 15, *supra,* this exemption can shelter either a specified amount ($15 million, indexed for inflation) of direct-skip transfers from immediate taxation, or a trust initially funded with the same amount of property from taxes on subsequent distributions and

* For a more extensive introduction to non-tax aspects of estate planning, see Lynn & McCouch, Introduction to Estate Planning (8th ed. 2026).

terminations, or some combination of direct skips and generation-skipping trusts. Married couples who plan to make significant generation-skipping transfers will want to be sure that each spouse makes optimal use of his or her own GST exemption. Accordingly, it may be important to ensure that each spouse has sufficient assets to make full use of his or her GST exemption. In this regard, if spouses elect gift-splitting treatment for gift tax purposes under § 2513, the election will automatically be given effect for GST tax purposes as well. I.R.C. § 2652(a)(2). Also, it should be noted that there is no counterpart in the GST tax to the "portability" provision which allows a decedent's surviving spouse to make use of the decedent's unused unified credit (discussed in § 78, *supra*). Because the GST exemption cannot be freely transferred between spouses, couples who do not wish to pay estate tax on the death of the first to die may wish to take advantage of the so-called "reverse QTIP" election under I.R.C. § 2652(a)(3). This allows the transferor spouse who establishes a deductible QTIP trust to allocate his or her GST exemption to the trust and to continue to be treated as the transferor of that trust for GST tax purposes even after the transferee spouse's death. Without the election, the transferee spouse would become a new transferor when the trust was included in his or her gross estate, and the original allocation of the transferor spouse's GST exemption would be wasted.

Also important for GST tax purposes is the zero inclusion ratio allowed by § 2642(c) for gifts that are exempt from gift tax by reason of the annual exclusion or the exclusion for educational and medical transfers.

Another potentially important provision allows a grandparent to transfer property to a grandchild free of GST tax if the child's parent in the intervening generation was dead at the time of the transfer. See I.R.C. § 2651(e).

Minimizing the GST Tax That Must Be Paid. Although in many cases the GST tax can be avoided entirely, some taxpayers will want to make taxable transfers to grandchildren or other beneficiaries at least two generations younger than themselves.

It will be important that they plan very carefully. First, they should try to use the GST exemption exclusively for transfers to skip persons, and avoid wasting the GST exemption on transfers to non-skip persons. As a practical matter, this means that a trust should be designed with an inclusion ratio of zero (totally exempt) or 100% (totally non-exempt), with no distributions from an exempt trust (including distributions on termination) to non-skip persons. Second, they should consider the benefits of transferring property in the form of a direct skip as opposed to a taxable termination or a taxable distribution. Direct skips, unlike the other types of generation-skipping transfers, are taxed on a tax-exclusive basis. Finally, in any type of generation-skipping transfer, it is possible to skip several generations in a single transfer with no additional generation-skipping tax liability. For example, a gift or bequest (or a distribution from a trust) to a great-grandchild is subject to the same GST tax burden as a similar transfer to a grandchild.

Estate or Gift Tax as an Alternative to the GST Tax. Generation-skipping trusts were originally designed to transmit wealth to remote generations without incurring *any* additional transfer tax after the gift or estate tax on the initial transfer. With the advent of the GST tax, the question in many cases has become not *whether* there will be a transfer tax but *which* tax will apply. In many cases, an estate or gift tax will be preferable to a GST tax, and in such cases it is often possible to design a generation-skipping trust deliberately to trigger estate or gift tax liability and thereby to escape a heavier GST tax liability. Consider the following comparisons. The estate and gift taxes give each taxpayer a unified credit that automatically offsets the tax on cumulative taxable transfers up to the exemption equivalent ($15 million, indexed for inflation); transfers in excess of the exemption equivalent are subject to tax at a flat 40% rate. The GST tax has no such credit, but does provide a separate $15 million exemption (indexed for inflation) which can be freely allocated to transfers made during life or at death. In the absence of any allocation of GST exemption, the GST tax applies to all non-exempt generation-skipping transfers at a flat 40% rate; a transfer that is partially but not fully covered by an allocation of GST exemption will be subject to tax at a blended rate between zero and 40%. The estate tax includes a credit for tax paid on prior transfers. I.R.C. § 2013. The GST tax does not.

At one time, generation-skipping transfers offered an easy method of circumventing the federal transfer taxes. Now many taxpayers will seek to expose at least part of their property to estate or gift taxation as a safe harbor from an even costlier GST tax. Given the range of factors affecting the timing of transfers, the choice of assets, and applicable rates and exemptions, it will be difficult to reduce the tradeoffs between the various taxes to any convenient formula or general rule. Often the optimal estate plan will involve judicious balancing of tax burdens and benefits among the estate, gift, and GST taxes.

The following example shows how powers of appointment can be used to manage the mixed use of the estate and GST taxes as wealth is transmitted through several generations.

Example: Grandmother leaves a $15 million bequest to fund a non-exempt trust for the benefit of her grandchildren. The bequest is subject to estate tax in her estate. It is also a direct skip to a trust and is subject to GST tax. Following the imposition of a GST tax at Grandmother's death, the trust will be treated for GST tax purposes as if the transferor (Grandmother) were only one generation above the grandchildren beneficiaries. (This generation reassignment occurs automatically under the "multiple skip" rule of I.R.C. § 2653(a), discussed in § 15, *supra*.) Since the grandchildren are now deemed to be only one generation below the transferor, they have ceased to be skip persons and subsequent distributions to them will not be taxable as generation-skipping transfers. If the trust eventually terminates at the death of the last grandchild and the trust property is distributed to the *great-grandchildren,* there will be a taxable termination at that time since the great-grandchildren will be skip persons relative to the transferor. (Note that two levels of GST tax must be paid in order to get property to the great-grandchildren. Had Grandmother made part of the transfer in the form of a direct skip to a separate great-grandchildren's trust, that part of the transfer would have been subject to only one level of GST tax.)

Alternatively, Grandmother could give a general power of appointment to the last surviving grandchild. The trust property would then be included in the gross estate of that grandchild (and possibly sheltered from estate tax by the grandchild's unified credit). The grandchild would then become the new transferor (see I.R.C. § 2652(a)(1)), so that the great-grandchildren would not be considered skip persons. The last surviving grandchild could even make provision for a substantial new trust for the benefit of *great-great-grandchildren* (and more remote generations) by allocating his own GST exemption to the trust property. Thus, by giving the grandchild a general power of appointment over the trust property so that he becomes a "transferor" at death, it may be possible to provide additional flexibility in the terms of the disposition and also reduce the total tax burden.

CHAPTER 16

REFORM PROPOSALS AND FUNDAMENTAL ALTERNATIVES TO PRESENT TRANSFER TAX SYSTEMS

§ 82 INTRODUCTION: REFORM PROPOSALS

In any constructive discussion of possible reforms of wealth transfer taxation, the first step is to consider what general qualities such a tax should have. Many policy analysts would agree that most or all of the following characteristics are desirable in taxing the transmission of wealth. First, the tax should produce a reasonable amount of revenue, without necessitating large administrative costs, which also means that it should be easy to understand and therefore comply with. This is sometimes called "fiscal efficiency." Second, the tax should impose significant restrictions on the passage of large amounts of capital to succeeding generations, without at the same time drastically reducing the incentives to accumulate such capital. Third, the tax should be perceived as fair, which entails treating similarly situated taxpayers alike, and not providing disparate treatment for transactions which are the same in substance and different only in form. Thus the tax should not interfere with a taxpayer's dispositive plans by imposing technical rules that favor certain forms, such as trusts, over other more or less equivalent dispositions. Like any tax, the tax on wealth transfers should be both "economically efficient" and as "allocationally neutral" as possible, in the sense of not interfering with taxpayer choices concerning investments, work effort, education, family, etc. Finally, a tax on wealth transmission should be consistent with, and mutually reinforcing of, the income tax, at least as long as the two taxes are kept separate.

By almost any measure, the present transfer taxes leave room for improvement. Despite the enactment in 1976 of a unified rate schedule, a single, cumulative base, and a unified credit for the estate and gift taxes, those taxes have never been completely integrated. This lack of coordination gives rise to inordinate statutory complexity, which has become even more marked in recent years as Congress has added more and more special rules aimed at promoting or deterring particular types of transfers. In some cases, transfers with similar economic effects produce dramatically different tax consequences due to minor differences in form. As a result, many taxpayers are prompted to engage in costly and elaborate schemes with little or no significance apart from potential tax savings. Although it would probably be unrealistic to expect enactment of an ideal transfer tax system any time soon, a number of thoughtful proposals for comprehensive reform have been forthcoming. In addition to those changes explicitly or implicitly suggested in previous chapters, the following specific reforms are among those discussed by commentators.

One area of perennial interest to reformers is the structure of rates and exemptions. The present estate and gift taxes share a unified rate schedule which appears on its face to be gradually progressive, with nominal rates ranging from 18% on the first $10,000 to 40% on transfers over $1 million. However, all of the low brackets are preempted by the unified credit, which in effect eliminates estate and gift taxes on the first $15 million (indexed for inflation) of cumulative taxable transfers. Thereafter, the marginal rate jumps abruptly from zero to a flat rate of 40%. On one hand, more gradual rate progression could be restored by converting the unified credit to a "zero bracket amount" (corresponding to the "exemption equivalent" of present law) and establishing relatively broad rate brackets for transfers exceeding the zero bracket amount. The rate bracket structure could be held at a constant level in real terms by indexing the brackets for inflation, thereby solving the problem of "bracket creep." On the other hand, a more steeply progressive rate structure would introduce additional complexity and encourage the development of new techniques for shifting tax liability from high-bracket taxpayers to low-bracket taxpayers.

Proposals to achieve complete integration of the estate and gift taxes have focused on two main issues. The first issue involves the definition of the transfer tax base. Under current law, the gift tax is computed on a "tax-exclusive" base, since the amount of a taxable gift does not include any gift tax incurred by the donor. In contrast, the estate tax is computed on a "tax-inclusive" base, which includes all property owned at death, including any funds used to pay the estate tax. Thus, notwithstanding the unified rate schedule, a lifetime gift is taxed more lightly than a similar transfer at death because the gift tax is payable with pre-tax dollars while the estate tax must be paid with after-tax dollars. For example, assuming a flat 40% tax rate, a person with $42 million can make a gift of $30 million and pay the resulting gift tax with the remaining $12 million. If the person transfers the same property at death, however, the estate tax would be $16,800,000, leaving only $25,200,000 for the beneficiaries. The disparity could be removed simply by requiring that the amount of a taxable gift be "grossed up" to include any resulting gift tax liability. (Alternatively, the amount of the estate tax could be allowed as a deduction in computing the taxable estate.) Adopting a uniform tax-inclusive base would remove one of the main tax incentives for large lifetime gifts and would thereby enhance both horizontal and vertical equity as well as economic efficiency or neutrality.

The second issue discussed in integration proposals involves the timing of transfers. Much of the complexity of current law stems from the disparate rules under the estate and gift taxes for determining when a transfer is deemed complete. In several instances, an inter vivos transfer may be drawn back into the gross estate at death due to some retained interest or power, even though the same transfer was treated as complete during life for gift tax purposes. In a completely integrated system, it would be possible to design a uniform completion rule to ensure that a particular transfer would be subject to tax only once. Several possibilities can be imagined. For example, under an "easy-to-complete" approach, a transfer of property would be subject to gift tax when made, except for any right to present possession or enjoyment (or a power to regain possession or enjoyment) retained by the donor; the donor would eventually be taxed on the remaining value, if any, of a retained interest or power upon a subsequent transfer or lapse during life or at death. At the other end of the spectrum, a "hard-to-complete" approach would hold the transfer open as long as the donor retained a substantial present or future interest in the property (or a power affecting beneficial enjoyment), with gift tax being imposed on any interim distributions of income or property to other beneficiaries. In an integrated system, the choice of one approach or the other, or some variant thereof, could turn primarily on considerations of administrative convenience. Under an easy-to-complete approach the taxpayer could file a single return at the time of the transfer, while a hard-to-complete approach would require periodic reporting of each distribution. The main advantage of a hard-to-complete approach is that it would make the valuation process simpler and more accurate and thereby reduce opportunities for abuse.

If the estate and gift taxes were fully integrated, the choice of a particular timing rule would become considerably less important. In general, if the tax rate remains constant, and the tax base is consistently defined and increases over time at the same rate as the general after-tax rate of return on investments, it can be demonstrated that the tax will have the same present value regardless of whether it is imposed immediately or at some later time. To see why this is so, suppose that both the gift tax and the estate tax are imposed on a uniform tax-inclusive base at a flat 40% rate, and that all property appreciates at an annual rate of around 7%, so that the dollar value of any asset will double in value every ten years. Under these (admittedly stylized) assumptions, a donor with $42 million could make a gift of $25,200,000, after paying a gift tax of $16,800,000. (Remember, in computing the tax on a tax-inclusive base, the amount given to the donee must be "grossed up" by the resulting gift tax.) If the donor retained the original property (including the amount not paid in gift tax) until her death ten years later, she would have $84 million at death, which would generate an estate tax of $33,600,000 and leave $50,400,000 for the heirs after tax. In present value terms, an immediate gift tax of $16,800,000 is equivalent to an estate tax of $33,600,000 payable in ten years. By the same token, an immediate gift of $25,200,000 after tax is equivalent to an inheritance of $50,400,000 receivable in ten years. Matters would be complicated, of course, by a progressive rate schedule, by special gift tax allowances such as the annual exclusion, and by the fact that rates of return can vary greatly due to market fluctuations and investment successes or failures. Thus, it appears that questions of timing would become less pressing in an integrated transfer tax system, even though they would not disappear entirely.

In addition to the grand project of integrating the estate and gift taxes, reform proposals have also addressed several specific problems. The gift tax annual exclusion, for example, has evolved from its origins as a de minimis allowance born of administrative necessity, and has emerged as the foundation of sophisticated planning techniques involving multiple lapsing powers of withdrawal. Some proposals would attempt to stem leakage in the tax base by reducing the amount of the per-donee annual exclusion or by imposing an additional per-donor limit on the aggregate amount of excludable gifts made each year. The present-interest requirement could also be tightened to disqualify transfers in trust and powers of withdrawal, so that the exclusion would be available only for outright gifts of property. Other proposals would move in the opposite direction and relax the present-interest requirement to allow the exclusion for any gift that would eventually be subject to gift or estate tax in the hands of the donee (or his estate), without regard to the timing of distributions. In a similar vein, building on the existing exclusion for educational and medical transfers, some proposals recommend a broad exclusion for gifts made for immediate consumption (to be distinguished from gifts of more durable forms of wealth).

Another perceived shortcoming of current law is the exceptionally lenient treatment given to life insurance. Life insurance proceeds can easily be put beyond the reach of the estate tax if all incidents of ownership of the policy are held by someone other than the insured person. For example, it is common practice for a life insurance policy to be held by the trustee of an irrevocable inter vivos trust. In addition, the proceeds are not subject to income tax on receipt by the beneficiary. It could be said in support of current law that no other property irrevocably transferred during life is drawn back into the transferor's estate at death. And yet no other type of property so abruptly increases in value by virtue of death nor so closely resembles a testamentary transfer.

The marital deduction has also drawn attention from reformers. The marital deduction has outgrown its original, limited function of neutralizing discrepancies in the tax treatment of married couples in community property and separate property states. Since the 1981 statutory amendments, the marital deduction has come to serve the broader function of allowing unlimited tax-free transfers between spouses. If the married couple is to be treated as a single taxable unit, the terminable interest rule could be made much simpler and less rigid. For example, an elective marital deduction could be allowed for the full value of any property in which the transferor's spouse receives a qualifying interest (which might be defined more flexibly than under current law), subject to a requirement that the property eventually be subject to gift or estate tax upon a subsequent transfer outside the marital unit. At the same time, allowing a marital deduction for the full value of property in which the transferee spouse receives less than absolute ownership (or an equivalent degree of beneficial enjoyment and control) might be perceived as reinforcing or exacerbating disparities between husbands and wives in the ownership and control of marital property.

For a sampling of reform proposals concerning the integration of the estate and gift taxes and related matters, see Staff of Joint Committee on Taxation, Options to Improve Tax Compliance and Reform Tax Expenditures 392–424 (2005); Task Force on Federal Wealth Transfer Taxes, Report on Reform of Federal Wealth Transfer Taxes, 58 Tax Law. 93 (2004); U.S. Treasury Dept., Tax Reform for Fairness, Simplicity and Economic Growth (1984); ABA Section of Taxation, Task Force Report on Transfer Tax Restructuring, 41 Tax Law. 395 (1988); Gutman, A Comment on the ABA Tax Section Task Force Report on Transfer Tax Restructuring, 41 Tax Law. 653 (1988); Dodge, Redoing the Estate and Gift Taxes Along Easy-to-Value Lines, 43 Tax L. Rev. 241 (1988); and Sims, Timing Under a Unified Wealth Transfer Tax, 51 U. Chi. L. Rev. 34 (1984). For earlier proposals, see U.S. Treasury Dept., Tax Reform Studies and Proposals, House Comm. on Ways and Means, Senate Comm. on Finance, 91st Cong., 1st Sess. (1969); American Law Institute, Federal Estate and Gift Taxation: Recommendations and Reporters' Studies (1969); and Advisory Comm. to the Treasury Department and the Office of Tax Legislative Counsel, Federal Estate and Gift Taxes: A Proposal for Integration and Correlation With the Income Tax (1947).

In recent years, the focus of debate has shifted from the question of how to improve the existing transfer taxes to the more basic question of whether those taxes are worth retaining at all. While most analysts would agree that the present system of transfer taxation leaves much to be desired, there is a sharp division of opinion over whether that system should be shored up or watered down or perhaps abolished altogether. Opponents insist that the transfer taxes are complex, wasteful, ineffective, and economically harmful—in short, that the present system is irreparably broken and should be discarded at the earliest opportunity. Defenders, on the other hand, maintain that the transfer taxes play an important role in making the overall tax system more progressive, backstopping the income tax, and restraining concentrations of inherited wealth. Rhetoric on both sides has become heated as the transfer taxes have moved to the forefront of a broader political contest over fiscal policy.

The debate over the fate of the transfer taxes came to a head in 2001 when Congress passed legislation providing for massive tax cuts, including a temporary one-year repeal of the estate and GST taxes (but not the gift tax) in 2010. In 2010, however, Congress reinstated the transfer taxes and made repeal optional for estates of decedents who died during that year. Beginning in 2011, the transfer taxes returned in full force, albeit with lower rates and larger exemptions. Most recently Congress raised the inflation-indexed exemption equivalent from $5 million to $10 million and then to $15 million, beginning in 2026. As a practical matter, the recent legislation has not sealed the fate of the existing transfer taxes; it has merely inaugurated a new stage in a longstanding debate over the proper role and structure of taxes on inherited wealth.

§ 83 FUNDAMENTAL ALTERNATIVES*

Lawyers tend to think "inside" the law, rather than to stand back and view it from a distance. This kind of thinking also characterizes some attempts by lawyers to propose revisions or alternatives to present laws, including tax laws. Perhaps lawyers do what they are best fitted to do, by training or by inclination or native ability, but it is worth noting that options for reform are by no means limited to incremental refinements of the existing transfer taxes. This concluding section introduces several fundamental alternatives to the taxation of wealth transfers.

The basic structure, characteristics, and problems of the estate, gift, and GST taxes have been explored in the preceding chapters. The preceding section then discussed some possibilities of further discrete changes to present law. In general, however, the main concerns about the transfer tax system as it now exists are its formidable complexity, which is, of course, only exacerbated by attempts at piecemeal reform, and its lack of neutrality. Tied to this complexity is the need to create ever more sophisticated schemes of disposition in order to take advantage of the many perfectly legal means of tax minimization. This in turn often induces taxpayers to depart from their natural and preferred plans and to adopt a different scheme of disposition in the hope

---

* The following passages are based upon and expanded from McNulty, Fundamental Alternatives to Present Transfer Tax Systems, in Death, Taxes and Family Property 85 (Halbach ed., 1977); excerpts are reprinted here with permission.

(sometimes but not always realized) of obtaining substantial tax savings. The transfer taxes as they stand thus may be viewed as overly intrusive into private affairs and yet unsuccessful in redistributing wealth, or distributing the tax burden, as fairly as could be.

This section, therefore, turns to fundamental and perhaps drastic alternatives to, rather than mere reforms of, the present transfer tax system. More dramatic, ambitious (and perhaps politically difficult) possibilities include: systems that attempt to measure and tax the "bequeathing power" exercised by the donor (such as the "Vickrey proposal"); proposals to tax more heavily or to confiscate inherited property over a period of several generations (such as the "Rignano proposal"); a so-called "accessions tax"; and, finally, a proposal to tax gifts and bequests as income to the recipient. Also mentioned are a wealth or net worth tax and the possibility of and arguments for not taxing gratuitous transfers at all.

Preliminary Note on Our Estate and Inheritance Taxes. Some salient features of the existing federal transfer taxes are: the transferor (or his executor) is treated as the taxpayer and is primarily liable for reporting and paying the tax; the tax is imposed on the value of the property transferred, under a single rate schedule which applies to cumulative transfers made during life and at death; taxation (or exemption) and valuation occur at the time of each transfer (rather than receipt); the same tax rates apply to all transferred property without regard to its source (e.g., earnings or inheritance); the rates do not take account of age differentials between transferors and transferees; and taxation is at positive and graduated rates that do not reach a confiscatory level (100%). Some of these characteristics have been viewed as deficiencies, for the correction of which other forms of transfer tax should be designed.

Inheritance Taxation. Although the federal death tax takes the form of an estate tax, a few states still use some form of an inheritance tax. Under an inheritance tax, the amount of tax paid would vary with the amount of a bequest or devise to a specific recipient, and perhaps would also vary according to the recipient's relationship to the transferor. Thus, rates would be progressive, or in any event different for smaller or larger gifts to a single recipient, possibly also differing according to degrees of closeness of the relationship, with higher rates of tax applicable to larger gifts and to gifts to more distant relatives or unrelated recipients.

The principal arguments for general reliance on the inheritance tax form rather than the estate tax are: (1) if the tax burden is viewed as falling on the successors, the inheritance tax form seems fairer in that it takes account of the number of recipients of a decedent's wealth and makes the tax depend on the size of their shares, rather than simply on the size of the decedent's estate; and (2) the inheritance tax structure facilitates preferential treatment of close relatives or other classifications of beneficiaries via varying exemptions and rate schedules. The main objections to the inheritance tax have been: (1) as contrasted with an estate tax, technical difficulties often result from the need to identify beneficiaries and value their interests, especially in cases involving discretionary trusts or contingent future interests; and (2) each inheritance is taxed separately, without regard to other gifts or inheritances received by the same taxpayer either contemporaneously or over a lifetime—a deficiency rather naturally handled by the accessions or income tax models to be discussed later.

Taxing the Exercise of "Bequeathing Power." Estate and inheritance taxes apply on the death of each transferor. Consequently, they create differential results, and some would say inequities, depending on whether a transferor uses "generation-skipping" transfers and depending in any event on how closely the death of each transferor is followed by that of a recipient. (Notice also that many generation-skipping transfers incur no GST tax because of its several exemptions.) Even if the impact of successive taxation is ameliorated by credits of limited amount or duration, as under the present federal estate and gift taxes, estates that are taxed at several transmission points end up being diminished more by greater taxes than are estates taxed fewer times during the same period.

To counteract these inequities and generation-skipping incentives, a succession tax structure could be set up to impose essentially the same tax burden on transmission of wealth from one individual to another without regard either to the number of steps or the time lapse involved. Notable among such proposals is the "bequeathing power succession tax" advocated by Professor William Vickrey in his Agenda for Progressive Taxation (1947). The purpose of the "bequeathing power" concept is to equalize the death taxes paid in two families in which the timing and sequence of deaths would otherwise produce heavier taxation in one than in the other.

Vickrey's mechanism would be complex in operation, but the goal and basic conception can be simply stated. "Bequeathing power" expresses a property owner's ability to place value in the hands of various transferees of varying degrees of remoteness. The tax on a transfer would be based on the "units" of bequeathing power used, reflecting differences in age (i.e., based on date of birth rather than generation) between the transferor and the recipient; the greater the differential, the greater the tax incurred by the transferor. As a result of this system, the value of an estate's bequeathing power (i.e., the power to benefit) with regard to any particular potential recipient remains constant as the wealth is passed from person to person, although the actual after-tax value of the estate declines with each transfer.

Unfortunately, like other transferor-oriented schemes that seek to equalize tax burdens regardless of the number of transmission points along the way, this proposal raises a host of administrative and technical problems that tend to recede in the transferee-oriented systems discussed below. In addition, like so many transfer taxes, it does not distinguish—as the next proposal does—between wealth the transferee inherited and that which he or she earned and saved.

Earned and Inherited Wealth Distinguished: The Rignano Proposal. In the view of some, it is inequitable or socially undesirable to tax the transfer of earned wealth as heavily as the transfer of wealth that was itself previously inherited. This is the idea underlying proposals such as one made by Eugenio Rignano, an Italian count, in The Social Significance of the Inheritance Tax (trans. 1924). Under his scheme, gifts and bequests of inherited wealth would be taxed more heavily than would transfers of wealth that the transferor accumulated from other sources. Thus, the rate of tax applied to property earned and saved by the decedent might be 5%, while that applied to property the decedent inherited from his or her parents and then transmitted to another generation might be 20%, and a still higher rate, say 50%, would apply to property the decedent had received from grandparents, and so on.

Such a proposal can be designed gradually, over several generations, to confiscate inherited wealth without discouraging work or saving. The rates in Rignano's own plan reached 100% on the further transmission of wealth that had been inherited from grandparents. Alternatively, the scheme can be diluted by more limited rate increases or by spreading them over a greater time span.

Serious administrative and practical problems inhere in distinguishing between inherited and earned wealth. Tracing and taxing the Count's family estate and vineyard as it passed through several generations might have seemed feasible; it would be quite another matter to trace the proceeds of its sale through securities, cash, reinvestments and secured transactions over two or three generations in the contemporary world. Also, even if based on the most sophisticated and complex tracing principles, the system would induce persons to consume their inherited wealth and to transfer only earned property.

A distinction between saved and inherited wealth could be introduced into other forms of transfer taxation. Such a proposal can be viewed as a palatable alternative to immediate confiscation of property that an owner attempts to transfer during life or at death. Analogous proposals have suggested allowing the first successor no more than an income or annuity interest in the property, or adding a "re-inheritance" duty to existing death taxes.

Heavier taxation of re-inherited wealth rests on the intuitively appealing proposition that human beings care more about leaving assets to their immediate heirs than to their remote heirs. Also, when final taxation is removed by two or more generations, the adverse effect on incentives for work and saving would seem to be minimized. The more favored position given to currently saved wealth (defined to include investment returns on inherited property and other capital, as well as earnings from one's own labor) could serve as an incentive for property owners to invest for maximum return and thus most efficiently from the viewpoint of the economy at large.

Nevertheless, any attempt to impose heavier taxes on the transfer of inherited wealth tends to be swamped by the formidable problems of identifying, tracing and valuing the inherited property, and of distinguishing it from the earned and saved (or more recently inherited) property.

An Accessions Tax—Built-In Unification, Simplification and Equity? The preceding chapters have pointed up the problems of a dual system of separate estate and gift taxes and the benefits of having a single, unified transfer tax system. Unification may take any of several forms. One of these is the so-called "accessions tax," which has been concisely described as "a progressive, cumulative tax on the total lifetime acquisitions of an individual through inheritances and gifts." The key feature of this tax is that it is not imposed on transferors but is instead levied upon, collected from, and calculated with reference to the transferees or recipients. In this respect it may seem to resemble an inheritance tax, but it differs in several important and fundamental particulars. The principal difference is the fact that it would be geared to the cumulative gratuitous accessions of a particular recipient from all sources during his or her lifetime and would be graduated accordingly. Also, at least in the form in which it is now most often proposed, it would come to bear at the time when property reaches the recipient, rather than when the recipient's interest is created; troublesome problems of valuing contingent future rights of unascertained beneficiaries are thereby eliminated. Thus, the timing of the tax will often differ from the usual estate, inheritance and gift taxes, which focus on the transferor's parting with the property; and the amount of the tax would not vary with the size of the estate of the transferor (as it does under an estate tax), nor would it vary so much with the amount of the particular receipt (the inheritance tax method) as it would according to the recipient's lifetime history of receiving gratuitous transfers from all sources.

The accessions tax for the current year would be computed by subtracting all accessions taxes paid in prior years from the total tax on all lifetime accessions through the current year. A lifetime exemption and a small annual exclusion would apply. Although rates and exemptions could be varied on the basis of the donee's relationship to the donor, such differentiation is not necessarily a part of an accessions tax. Also, it could be designed to deal simply and effectively with the generation-skipping problems posed by the varied array of trusts and similar arrangements that have proved so troublesome under the present system. By its very nature, it is a unified transfer tax, thus avoiding the problems of a dual system with separate exemptions and rate schedules.

One Accessions Tax Model. A fully elaborated model of an accessions tax was developed by Professor William Andrews in The Accessions Tax Proposal, 22 Tax L. Rev. 589 (1967). By his definition, an accession occurs only upon receipt of a gift or inheritance—that is, for example, not upon the creation of a trust but rather when the trustee makes a distribution, whether of income or of corpus.

Professor Andrews' proposal included an annual per-donor exclusion for gifts up to $1,500, a lifetime exemption of $24,000, and a complete exclusion of interspousal accessions and of accessions for current consumption. It also dealt efficiently, though bluntly, with the problem of generation skipping by providing a deduction equal to 40% of the amount of any accession from "immediate relations" (defined to include parents, parents-in-law, parents of a deceased parent, siblings and children), thus making the effective rate of tax lower than on accessions from other sources ("remote accessions"). A later version of an accessions tax, with different solutions to some of its problems, is described and analyzed in Halbach, An Accessions Tax, 23 Real Prop., Prob. & Tr. J. 211 (1988).

Consequences of Taxing Recipients Instead of Transferors. One of the most powerful arguments for an accessions tax approach is that of enhanced equity. That is to say, if the burden of a tax on transfers at death falls primarily on the decedent's successors, the burden is appropriately correlated with each recipient's ability to bear the tax, or at least with his or her total overall benefits from donative acquisitions. The accessions tax is not concerned with the size of the transferor's estate (the estate tax approach) or merely with the size of the particular accession apart from all others (the inheritance tax approach). In this respect, it appeals to many of the same notions of equity that are sought in the income tax: horizontal equity requires that people in an equal position (i.e., similarly situated) pay an equal amount of tax; vertical equity requires that those in a better position pay a larger tax (either proportionately or progressively). One consequence of the focus on transferors under the present transfer taxes is that the tax on a specified amount received is often greater in the case of a recipient who takes from one transferor than for a person who receives the same amount from several transferors. Also, the amount of the tax depends on the size of the estate or the transferor's donative history, rather than upon the lifetime receipts of the transferee—that is, under a transferor-oriented tax, one who inherits a given amount as one of several heirs bears a heavier burden than one who receives the same amount as a sole heir. In contrast, an accessions tax is neutral with regard to the number of other successors, the number of transferors, and the size of the estate or the donative history of the transferor. It is concerned with the overall, lifetime accessions position of the one who bears the tax, the transferee.

More Advantages and Disadvantages. As noted earlier, the accessions tax by its very nature unifies the transfer taxes and avoids the problems of a dual tax structure. It thereby avoids the problem of how to tax gifts arguably made in contemplation of death. It lends itself to dealing effectively with generation skipping, and it easily resolves many of the technical problems that have plagued other systems. In many respects it copes effectively with the tax problems presented by trusts, particularly discretionary trusts, but it does offer possibilities of tax deferral—even though at a high cost that may make the delay in tax payments neither worthwhile to the taxpayer nor harmful to revenue in the long run. The accessions tax offers greater neutrality and therefore greater equity with regard to estate and gift splitting between married individuals.

Some Questions. Probably most controversial and difficult to assess are arguments concerning revenue production and about the extent and desirability of redistribution of wealth under an accessions tax. The questions are significantly interrelated.

It is often said that an accessions tax probably would not raise as much revenue as the present transfer taxes do, unless rates were raised and exemptions lowered. It is not as clear as it might seem at first, however, that this argument is entirely valid, even if taxpayers were to engage in "planned dispersion" among numerous recipients in several generations, for the effect could largely—although not entirely—be counteracted by a combination of cumulation over a lifetime of receipts from an increased number of transferors and differential rates to handle the generation-skipping element involved. As the number of descendants multiplies when generations are jumped (e.g., in addition to two children, each pair of husband-wife transferors is likely to have four grandchildren), so does the number of ancestors from whom accessions are received and cumulated over a lifetime (e.g., each such grandchild has four grandparents as well as two parents). In addition, an associated element of what might be called "accession-splitting" between a natural donee and his or her spouse can be handled by an aggregation rule, though not without injecting an element of complexity into the system. With regard to the problem of tax deferral resulting from taxing trust distributions rather than trust creation, it is important to note that such a tax does not involve the "interest-free loan" element that is present in the income tax but rather is compensated for by the enlarged tax base that is reached by an accessions tax that has been postponed, only to be levied on distributed or accumulated income as well as on the original trust corpus.

Supporters of the accessions tax argue that it would produce greater, earlier, and more desirable redistribution of wealth, as well as greater equity. Because property tends to be kept within the immediate family anyway, however, the extent to which this is true and the results and benefits of such redistribution are highly speculative, as is the distribution of transfer tax burdens.

Some Further Questions. One of the greatest attractions of an accessions tax is its apparently close coordination between the amount of the tax and the ability to pay of those who are viewed as bearing the burden. However, the question of who bears the burden may be more complicated than it appears at first glance. Are the bearers necessarily the beneficiaries who receive some property (though perhaps less than they would have but for the tax), or might the burden be borne by omitted beneficiaries who would have received transfers had the transferor not recognized that his or her distributive wealth would be diminished by transfer taxes? No definitive answer can be given at present, nor is it possible to know how much the anticipation and presence of the tax would affect a transferor's inclination to work and save as compared with a disposition to forego earnings and to consume existing savings. Consequently, a comparison of the equity of various transfer tax regimes, including—but not limited to—the accessions tax, must now proceed based on informed speculation rather than objective certainty concerning who bears the tax.

In addition, the argument that the burden of an accessions tax corresponds to ability to pay is true only in the limited sense that the tax relates to the recipient's lifetime history of benefits from *donative* transfers. The income or other wealth of the recipient is not taken into account. Whether the progression of rates based solely on donative transfers under this and other forms of wealth transfer taxes is desirable deserves further analysis. If it is thought desirable to take into account overall taxpaying ability, including income, then other tax structures may be more appropriate. These might include a periodic, comprehensive wealth tax or an income tax that includes donative receipts in its base.

A Tax on Wealth (Rather than on Transfers). An alternative, or possibly even a supplement, to a transfer tax could be a wealth or net worth tax, levied periodically on a comprehensive base of the taxpayer's net worth (wealth minus liabilities). The timing and frequency of the levy would depend on the rate of the tax and its revenue or redistribution goals.

Since such a tax is imposed without regard to a transfer, it would pose problems of periodic liquidity, probably requiring increased holding of assets in liquid form, and would involve wealth being steadily eroded by taxes while property remains in the hands of the same (increasingly unhappy) owner. For a sense of some other issues and questions about the impact of such a tax on risk-taking, investment, and other aspects of economic behavior, assume that property produces an annual investment return of 6% and consider an ad valorem tax levied at the annual rate of: (a) 3% (half of annual return); (b) 6% (entire annual return); or (c) 18% (three times annual return). One might also consider whether some effort should be made to value and tax human capital, for omitting such "wealth" from the tax base may make a wealth tax inequitable and allocatively biased, although some may think that this form of "investment" should be encouraged by leaving it exempt.

For thoughtful discussions of wealth taxation, see Cooper, Taking Wealth Taxation Seriously, 34 The Record 24 (1978); and Shakow & Shuldiner, A Comprehensive Wealth Tax, 53 Tax L. Rev. 499 (2000).

Simple Repeal of the Federal Transfer Taxes. There has been much talk in recent years of repealing the existing transfer taxes altogether and enacting nothing to replace them. They raise a relatively small proportion of total federal revenues, and their redistributive effects are uncertain. They involve significant costs of administration—though those costs are probably no higher in proportion to the revenue they produce than in the case of the income tax. Also, substantial costs of compliance or legitimate avoidance are borne by taxpayers, and tax-motivated planning involves more than transaction costs—it also produces intrusions, distortions, and apparent inefficiencies in the allocation of economic resources, not to mention inequities among taxpayers depending on whether they can avail themselves of expert advice. (Much the same could be said, of course, about the income tax.) Evidence that the transfer taxes have served to redistribute or equalize wealth or to break up concentrations of economic power is hard to come by; perhaps the most that can be said is that inequalities of income and wealth might have become even more marked in recent decades if these taxes had not been in effect.

Equity, with respect to transfer taxation as in many other areas of tax policy, is largely in the eye of the beholder. In terms of horizontal equity, the present transfer taxes are open to criticism on the ground that they favor consumption relative to saving—a person who manages to consume all of his accumulated wealth will never incur a transfer tax, whereas a person who consumes little and accumulates a fortune will eventually become subject to tax. In addition, to the extent that the tax bears unevenly on different types of property or forms of disposition, it may be viewed as failing to provide equal treatment for similarly situated taxpayers. In terms of vertical equity, however, the case for the transfer taxes is considerably stronger. From the perspective of *recipients,* the taxes tend to reduce inequality of inherited wealth and enhance equality of opportunity. More generally, due to the structure of rates and exemptions, the transfer taxes represent the single most progressive component of the existing federal tax system. Simple repeal of all taxes on wealth transfers would not only represent a retreat from progressive taxation, but would accentuate the disparate treatment of realized and unrealized gains under the present income tax. Without the estate tax, unrealized appreciation at death would escape tax altogether. Since such appreciation is functionally equivalent to taxable gain realized during life, and is disproportionately concentrated in the hands of wealthy taxpayers, the resulting situation would violate both horizontal and vertical equity.

One possible response, of course, would be to require that all unrealized appreciation in property owned at death be included in gross income on the decedent's final return. A deathtime gains tax, if properly designed, would rectify a serious and longstanding gap in the income tax base, and would at least partially offset the erosion of the estate tax caused by recent increases in the exemption equivalent. A deathtime gains tax might even be considered not merely as a supplement to, but as a replacement for, the existing transfer taxes, although the distributional effects of such a tax as well as its incentive effects would merit further study. Compared to the ill-fated experiments with carryover basis in 1976 and 2010, a deathtime gains tax would raise far more revenue and would be considerably easier to administer. For a lucid elaboration of this approach, see Zelenak, Taxing Gains at Death, 46 Vand. L. Rev. 361 (1993).

Perhaps the most serious charge against the transfer taxes is that they stifle capital formation and impede economic growth, due to their negative effects on incentives for work, saving, investment, and entrepreneurial risk-taking behavior. This charge deserves to be taken seriously, as far as it goes, but the picture is a good deal more complex. It is certainly plausible that a parent contemplating a heavy estate tax burden may be inclined to retire early and consume his or her accumulated wealth in order to beat the tax, but the opposite result is equally plausible; the parent may be spurred to work harder, save more assiduously and invest more aggressively in an attempt to meet the tax burden. Moreover, it may be that the transfer taxes actually encourage work, saving and investment on the part of *recipients* whose inheritances are reduced by the tax. In other words, if the taxes were repealed, recipients of larger inheritances might opt for more leisure and higher consumption. Given the inconclusive state of theoretical and empirical research concerning the incidence of the transfer taxes, the behavioral responses of wealthy individuals, and even the dominant motives for making gifts and bequests, it should come as no surprise that the economic effects of the taxes cannot easily be measured or evaluated. All in all, it seems likely that a transfer tax imposed at death has somewhat smaller disincentive effects on work effort and saving than, say, a revenue-equivalent income tax imposed during life. For an excellent discussion of these and related issues, see Gale & Slemrod,

Overview, in Rethinking Estate and Gift Taxation (Gale et al. eds., 2001).

It can certainly be argued that taxing transfers of wealth is simply not worth the price paid in complexity, transaction costs, allocative inefficiency, incentives to earn and save, and in the employment level, which depends on the capital base. From a tax policy perspective, though, the important question is not whether the present transfer tax system, viewed in isolation, is complex or burdensome, but whether there are better alternatives. Simple repeal would reduce federal revenues by at least $30 billion a year, and the lost revenue would presumably have to be made up from other taxes imposed either currently or in the future; it seems unlikely that the lost revenue would be completely offset by a reduction in public outlays. Nevertheless, the possibility of repealing wealth transfer taxation as a separate revenue source could provide an opportunity to replace it with another form of taxation that might operate more simply and fairly, be easier to administer, impose lower transaction and compliance costs, yield substantial revenue, reduce concentrations of wealth, and produce a more neutral or otherwise more desirable influence on the allocation of resources. An alternative that may offer some or most of these advantages is considered in the following paragraphs.

Taxation of Gifts and Bequests as Income. An elegantly simple and economically attractive alternative to the present mode of taxing gifts and bequests would be to stop applying special transfer taxes to either transferors or transferees and merely tax the latter as having received income. Technically, at the federal level, this proposal consists of repealing the estate, gift, and generation-skipping transfer taxes and also repealing I.R.C. § 102, which excludes property acquired by gift, bequest, devise, or inheritance from the recipient's gross income for income tax purposes.

One goal of such a change would be simplification of the tax law. In its basic form, the proposal would add nothing to existing law on the books; in fact, it would repeal many sections of the Internal Revenue Code. Some changes in the income tax law probably would be necessary, however, to deal with particular problems to which reference will be made shortly. (Moreover, some theorists would even insist on a new deduction for the donor if the donee is to be taxed on a gift as income; others would vehemently disagree.)

Why tax gifts and bequests as income? A gift or inheritance enlarges the recipient's power to consume or invest, just as does other income, which economists have long defined as any accretion in wealth or any net receipt. In the standard von Schanz-Haig-Simons definition, income is the sum of the value of rights exercised in consumption plus the change in the value of the store of property rights between the beginning and the end of an accounting period. Probably for this reason, reputable tax reform proposals (such as Canada's Carter Commission Report, 1966) have recommended that gifts and bequests be included in the income tax base.

From the inception of the federal income tax in 1913, the statute has expressly excluded gifts and bequests from the recipient's gross income. The exclusion may be based in part on a limited concept of income (as the term was used in the Sixteenth Amendment), which the Supreme Court defined in an early case as "gain derived from capital, from labor, or from both combined." Since then, except for cases of specific exclusions, the judicial definition has gradually expanded to include any "undeniable accessions to wealth, clearly realized, and over which the taxpayers have complete dominion." The present statutory exclusion of gifts and bequests may also have been designed to keep the tax collector "out from under the Christmas tree." And, of course, inertia has probably been a major factor in continuing the income tax exclusion after enactment of the estate and gift taxes.

Some Advantages of Taxing Gifts and Bequests as Income—Fairness. To tax gifts and bequests as income would be to expand the base of the income tax and to comprehend within its single set of graduated rates, its annual accounting period, and its other structural characteristics these important items of accretion to one's ability to pay tax as well as to consume or to invest. The result has the advantage of fairness, at least to those who view the federal income tax in its basic provisions as the fairest tax in the federal system, especially because the proposed inclusions would enable it even better to "get at" overall ability to pay. The proposal would also do away with the different tax rates and exemptions applicable to gifts and bequests—as we have seen, disparities that give rise to much tax planning, controversy, and ultimately inequity. Finally, although it is premature to advance a definite conclusion about redistributive effects, a likely surmise is that taxing gifts and bequests as income would lessen concentrations of wealth both by better gearing the tax to ability to pay and by inviting wider lifetime and testamentary distributions of property to lower income taxpayers, as the present transfer taxes do not.

Preventing Tax Avoidance—Another Aspect of Fairness. The federal transfer taxes are well known as taxes that can be avoided or at least greatly reduced, legitimately, if competent tax advice is available, and the gift tax is one that often goes unpaid even when due. Consequently these taxes both produce little revenue and quite unevenly burden similarly situated taxpayers. The costs of administering and enforcing the existing transfer taxes, and those of complying with or minimizing them, as noted earlier, can be substantial. Private dispositions of wealth may to some extent be deterred or accelerated or otherwise distorted by the transfer taxes. While a system of taxing gifts and inheritances as income would not be entirely free from these costs, the costs might well be lower.

Some Concerns and Possible Solutions. One concern in taxing gifts and bequests as income is that a taxpayer might in one year receive a large inheritance all of which would be taxable at once and at graduated income tax rates. The unfairness to such a person is obvious in comparison to another who receives a like amount over a number of years. One solution for this problem of "bunching" would be to allow "income averaging" over a period of, say, five years or more.

Another concern is the necessity for reporting birthday gifts and many other small transfers that would heavily burden taxpayers or else go unreported. The answer to this problem is to include in the income tax law an annual or lifetime exclusion of a certain amount, or both, as in the present transfer taxes.

Another major problem would arise from the need to value many more taxable gifts, if income tax exemptions were set lower than present transfer tax levels.

It is likely that some additional statutory enactments would be necessary in order to cope with the multifarious and complicated devices that taxpayers have learned, or tried, to use to minimize or avoid the present transfer taxes. These include powers of appointment, revocable and amendable transfers, annuities, life insurance, gifts disguised as loans, and many other matters now dealt with by the transfer tax law. Some other questions that will undoubtedly arise can also be handled without undue complexity; these include whether a special exclusion should be afforded to surviving spouses and children, whether the basic taxable unit should be the individual or the family (including dependent children, as in the Carter Commission Report), and whether the donor should realize gain or loss on disposing of property by gift. Unduly heavy taxation of estates that are subject to multiple transfers in quick succession could be handled by a graduated credit, exemption, or other allowance. Generation-skipping transfers and discretionary trusts, however, would present more serious problems, and the solutions to these problems might restore some significant complexity to the law, since the income tax approach, unlike the accessions tax, does not inherently tend to correct for them. Other current issues will be less of a problem. For example, the question of what is a "gift" or "bequest" under the present I.R.C. § 102 exclusion would be of less significance. Taxing gifts and bequests as income also bypasses the problems of integrating a gift tax with an estate tax.

Broader policy questions are also involved. An income tax approach would tend to invite distribution of gifts to low-bracket recipients—the very young, the very old, or those having low income years to average with the year of receipt. These incentives and the equity of results among taxpayers would differ somewhat from those created by an accessions tax, where gifts to low-accession recipients make later gifts to those same recipients, by the same donor or others, taxable in higher brackets. No lifetime cumulation of that kind would be likely to find its way into the income tax model—although it could.

The allocational economic effect of an income tax approach, in the private sector, must not be ignored. If incentives are created for different distributions of wealth, effects on capital accumulation and spending can be expected to follow from differences in the marginal propensities of taxpayers to save or consume. Both the altered tax base and changes in distribution and wealth holding patterns may in turn affect the progressivity (or regressivity) of taxes on the transferred property and on its future income.

Revenue Losses or Gains? Reliable estimates of the revenue impact of the proposal to tax gifts and bequests as income are not readily available. Such admittedly rough estimates as have been made, however, offer some general impression of the order of magnitude of revenue that might result. Based on certain assumptions about rates and exemptions, and assuming (for want of a reliable basis for any particular contrary assumption) no change in behavior as a result of a different tax law, it appears that including gifts and bequests in income would produce substantial revenue, perhaps at least as much as the present transfer taxes.

Economic and Social Effects. The redistributive effect of taxing gifts and bequests as income, rather than under a separate transfer tax system, might well be positive, but the available data and analysis are insufficient to demonstrate or quantify this point.

Both the income and accessions tax models shift the focus from the transferor as taxpayer to the recipient, and, more importantly, the income tax model would no longer differentiate donative acquisitions from earnings and the like. These changes would alter society's property and reward structure, especially viewed from the transferor's perspective. They might also involve an actual shift of tax burden, in the sense of incidence and "who pays the tax." Important effects might follow from simply removing amounts of funds from different pockets or from creating different incentives to which both potential transferors and recipients would respond differently—in working, saving, or consuming—than they would to a separate transfer tax. The results could be expected to appear in allocation of national resources, distribution of wealth, consumption patterns, formation of capital, employment levels, and productivity. Beyond the economic issues lurk significant social and moral questions about what roles the transfer taxes play which may differ from the roles best served by an income tax model.

Taxation as Income—Conclusion. The structural reform that would result from taxing gifts and bequests as income to the recipients and repealing the present transfer taxes would produce a simpler federal tax law, a law less costly for the government to administer and for taxpayers to comply with. It would produce a fairer tax, because it would coordinate the tax liability with ability to pay—as measured by all income, not just donative receipts. Although income may not be a perfect measure of a person's ability to pay tax, it seems to be the best measure the federal tax system has come up with so far, and it would be made more comprehensive if it included gifts and bequests. Consequently, this structural reform would produce a fairer taxation both of gifts and bequests and of other items of income.

Conclusion. To propose drastic alternatives to the existing federal estate and gift taxes may seem to invite trouble, in part because of the many unknown effects and costs attached to employing taxes with which we have little or no experience. To stay with the familiar forms, and to attempt incremental adjustments to perfect them, seems less disruptive.

Nevertheless, so little is known about the real economic and social effects of our present transfer taxes, and even today there is so much litigation and dissatisfaction, that a shift to some new structure may not be nearly as difficult as it would at first seem. If major gains in simplicity, equity or allocative efficiency were likely, a change could well be worth the risk and costs. Among the main alternative forms explored, the accessions tax and the taxation of gifts and bequests as income have the most to recommend them in principle and relatively few political and legal obstacles as a practical matter. Each merits further study and serious consideration as an alternative to the endless tinkering and complexifying tax "reform" efforts that have so preoccupied Congress in recent years.

INDEX

References are to Sections